D1591026

As Free As An Eagle

The Inmate's Family Survival Guide

by Daniel J. Bayse
Certified Family Life Educator

Dedication

This book is dedicated to four very special people in my life who made this work possible: to my wife Linda, whose many hours of working overtime and days of editing the manuscript allowed it to be created; to Justin, my son and favorite little boy, who donated many hours of "daddy time" so I could sit at the computer; and to my parents, Gladys and Justin Bayse, who taught me by their example that man's highest calling is to serve others.

Director, Communications and Publications: Patricia L. Poupore
Publications Managing Editor: Elizabeth Watts
Editorial Assistant: Becky Hagenston
Cover Illustration: Jane E. Jacobsen
Cover Design: Leonard Righter

Reprinted in the United States of America by Graphic Communications, Inc., Upper Marlboro, MD.

ISBN 0-929310-63-2

This publication may be ordered from the:
American Correctional Association
4380 Forbes Boulevard
Lanham, MD 20706-4322
1-800-222-5646

For information on publications and videos available from ACA, contact our World Wide Web home page at: http://www.corrections.com/aca

Acknowledgements

This book combines the information found in the three family life education courses that I created with the cooperation of the Alabama Department of Corrections' Treatment Division and Auburn University's Department of Family and Child Development for use in Alabama's prison system: *How To Keep Your Family Alive While Serving A Prison Sentence; How To Reenter Family Life And Society After Completion Of A Prison Sentence;* and the seminar for inmates and their families; *What In The World Are We Going To Do With Him?*

Although the book lists one author, I did not write it without the help of many other people. Besides the prior research and work by the authors of the books, journal articles, and research projects listed in the bibliography, there are several people who have made special contributions to this book.

Byron W. Lindholm, Ph.D., helped me start this project. Paul H. Van Wyk, Ph.D., director of mental health services for the Bullock County Correctional Facility, Union Springs, Alabama, spent many hours editing the rough drafts, provided valuable insights into the special needs of inmates, and gave encouragement.

Scot M. Allgood, Ph.D., associate professor, Department of Family and Child Development, Marriage and Family Therapy Center, Auburn University, provided hours of supervision, editing, and encouragement.

Merle R. Friesen, Ed.D., director of treatment, Alabama Department of Corrections, Warden Lionel Davis, and the entire staff at the Bullock County Correctional Facility made sure that inmates could attend the classes and participate in the research that later became this book. They are the most cooperative people that I have ever worked with. And, to the inmates who were part of the classes where this material was first taught, thank you for your input.

The professional community has been extremely helpful in the preparation of this book. Staff members from Prison Fellowship and the National Council on Family Relations provided needed ideas, contacts, resources, and encouragement. Prem Gupta, Ph.D., Guelph Correctional Centre, provided some valuable insights about inmate rehabilitation. J. Michael Burns, Ed.D., taught me how to teach without sounding "preachery."

Thanks also to Elizabeth Watts, my editor at ACA, for her excellent job of polishing the manuscript.

The title of this book was inspired by an illustration used by Jerry W. Lee, Th.D., in a class at Florida Baptist Theological College.

To all of these and others who made this work possible: "Thank you!"

Foreword

Study after study shows that inmates who can hold a job, stay off alcohol and drugs, and have a strong family relationship are those that stay out of prison. Unfortunately, many inmates start new lives out of prison with disintegrated family relationships.

In this self-help guide for inmates and their families, Dan Bayse shows inmates how to take responsibility for their own actions, repair their family relationship, and stay out of prison. Using simple language and examples that inmates can relate to, Bayse discusses some of the ways to break the chains that bind them to their hard-living lifestyle—the one that got them into prison—and adopt the new lifestyle of settled living.

The effectiveness and appeal of Bayse's approach have been demonstrated by the fact that both the Alabama and Oklahoma Departments of Correction have adopted his program for systemwide use. Inmates, counselors, chaplains, and inmate family members can all benefit from this helpful book.

The ACA wants to spread the word about this and other programs that are working to help inmates across the country. Contact our Communications and Publications Division with information about your program.

Anthony P. Travisono
Executive Director

Contents

Foreword v

Introduction 1

Chapter 1: How Did I Wind Up Here? 3

Did you get more than you bargained for? 5
Your family was there because they loved you 7
"Prison house blues" 7
Why inmates return to prison 8
Why people violate the law 11
Debts must be paid 12
"What about me, I'm innocent!" 14
Admitting the facts about who you are 16
Admitting that you asked to be placed here 18
The law of the harvest 20
How to successfully end your sentence 21
Where do I start? 23

Chapter 2: "Daddy, Why Did You Have To Go Away?" 25

Mayberry only exists on TV 26
Looking out for Number One 28
One big unhappy family 32
Prisonization and its effects on inmates 33
How to prevent prisonization from happening to you 36
How families work 37
As the twig is bent, so grows the tree 41
You can't blame your parents for your actions 44
Look at the legacy you are leaving your children 46
A letter to your child(ren) 48

Chapter 3: "Quick, Throw Me A Lifesaver" 52

What's a lifesaver? 53
Your invisible chain 55
Every generation is linked by chains of loyalty 57
How to draw a family tree 60

Contents

Where did the chains come from? 65
You accepted the chain that binds you to your past 69
The family bank account 71
Removing the chain that binds you to your past 75
An exercise 77

Chapter 4: CPR For A Dying Relationship 80

Many relationships appear to be dead or dying 82
How can you tell when a relationship is dead? 83
How your family relationship got sick to begin with 86
Failing to discipline children is an abuse of power 87
Understanding what you owe your family 88
Giving yourself and your family good self-esteem 90
What is love? 92
How to communicate your true feelings to others 93
Forgiveness is not forgetting 96
How to develop and use problem-solving skills 97
Start dreaming about getting out 101
Differences between growing and dying family relationships . . . 103
How to keep your family alive while you're in prison 105

Chapter 5: So You Want To Get Out, Or Do You? 109

Inmates dislike prison, yet return 110
Common stresses of reentry into family life and society 112
Learning how to live as free as an eagle 114
"Hard living" will cause you to return to prison 116
Alcohol or drug dependency contributes to hard living 117
The road back to prison 122
The way to keep from returning to prison 123
Using problem-solving skills to balance your life 125
Developing a new way of life called settled living 127
Giving your family the gift of love 129
Here are your keys to freedom 131
Do you really want out? 132

Chapter 6: What's In A Name? 133

The meaning of a person's name 134
People see different qualities in the same people 135
Rebuilding your name means learning to control your temper . . . 137

Rebuilding your name means developing goals 138
Rebuilding your name requires a commitment to change 140
Seven things that will keep you from changing 142
Guilty or Not Guilty? 145
A resource that will make your life incompatible with crime 147
Have you forgiven yourself for what you've done? 148
Building a new image for yourself 150
Making your new name stick 152
But what if "everything" goes wrong? 153

Chapter 7: "Hey Man, I Need To Feed My Family"
(And other ways to find a job that don't work) 154

You have not lost your rights to employment 155
Your state employment service is willing to help you 157
Using problem-solving skills to find the right job 158
A short description of the job search 159
Ask not what your employer can do for you 160
How should I dress for the interview? 161
What will a prospective employer ask during an interview? 162
How to handle rejection 164
Employers have legitimate concerns about you 165
Taking the hard-living road to work 167
The settled-living road to freedom 168
Using the keys to freedom at work 170
Avoiding the pitfalls 172

Chapter 8: ". . . And They Lived Happily Ever After"
(And other fairy tales that are not true) 174

The real ending to the fairy tale 175
The moral of the story 176
Living "happily ever after" is a decision 177
Things you need to consider before going home 180
Facing their unresolved anger 181
Stresses of reuniting with your family 182
Giving your children a chance to be successful 184
The purpose of discipline 187
Effective methods to discipline children 189
The proper use of anger 191
How to decide if something is worth fighting over 193

Contents

Violence in homes 194
Differences between how happily married and unhappily
married couples communicate 195
The kind of husband your wife needs 198
And he lived happily ever after? 199

A Message to the Families of Inmates 200

Chapter 9: "What Are We Going To Do With Him?" 201

A modern parable 202
The criminal mentality 204
The kind of family an inmate really wants 207
Families are victims of his crime 209
Helping each other to get over the pain 211
Dealing with increased discipline problems 213
Dealing with the family's physical needs 213
Dealing with your emotional needs 215
Finding true friends 216
Working with the prison system 218
Forming support groups 220
Finding transportation to visit the prison 221
Practicing ethical living 221
Teach your inmate to see how he has hurt you 223
Getting ready for his return 225

Nationwide Resources 227

Suggested Readings 229

Bibliography 230

Introduction

I f you are presently sitting in a jail or prison cell or have a family member in prison, this book is written for you. The first eight chapters are written for the inmate. The last chapter is written for the family, including the inmate. The goal of this book is to teach inmates and their families how to live as free as an eagle with the ability to soar over life's problems.

This book may have a significant influence on your future success. Over fifty years of research repeatedly shows that having a strong family relationship to return home to and the ability to stay on your first job for one year are the keys to parole success. Inmates who fail these tasks have a tendency to return to prison. This book teaches inmates and their families how to help end the inmate's criminal career.

Believe it or not, being in prison does not mean that your family relationship must die. Actually, it is possible the family relationship can continue and become even stronger while a member is in prison. Many inmates and their families have already been helped by this book. You may be able to say the same when you finish reading it.

The first part of this book focuses on helping you dream of keeping your family alive while in prison. The next part will focus on teaching you methods to make your dream of having a successful reentry into family life and society come true. As you have seen, many inmates never achieve that dream. They walk out the front gate, try to fly on their own, and then crash right back into prison. This does not have to happen to you!

The choices that you make will determine whether you fly or crash. Once you are ushered out of the front door and the warden slams it shut behind you, you will be at a crossroads. In front of you will be two roads. The road that looks the most familiar is actually a loop. Recently released inmates who take that road will find themselves right back in prison, usually within one year. The other road is a little harder to travel and requires newly released inmates to learn new ways of doing things. It's worth the work because this road leads to a successful reentry into family life and society and true freedom.

Why do inmates choose the wrong road? Because they have never learned how to read the road signs. Many recently released inmates think they are on the road that leads to freedom. Then after it's too late, that discover they were riding along the loop and wind up back in prison.

Consider this book your own personal road map. It will show you how to read the road signs so that you will take the road that will enable you to get out and stay out. You will learn how you can fulfill your dream of creating a good reputation in your community and how you can sell yourself to an employer so that you can find a good job and become a provider for your family. You will learn the causes of anger and violence and more about effective methods of communicating.

And more importantly, this book will teach you how to rejoin your family with a minimum of difficulty. There is a right way to accomplish this and a wrong way. You will see the difference between happily married couples and unhappily married couples. Although there is no guarantee that your family relationship will remain intact after you get out, this book can give you some tools that will give you a greater chance of success.

The goal of this book is to help you get this time of incarceration behind you, to help you end your criminal career, and to help you become a useful member of family life and society. It is my dream that, after reading this book, you will be able to live the rest of your life *as free as an eagle*.

—*David H. Olson, Ph.D.*
Professor, Family Social Science, University of Minnesota
Past-president, National Council on Family Relations

Chapter 1
How Did I Wind Up Here?

Have you ever found yourself somewhere or involved in something, and suddenly you realized that you did not belong there or that what you got is not what you expected? We all do, and when this happens it is only natural to wonder how or why we ever got there.

Many "macho" men talk about their wild experiences in singles bars where they have gone to pick up women. Invariably, each of these men will have a similar story to tell. The details will be different; the cities will be different, and sometimes the guy will say that this incident happened while he was in the military, or on a sales trip, or on a vacation, or whatever. Like fish stories, these stories are never told the same way twice, and the details get more exciting each time they are told.

One story comes from a young sailor who was stationed aboard a submarine homeported in Norfolk, Virginia. He had just returned from a long nine-month cruise to the Mediterranean. For the last three months he

Chapter 1

had been under the Atlantic Ocean. Then, after what seemed like an eternity, the sub surfaced off the coast of Virginia.

He manned the rails as the captain eased the sub into its berth. The Navy band blasted their welcome as the ropes pulled the ship tight against the dock. Children perched on their mother's shoulders were wildly waving little American flags while straining to catch that first glimpse of their daddies. Wives and families had tears in their eyes as the men began to run down the gangplank.

The sailor was a single man whose family lived halfway across the country. Even though he wanted desperately to be with his family, he was told that he would be in the second group to be given enough leave time to return home. However, he had been allowed a long weekend and did not have to be back aboard the ship until Monday morning. So off he went, bouncing down the gangplank with nine months of pay bulging in his pockets. He flagged down the first cab he could find and headed straight for Virginia Beach.

There he checked into the Hilton. "After all," he thought, "I just spent nine months at sea, I've got all of this money in my pocket, and I deserve the best." The first thing the young sailor did was to take a long, hot shower in the privacy of his own room. He had gotten so tired of taking lukewarm showers in that open shower room with a bunch of scruffy-looking men who got an erection every time they washed "it" because it had been so long since they had gotten any.

After he stepped out of the shower and dried himself off, he plopped down on the quilted bedspread of the soft, spacious, king-sized bed while lazily listening to the music coming out of the stereo. It felt so good to have the radio set to the station he liked and playing at the volume he preferred for a change.

His room was on the top floor and faced the ocean. How happy he felt as he laid sprawled across the bed looking out of the large sliding-glass balcony door with the breeze gently blowing the curtains and the saltwater air permeating his lungs. He was glad, and felt a sense of relief that he was looking at the ocean instead of traveling under it, trapped in a submarine. He felt ecstacy at finally being free to enjoy the world. How much he had looked forward to his first night of freedom after being cooped up in that submarine for such a long time!

That evening he walked from bar to bar, lounge to lounge, and listened to the bands. At each place, he tried their drinks and looked at the women that were there. He continued his search until he found what he considered to be the perfect spot to spend his first night of liberty, a place called "Sir Macho's Lounge." What made this lounge so perfect was a beautiful blonde whose big brown eyes completely captivated him the minute he walked through the door.

As their eyes met for the first time, he just knew that they were right for each other. And so they drank, and they danced, and they drank some more. Her voice was so sweet, and so soft. And best of all, she liked the idea of spending the night in the Hilton, standing on the balcony of a top-floor room overlooking the ocean, underneath the light of a shimmering moon. She liked the idea of feeling the warmth of his body pressing against hers in the gentle breeze while listening to the rolling waves pound the seashore. And so they did, and did, and did, and then did it some more.

Morning came, and the softness of the moon's flattering light was replaced by the harsh glare of the morning sun. When the sailor woke up someone was playing big drums inside of his head. He swore that the seagulls outside of his window were using megaphones.

But worse yet, he saw this strange woman sleeping in his bed that he swore that he had never seen before. The beautiful blonde was no longer there. In her place was a woman who was so ugly that she made the Wicked Witch of the West in *The Wizard of Oz* look like a perfect 10. This woman was old, and wrinkled, and grey. Only then did he see the blonde wig on the pillow.

As the breeze blew across the bed and into his face he suddenly realized that not only was she old and wrinkled, but she had not had a shower recently. This sent him running to hug the toilet.

The sailor grabbed his things and ran out of the room, out of the hotel, and back to the ship as fast as he could go. He thought to himself over and over, "How could I have been so blind, and so stupid?"

A couple of weeks later he was at sick bay because "it" had started to drip. The doctor told him that not only did he have the clap, he also had herpes.

Did you get more than you bargained for?

Now that you are here in prison, do you feel sort of like that sailor felt when he saw what his prize was really like? Can you identify with how that sailor must have felt now that you realize that you got more than you bargained for?

Chapter 1

Just like that young sailor's, your life changed suddenly, completely, and in such a short period of time. You worried for so long about what was going to happen, hoping that at each stage of the proceedings that your case would be dismissed, for any reason. You didn't really care why, you only hoped that somehow someone would say some magic words and your case would suddenly disappear.

Your preliminary hearing came, and the case was certified to the grand jury. During the proceedings you wondered why your lawyer did not even try to win that trial. No one told you that this wasn't really a trial, that you would not have a chance to testify, or even that this was the way it was supposed to be. No one told you that this portion was simply to determine if the state had enough probable cause and enough evidence to present your case to the grand jury. No one told you that at the end of this proceeding that you would not know your fate.

You were told to be in court on the day your case was to be presented to the grand jury. Did you want to talk to the members of the grand jury and tell them how innocent you were or about the special circumstances that made your case different from all the rest? But you weren't even allowed to see them. Only the police officers and maybe some of the witnesses were allowed in that private room. Your lawyer wasn't even allowed to listen. After all of that secrecy, did you feel like you were in a "kangaroo court" when the members of the grand jury suddenly appeared and announced that they had certified your case as a "true bill?" And again, no one told you that this did not mean that you were guilty. No one told you that all this meant was that the state had proven to the grand jury that they had enough evidence to support the charge and that finally a date could be set for your trial.

Finally your big day came. You arrived at the courthouse and sat there in your finest suit waiting for the judge to enter and your case to be called. Did you wish that your trial was just a bad dream and that soon you would wake up and it would be gone? Do you remember the struggle that you went through deciding which way to answer the question: "How do you plead: Guilty or Not Guilty?"

That was a hard decision. Your lawyer was probably pulling you one way and the prosecutor pulling you another. You were really scared, and you knew that there were only three choices: (1) to plead guilty and hope for mercy, (2) to plea bargain for the best sentence, or (3) to plead Not Guilty and take your chances before the judge and jury. As you made that decision, in the back of your mind was the gnawing realization that the rest of your life would be affected by the decision that you made.

Your family was there because they loved you

If your family was there at your trial, it was because they loved you and wanted to support you during your darkest hour. And no matter whether your trial lasted fifteen minutes or three weeks, suddenly it was over. If you had a jury trial, you can remember the knot in the pit of your stomach when you heard the words, "The jury has reached a verdict." Jury trial or not, you can remember how the knot jumped up in your throat as the judge told you to stand. Then the words, "Guilty as charged" rang in your ears. And as quickly as it started, it was over.

The judge had hardly pronounced sentence when the officer grabbed your arm and whisked you away. If you were one of the lucky ones, the officer allowed you a brief moment to give your wife or mother a quick hug. But more than likely you were led quickly out of the courtroom without even having a chance to tell them good-bye.

Suddenly, you saw your family being torn apart right before your eyes and replaced with steel bars, open showers, fences, and a prison "family."

Can you remember this old nursery rhyme?

Humpty Dumpty sat on a wall.
Humpty Dumpty had a great fall.
All the king's horses
And all the king's men
Couldn't put Humpty
Together again.

If you are like many of your fellow inmates, you now see your family as being like Humpty Dumpty; sitting, wobbling, on the wall, afraid that soon it will fall off and be broken into pieces—never to be put back together again.

"Prison house blues"

And now, here you are in this awful place. If the truth was known, there are probably many things that you would rather be doing than sitting here, reading this book, in the middle of a lonesome prison that sits out in the middle of nowhere.

Chapter 1

Have you ever heard Johnny Cash's song, "Folsom Prison Blues?" The song describes a prisoner who hears a train whistle blowing in the distance. He dreams of being on the train and it carrying his blues away. Is that you that Johnny Cash is describing in his song? Do you strain to listen to the train as it rolls across a distant track? Do you watch every airplane that crosses the sky wishing you were on it? Do you ever stay awake at night just to listen to the occasional car or truck that passes the prison during the night? Do you ever dream of walking out the front gate of this prison just as one of those fancy cars drives up, whisking you away, never to return?

Well, that will probably happen some day. All inmates have something in common: Every inmate, including those sentenced to life without parole, plan to leave the prison some day. You, too, plan to have the opportunity to put this time of your life behind you.

But for many of you, when you get out your time of freedom will be short-lived. Studies conducted by researchers between 1984 and 1988 indicate that approximately 35 percent of the inmates released from prison each year will be returned within three years. Becoming involved in alcohol or drug abuse after your release increases your chances of returning *within one year* to 62 percent. And if you stay on your first job for less than one month after your release, your chances of returning to prison increase to 86 percent.

On the other hand, research shows that men who stay off alcohol and drugs, work regularly, and return to strong, healthy family relationships are the ones who consistently get out and stay out. In 1984 Robert Homant published a study that followed ex-offenders for ten years after their release. In that study, *none* of the men who stayed on their first job for one year were arrested during the entire ten years of the study. James Boudouris followed 468 men after their release from Iowa prisons. Again, those who maintained a healthy family life and a steady job were less likely to return to prison.

What this means is, if you want to stay out when you get out, you need to repair your family relationships while you are in. Or, you need to keep your family ties strong while you are in. If you wait until it's time to get out, it will be too late.

Why inmates return to prison

Have you already noticed that the inmates that return to prison are those that returned to their old ways of doing things once they got out? They are

the ones that did not learn anything while they were in. They are like that young sailor mentioned earlier. They leave prison and immediately start looking for a good time. They seem to think that they have some catching up to do. They have to go to all of their old hangouts to meet their old friends, find out what booze tastes like again, and of course, teach all the women that the "world's greatest lover" has returned.

The guys that return to prison are like the young sailor who forgot that it only takes one moment of yielding to his own desires without thinking about the consequences to do something that will tarnish him for the rest of his life. The guys that return are those that look out only for themselves. That's called "Looking out for Number One." You can always tell a person who is looking out for Number One, you just can't tell him much! He's the one that struts around like the only rooster in the hen house. He's the one who's words and actions say:

I'm NUMBER ONE!
I can do anything I want!
Say anything I want!
Anytime I want!
Anywhere I want!
To anyone I want!
And there is nothing that you or anyone else can do about it,
PERIOD!

And he looks you right in the eye as he says it, sticks out his tongue, gives you a great big "raspberry," sprays his spit all over you, and dares you to do anything about it. He's the one who is always getting written up by the correctional officers. That's because he just cannot seem to obey the prison's rules. If you think you are Number One you also think that the rules don't apply to you, which means that you can live by your own rules. But if you can't live by the silly rules in this place, how are you going to live by the silly rules on the outside?

Can you see why people get out and come right back? Their old, hard-living lifestyle is what got them in this prison to begin with. And since they think of themselves as being Number One and the most important person in the world, they think they can do anything they want; say anything they want, anytime they want, anywhere they want, to anyone they want; and there is nothing that you or anyone else can do about it, PERIOD!

When these guys get out, they go back and start drinking, drugging, and running with the wrong crowd. Soon they are back to their hard-living criminal lifestyle. And then when they mess up, they will try to blame the "crowd" or someone else for what they did.

Well, here's something to think about: There isn't anyone in the entire world that can make you do anything. Everything that you do involves making a decision. You have to decide to do it. And you are responsible for your every word, thought, and action.

You're probably thinking, "This guy's nuts, people make me do things all the time."

Here's an illustration. Suppose that right now a correctional officer orders you to put this book down, get up, and leave the room. He cannot *make* you do it. He can call some help if necessary and pull the book out of your hands and drag you out of the room, but he can't *make* you leave. If you get up and leave it will be because you have thought about what he said and decided to do what he asked. You can also decide to refuse, and that decision has consequences that are a natural outcome of your decision.

People who are looking out for Number One start pushing their wives and children around because they get tired of hearing their racket, nagging, and complaints. They don't consider the needs of their wives and children to be important, only their own needs. And of course, they won't even consider that the reason that their families are in such turmoil is because of their own actions. Notice that it is always their family's fault for the problems they are having.

These people carry this same attitude to work. People who are looking out only for themselves get frustrated when someone tells them to do something. If you think that you are truly Number One, then you will feel that you are your own boss. And if you are your own boss, then nobody can boss you around. People who are looking out only for Number One will then blame their bosses for their troubles at work and say things like, "If only that stupid jerk wasn't so unreasonable, I could have continued to work there." Notice how they always blame others for their own decisions.

People who are looking out for Number One will say that the boss gave them an unreasonable task to do. The truth is that they decided not to comply with the boss's instructions, and rather than do the task, they either quit or got fired. Then out of their frustration and anger because their life is not going the way they want it to go, they do something to prove to themselves that they are the one in power. The ultimate in proving to yourself that you are truly Number One and that you have the power to create your own rules and laws is to break society's rules and laws.

Why people violate the law

To violate the law takes a conscious decision on your part. You can continue to give all of the excuses in the world to explain your involvement in criminal activities. But your excuses are just that, excuses. The fact is that you did your crime because you decided to do it and probably enjoyed your crime while you were committing it.

At the moment that you did your crime or crimes the only thing that you were thinking about was what your needs were at the moment and what you wanted to do to meet your needs. You decided to satisfy your needs regardless of how it affected others. You were looking out for Number One. You decided that you could do anything you wanted; say anything you wanted, anytime you wanted, anywhere you wanted, to anyone you wanted; and there was nothing that anyone could do about it, PERIOD!

For example, if burglary or robbery was your crime, you forced someone to give you their property, either by breaking into their property and taking it without permission or by having "Mr. Smith and Mr. Wesson" do the asking. You declared that the laws pertaining to property did not apply to you and that you had the power to take what you wanted without having to pay any penalty.

If you are in for a sexual crime, you enjoyed your self-proclaimed power to pick any man, woman, or child and then require them to have sex with you. A person who thinks that the ability to overpower someone proves strength will also think that using ropes to tie someone up or a knife or a gun to gain compliance will also prove himself even more powerful. And if the ability to physically overpower smaller people proves power, the most powerful men in the world would be those who require children, even their sons and daughters, to submit to sex.

The simple truth is that when you or anyone else commits a crime it proves that you did not care about your victim's feelings. Regardless of what your crime was, when you made the decision to commit it, the truth was that as you committed it you did not care about your victim's feelings. You were looking out for Number One. At that point, you declared that your needs were more important than anything else in the world. You saw something that you did not have the right to have and abused your power and took it. And when you abused your power simply to get what you wanted, you proved that you could not be trusted.

For example, if you are in prison for killing someone, you made yourself a god and decided that your victim was of no value to society and should be removed. You also decided that you had the power and authority to carry out your decision.

You may say, "Wait a minute, that doesn't apply to me. I was involved in an automobile accident where someone was killed." Were you drinking or drugging? If so, when you decided to get behind the wheel you decided that your need to get where you were going was more important than the safety of all of the others on the road. You didn't have the right to drive, but you abused your power and did it anyway.

If you are in prison for selling drugs, you probably enjoyed making more money than all of your straight friends who slaved all day and made peanuts. You enjoyed the power that came from having something that people would beg you for. Before you can sell drugs, you must reach a point where you do not care if your customers get hooked and have to steal to pay for their day's supply, or have to drop out of school because they can't concentrate, or die from an overdose. Before you can sell illegal drugs, you must reach a point where your desire to make money is more important than the damage it does to the neighborhood.

This is because you thought that you were Number One. You were the king of the hill. You could do anything that you wanted; say anything you wanted, anytime, or anywhere you wanted; and there was nothing anyone could do about it, PERIOD!

One of the problems with these methods of proving how powerful you are is that they are socially unacceptable. Your trial was a continuation of the struggle over who really had the authority to decide what the law was going to be. Your trial was to determine who was really in power, you or the state.

Before you can become a criminal, you must declare that society does not have the authority to tell you what to do. You must declare that society has no right to require you to control your urges. You must declare that you are in fact the "ruler" of your own little world who can create his own laws and not have to worry about punishment.

Debts must be paid

The ability to get this time behind you and keep your family alive while you are here so that you are someday able to reenter family life and society starts when you can admit the facts that surround your particular case. First,

How Did I Wind Up Here?

you need to realize, and admit, that you are here because you earned your right to be here.

When you work for an employer, that employer is indebted to you for the price that the two of you agreed on in exchange for your labor. It is a legally binding debt that must be paid. The accepted method of paying that debt is by issuing you a paycheck each time that you have worked the agreed number of hours or completed the agreed task. Your employer is not relieved of that debt until he or she gives you your paycheck.

Suppose you are a world-famous chef and considered to be one of the best cooks in the world. The owner of a plush restaurant needs someone like you to run the kitchen. You agree to work for the restaurant in return for a salary of $1,000 per week. After all, since you are the world's greatest cook, you are worth it.

Suppose your first week is over and it's now payday. The owner calls you in and tells you that you will have to wait until next week to be paid because he has decided that he's going to use your $1,000 to buy some new clothes. You would probably protest very loudly. You would talk about the bills you have to pay, about the family you need to feed and buy clothes for. If that didn't work, you would simply state a fact: "You owe me $1,000: pay up!" And if that didn't work, you would quit, then take the restaurant to court. At that point it would be stupid for the owner not to pay you the money he owes you because the judge would say that your salary was a legally binding debt that must be paid.

Let's look at another example. You own a car and bring it to "Fly-by-night Auto Repair" to have some repairs done. You tell the mechanic, "There is a noise in the front somewhere, there's something wrong with the tires, the seat cushions are dirty, the paint has become dull, and I don't like the quality of the sound coming out of the radio. Fix it, no matter what it takes or what it costs!" To which the mechanic would reply, "Yes sir, we'll gladly make your car like new again and have it ready tomorrow afternoon." You hand the mechanic the keys, tell him to do the repairs, and walk away.

Tomorrow afternoon comes and you arrive at the garage to pick up your car. You discover that the mechanic has installed a new engine; replaced the shocks, the ball joints, and the steering system; installed four new tires; replaced the fabric in your seats; and repainted the car. The sound problem was cured by replacing your car radio with the best stereo system and speakers that money can buy. The mechanic proudly tells you, "I kept my promise, you car is now like new" and hands you the bill: $6,382.

If you wanted your car back you would have to pay the bill. Anyone

Chapter 1

dumb enough to tell the owner of "Fly-by-night Auto Repair" to use his own judgement and fix the car "no matter what it takes or what it costs" owes a legally binding bill that must be paid. And if the mechanic had to go to court to collect the bill, you would discover that the time to negotiate about how much work would be done and the price to be paid for that work is before the work is done and not after.

Just as an employer is indebted to you until he gives you your paycheck and you are indebted to the mechanic when he fixes your car, when you committed your crime you created a debt to society for the harm that you caused through your criminal activity. Each state's law books spell out the amount and method of payment required for each violation of its rules.

The debt is created the moment the crime occurs. This means that when you choose to violate the law, you have created a legally binding debt to society that must be paid. The debt is not created when the case comes to court; that's simply the place where they total up the bill.

For some crimes, a fine will pay the debt and balance the books. For others, it takes a prison sentence. For others, society says that the person must forfeit his or her life, either by spending the rest of it in prison or by execution, to pay for what they have done.

The truth is that by committing your crime you earned your right to be in prison. And you must stay here until that debt is paid or until the debt is forgiven. And unfortunately, most inmates are like the man who took his car to the "Fly-by-night Auto Repair" who didn't even consider how much of a debt would be created until after the deed was done.

There is a bright side to this dark picture. Each day that you spend here you are one day closer to having that debt paid; and when you finally gain your freedom again, your debt will be paid in full.

"What about me, I'm innocent!"

Some of you are probably screaming, "Wait a minute, I'm innocent! I did not get a fair trial!" This is like a cartoon that showed an inmate talking to a correctional officer. "I want to see the warden," the inmate says. The correctional officer replies, "Let me guess: You are totally innocent of the made-up charges that put you here. The judge was crooked, and the police officers and witnesses lied on the witness stand. And besides that, your attorney did not represent you properly." "Hey," the inmate exclaimed, "I see that you have already heard about my case."

How Did I Wind Up Here?

By the time you get to prison, it does not make any difference if anyone believes you are guilty or not. What people believe *will not* change your prison sentence. Continuing to deny your guilt will not make your sentence go away, and admitting your guilt for the crime you were found guilty of won't increase your sentence. Your trial on that charge is over, and the sentence is set.

Unfortunately for you, people who work with inmates are used to being told about how they were framed, or how innocent they are, or about the circumstances that forced them to do their crime. Also unfortunately for you, many inmates are compulsive liars who would just as soon lie as tell the truth. Here is a true story that illustrates this. It happened when I was a member of the Virginia State Police.

One morning about 2:00 a.m. on Interstate 95 just south of Richmond, I stopped a man for driving under the influence. He begged me not to arrest him because he was going to his mother's funeral, and if I arrested him, he would not have time to drive to South Carolina in time to be at her funeral.

I arrested him in spite of his cries, and I listened to him repeatedly tell his sad story about having to miss his mother's funeral all the way to the police station; during the breath test; and again as he begged the magistrate to release him on his written promise to return to court.

He didn't have any more luck with the magistrate than he did with me. The bond was set, and he was taken to jail. He was allowed to make his one phone call. Guess who he called? You got it, his mother! He made a long-distance, collect phone call to his mother and said, "Mama, I'm in jail, can you send me the money to make bond?" Later that morning she sent the money to get him out of jail.

Ask yourself this question: "Am I really innocent?" Some of you may say, "The law says I'm innocent until proven guilty beyond a reasonable doubt." Legally, that is exactly right, that is what the law says. But the truth is that at the moment you commit a crime, you have in fact become guilty of that crime and have created a debt that needs to be paid.

Suppose that one morning you walk into the First National Bank with a gun in your hand. Before anyone has a chance to notice you, you open fire into the wall just above the teller's heads. As everyone squirms on the floor, you jump the counter, scoop up all of the money in the cash drawers, spray the walls with another burst of fire, and run out. Then, while the police are responding to that robbery, you walk into the Second National Bank and do the same thing. Knowing that the police department is probably completely overwhelmed by two bank robberies, you walk into the Third National Bank and do the same thing again. Naturally, since each bank had their video cameras working and since your face appears on each of them, you get arrested and charged with three counts of bank robbery.

Suppose that the police department stored these tapes in their evidence room on top of a set of stereo speakers until the date of your trial. And suppose that the police officer assigned to the evidence room played the stereo every day not knowing that the magnets in the speakers were slowly erasing your image from the three videotapes.

Your trial date arrives, and you plead Not Guilty. The district attorney smugly puts the video cassette into the VCR and pushes Play, only to discover that all three tapes have been erased and all he sees is snow. To his dismay, he also discovers that because the tapes were so conclusive, the police department failed to collect any other evidence. Your case will be dismissed. You will be found Not Guilty.

Does this mean that you are not a bank robber? Of course not. You became a bank robber the minute that you walked into the door of the First National Bank and opened fire. At the moment that you robbed each bank, you created a debt to society that needed to be paid. In this case, the incompetence of the police department meant that you could not be found guilty in a court of law, but did not change the fact that you are a bank robber who should have been found "Guilty as charged."

Admitting the facts about who you are

The prison in which you currently reside is an exclusive clubhouse. To gain entrance, you must be tried for a felony and convicted of that crime. Your warden will not allow just anyone to walk up to the front gate and live here for a while. Your warden, as all wardens do, requires that you earn your right to live here.

You had your trial. The evidence was presented and you had the opportunity to present your case. Your very presence in this prison makes it obvious that you were not able to convince the judge and/or the jury of your innocence. If you were unable to convince them, why should anyone in the prison system, or anyone else, believe you now? Unless you pled guilty, the court heard both sides of the story. In prison, we can hear only one side of the story: yours. And unfortunately, many inmates are compulsive liars who would not know the truth if it stared them in the face.

What difference does it make anyway if they believe you or not? No prison official has the power to change your sentence. If you have any hopes of getting out of here early, the prison officials and parole board are looking for the following:

1. Inmates who know that what they did was wrong.
2. Inmates who realize why they did what they did. This can be as simple as admitting that "I saw something that I wanted that I was not entitled to, declared that society had no right to require me to control my urges, and decided to abuse my power and take it."
3. Inmates who know the changes that they have already made in their lives to assure that it does not happen again. In other words, exactly what have you learned while you have been in prison that would keep you from making the same mistake again?

Your life will begin to change when you can admit the facts about who you are and can admit to yourself and others that you are a convicted criminal. Here is one of the most important statements that you will ever read:

ADMITTING THAT YOU ARE A CONVICTED CRIMINAL SAYS SOMETHING ABOUT YOUR PAST. IT SAYS NOTHING ABOUT WHAT YOU ARE NOW OR WHAT YOU WILL BE IN THE FUTURE.

Admitting that you are a convicted criminal simply admits the facts about something that has already happened in your past, and it is public record. You will have to decide if you will be a criminal in the future, and you alone are responsible for that decision.

Admit that you are here in this prison because you were *convicted* of violating the law. Repeat these words:

"I AM A CONVICTED CRIMINAL. I AM HERE BECAUSE I WAS CONVICTED OF THE CRIME OF __(fill in the blank)__."

Some of you are having trouble saying those words because you feel that you are innocent of some or all of the charges that put you here. This may sound harsh, unloving, and uncaring, but at this point in your life, what difference does it make if you are innocent or not? The fact is that you were convicted of specific crimes and given a specific sentence as payment for those crimes. And continuing to deny these facts will not change anything.

Admitting that you have been convicted of specific crimes simply shows that you are willing to admit to the facts about yourself, not that you agree with the charges. The longer that you deny the facts about yourself, the angrier and more bitter you will become.

If you want to learn how to be someone different than what you are today, you must learn how to take the sour lemons of life and make lemonade out of them.

Try it again and see if you don't feel a little bit better about what you are saying.

"I AM A CONVICTED CRIMINAL. I AM HERE BECAUSE I WAS CONVICTED OF THE CRIME OF___(fill in the blank)___."

Remember, what you have just admitted to yourself says something about your past and nothing about your future. You can't change what has happened in the past. You have a permanent criminal record, and there is nothing that you can do about it. You made a mistake, and you are paying for that mistake. You can't change your past, but you can change your future. You must decide: Are you a criminal or an ex-criminal? It is your decision. You and only you are responsible for the decisions you will make in the future. You must decide if you are going to remain a criminal or not. And you alone are responsible for that decision.

Admitting that you asked to be placed here

Part of the healing process that will enable you to successfully end your criminal career comes when you can admit that you asked to be placed here. Some of you are thinking, "This guy is nuts—nobody in their right mind would ever want to live here." True. However, the laws of society plainly state the penalties for violation of those laws, and when you chose to violate the laws you also chose to accept the penalty that goes with the violation.

When you commit a crime, you are also asking for the penalty that is the logical and proper wage of that crime. For example, if you decide to exceed the posted speed limit, you are asking for the state to catch you, collect a fine, and possibly take away your privilege to drive. The moment that you decide to assault someone, you are asking the state to put you in jail for up to one year and allow you to pay a fine of up to $1,000. The moment that you decide to commit a felony, you are asking to be sent to prison. And what if you decide to commit murder? Depending on the state and the circumstances, you may have just asked the state to execute you.

If, during your trial, you asked for leniency, what you were really doing was asking not to be required to pay as much of a debt to society as you earned. If you tried to get off because of some loophole, what you were really doing was asking your attorney to find a way for you not to have to pay the debt to society that you earned. You can continue to ask for leniency or to use the legal loopholes, but what you are really doing is asking not to repay the penalty that you earned.

Suppose that you are in an airplane loaded with four tons of Columbian Gold. (For the naive ones reading this, that's a high grade of marijuana.) The minute that you loaded the plane in Columbia you became guilty of possession of drugs with intent to distribute and earned a prison sentence. As you were committing your crime, you were also asking the state to catch you and put you in prison. And even if you don't get caught, you are still in fact a drug smuggler and guilty of the crime.

Suppose that police officers are waiting for you when you land the aircraft. You are arrested, tried, and found guilty. Then suppose a federal judge reverses your conviction because he agrees with your lawyer's contention that not having the same percentage of women on the master jury list as there are in the county prevented you from getting a fair trial. The truth is that if you are still a drug smuggler who is guilty of the charges. Your lawyer has just found a way for you not to receive the wages—the penalty—that you earned when you loaded the airplane with the marijuana.

You, in fact, become a thief the moment that you break into a house, regardless of whether or not you are ever caught or what the verdict of a court says. You, in fact, decided that you wanted to go to prison the moment you committed your crime.

You have decided that you want to go to prison the minute that you decide to abuse your power and force someone to have sex with you. You have also decided that you want to go to prison the minute that you put a gun in your pocket and head out of the door to rob a business. And the list goes on and on and on.

You will not be ready to reenter family life and society until you can admit the facts surrounding your case and stop making excuses about your past. You will not be ready to reenter family life and society until you realize that you asked to be put here by committing criminal acts. You will not be ready to reenter family life and society until you realize that if you ever commit any additional criminal acts, at the moment you commit the crime you will have created a new debt that will need to be paid.

Before you gripe too much about the length of your sentence or the unfairness of your trial, ask yourself: How much time would you have to serve if you had been caught for every crime you have ever committed and had to pay for all of the debt you had created? Would you ever be released from here? You will not be ready to leave this prison until you realize that you earned your right to be here and are receiving what you earned.

The law of the harvest

There is a natural law called the law of the harvest that applies to all of life's decisions. The law of the harvest simply states, "You reap what you sow." This law applies to all of nature, including humans. For example, if you plant an apple seed it will become a tree that will give you apples. If you plant corn, soon you will have ears of corn to cook. But you can't grow pineapples on a pine tree or roses on a blueberry bush. What you plant is what you will get in return, and what you get in return will be more than what you planted. What this means to you and your family is that if you plant "seeds" of violence in your home you will grow violent children. If your actions, values, and behavior patterns plant "seeds" of doubt and suspicion in your home, you will grow a family full of people who doubt each other and are always suspicious of each other's motives. The longer that the "plants" of doubt and suspicion grow, the stronger the feelings will be. And then when your children are grown, they will be full of doubt and suspicion, and the chain will continue.

On the other hand, if your actions, attitudes, and behavior patterns plant seeds of trust and loyalty in your home, as the plant grows, you will see your family begin to trust each other more. This in turn will create a greater desire for the members of the family to show increased loyalty to each other. When this occurs you have begun to reap the harvest of the seeds of trust and loyalty that you planted earlier. You reap what you sow, and what you sow is your decision.

Every giant oak tree that spreads its branches tall and wide and provides shade begins with one little acorn. It only takes one impulsive act on your part to "grow" into something that will damage you and/or your reputation for the rest of your life. The law of the harvest: You will reap what you sow.

Should that young sailor have been surprised when he woke up next to the "wicked witch of the west"? With all of the information available today, should he really have been surprised when he wound up with sexually transmitted diseases? During that one moment of indiscretion he wound up with the clap and herpes. And because of his one night of "pleasure," he will be scarred for the rest of his life. He reaped what he sowed.

How Did I Wind Up Here?

In order to successfully reenter family life and society on completion of your prison sentence, you are going to have to make some changes. You are going to have to learn how to plant different "seeds" in your own personal life and in the lives of your family members.

Start by not allowing yourself to become a career criminal. Did you know that there are a bunch of crooks here in this prison? Do you realize that this place is filled with people who are looking out only for who they consider to be Number One, themselves?

As you associate with your fellow inmates and listen to what they say and are asking you to do, remember the law of the harvest. During your stay with this "prison family," if you only look and listen to the other inmates and allow them to plant their ideas into your head, soon they will grow and change your way of thinking into the "prison mentality." This is called "prisonization" or becoming "institutionalized."

Prisonization happens when you allow yourself to become part of the criminal subculture and begin to think of yourself as a criminal. The problem with this is that if you begin to think of yourself as a criminal, you will become one. What you think of yourself is what you will become. It is important that you focus on what you plan to do with your family and with your life when you get out. It is also important for you to remember that you can admit that you are a convicted criminal without fear because you now know that this says something about your past and nothing about your future. You must decide what you are going to be in the future. Only you can answer this question: "Are you a criminal, or an ex-criminal?"

How to successfully end your sentence

People who are able to successfully reenter family life and society after the completion of a prison sentence have two traits: settled living and close family ties. Settled living can start right now, right here in this prison. This starts when you make—and keep—a commitment to make your part of the world a better place, simply because you are there, no matter where you are or what circumstances you find yourself in. You can start living this way by doing things to make this prison a better place to live simply because you are here. Find the groups that you can get involved with here in the prison that do good things and become part of them.

Settled living includes ethical living. This means living in such a way that you never have to look over your shoulder wondering who is watching what you are doing. This means living in such a way that you never have to worry about a shakedown or a sudden inspection or when the correctional officer tells you to "fill the cup."

Settled living means that you have decided to become someone who is dependable and trustworthy. Settled living means living in such a way that you can be trusted to do the tasks that you are assigned to do. And since this has become your goal, you develop ways to make this happen.

Settled living means controlling your drinking and drug habits. Alcohol and drugs affect your ability to distinguish the difference between right and wrong. Think about it: How many of your fellow inmates used alcohol or drugs to give them the "courage" to do their crime? Did you? It was false courage. You have a chance to dry out while you are here. Take advantage of it. Learn how to live without alcohol or drugs, if for no other reason than when your sentence is up you will be able to stay out of prison.

Part of the settled living lifestyle means learning how to have healthy and close family ties. This means that your life will revolve around your decision to live in such a way that your family can trust you. This means that you will always consider their feelings and needs in everything that you do. This means that you will always treat them like you would like to be treated. This also means living the rest of your life learning how to communicate with your family so that everyone can share their true feelings with each other.

A very important aspect of settled living means developing problem-solving skills that will enable you to deal with life's challenges. People with close family ties have learned proper problem-solving skills so that the normal—or not so normal—stresses of life do not wreck their lives.

Before you can have any hope of repairing the damage that you have done to your family relationship and to create or maintain close family ties you are going to have to learn (1) how to love, (2) how to build your own and your family's self-esteem, and (3) how to give your children a better example to copy than you have in the past.

The most important thing that you can do to enable you to successfully reenter family life and society after the completion of your prison sentence is to keep your family intact while you are here. Believe it or not, family relationships do not have to die simply because you are in prison. In fact, you can actually make your relationship with your family better while you are here. It will take some hard work on your part. It will require you to settle some debts that you have with them. It will require you to make some hard changes and to teach your family a new way of doing things.

How Did I Wind Up Here?

The reward for that hard work will come when you leave this place. By doing the hard work required to patch up your family relationship, you will give yourself the ability to leave this place and have a better chance of ending your criminal career.

Where do I start?

Sit down and write a letter to your wife, girlfriend, or mother and tell her what you learned while reading this chapter. In this letter, tell her the specific facts about your crime. Do not include the details of how you committed the crime; instead talk about what you now realize is *the reason why* you committed your crime and what you earned when you committed your crime. Tell her about the people who influenced you to commit your crime and how you were able to convince yourself that it was alright to do it.

You may not want to mail the letter, and then again you might. The purpose of this assignment is to teach you how to share your true feelings. As you write this letter, think about the things that the parole board will be looking for when you talk to them.

This letter may be one of the hardest things that you have ever done, but it may start the change that you have been looking for in your family relationship. What do you have to lose?

Here is an example of how you might write this letter if you were in prison for breaking into a house:

My dearest wife,

This is a very hard letter to write, but it is something that I have needed to write for a long, long time. I have started reading a book called As Free As An Eagle: The Inmate's Family Survival Guide, *and it made me realize some things about myself that I have never realized before.*

Until today, I never realized that at the moment I decided to break into that house that I was asking to be sent to prison. I never realized that as I went through that window that I created a debt to society for the harm that I did and earned my right to live here in this prison.

What I realize now is that all I cared about was what I needed— something that I could sell so that I could buy some drugs to take care of my needs—and I didn't care about the harm I did to you or my victim.

Chapter 1

I'm the one that decided to do it, and I am responsible for my own actions. But instead of doing what I knew was right, I decided to be like other family members who drank too much and followed the example of friends who thought it was cool to steal. Was I ever wrong. They never told me that you reap what you sow and that eventually it would catch up with me.

Dear, I'm trying to change, and I have a long way to go. I've signed up for the substance abuse program, and I found a church group here that I feel comfortable in, and I am going every week. I'm reading everything that I can get my hands on that might help me learn a new way of life.

Thank you for standing by me. I appreciate that so much. Thank you for your love. I hope that as I continue to grow you will begin to see a "new and improved" me.

Your loving husband,

Chapter 2
"Daddy, Why Did You Have To Go Away?"

O ne of the results of a 1989 research project conducted in an Alabama prison revealed that inmates, whether married or not, had an average of two children. In every prison, inmates ask how they should respond to their children when they ask, with tears in their eyes, "Daddy, why did you have to go away?"

This is a question that cannot be ignored. The answer you give them may affect whether they copy your actions, values, and behavior patterns or not. Remember that children want to be "just like daddy," and your answer can make a difference in the path they choose to follow when they reach adulthood.

Many centuries ago, a wise man named King Solomon said, "Train up

Chapter 2

a child in the way he should go: and when he is old, he will not depart from it" (Proverbs 22:6). The answer that you give your children to that question is part of the training.

Like it or not, we all are a product of the family that we grew up in. We tend to repeat the attitudes, values, and behavior patterns of our parents, grandparents, and even our great-grandparents whom we probably never even met. Unless you want your children to grow up just like you and make the same kinds of mistakes you have made, you need to teach them not to copy your mistakes.

The goal of this chapter is to (1) help you to be able to identify where you got the attitude that it was okay to do the crime that you did and (2) to show you how you can teach your children not to make the same mistakes that you have made. You may think you already know how to do this, and maybe you do. However, until you have learned to identify the actual mistakes that you made in the past and why you made them, you can't teach others how not to make those same mistakes.

Mayberry only exists on TV

Remember *The Andy Griffith Show*? The reruns of this show are still popular today. In this show, Andy Griffith played Andy Taylor, the loving, benevolent sheriff who always had the right answer and the ability to set things straight. He kept the town running so smoothly that he didn't even need to wear a gun. Wasn't it nice that regardless of how busy he was at his job he always had time to take his son, Opie, fishing?

Then there was Barney Fife, the bumbling deputy. He was so inept that he was only allowed one bullet, which he had to keep in his shirt pocket. Every time he put it in his gun he would almost shoot his foot off trying to put the gun in his holster. But that was okay because life in Mayberry was so quiet that he rarely needed to use his gun.

And of course there was dear Aunt Bea. She was so loving and caring and of course made the perfect home for Andy and Opie.

Then there was Mayberry itself. It was a small, quiet town where everyone had their place and everyone got along together peacefully; except, of course, for an occasional squabble down at the barber shop. People in Mayberry did not even have to lock their doors at night because everyone in town could be trusted. The town drunk even brought himself to jail when he had too much to drink and locked himself in for the night.

"Daddy, Why Did You Have To Go Away?"

In one particular episode, the town scrooge kept doing things on Christmas Eve that would ordinarily cause a man to be put in jail. Andy kept fussing at him and telling him to go on home. Finally, Andy realized that the scrooge was simply trying to find a place to be for Christmas so that he would not have to be alone.

Understanding Andy put the man in jail for the night. Then he called the jail's cook—Aunt Bea of course—and had her bring Christmas dinner to the jail where Andy, Opie, Aunt Bea, Barney, Andy's girlfriend Ellie, and the scrooge sat down and shared the meal. Pretending to have to leave to answer a call, Barney excused himself and returned dressed as Santa. He brought everyone, including the scrooge, presents. All of this was done just so the town scrooge would not have to feel alone on Christmas Eve.

Everyone in Mayberry had their own place and their own identity. Everyone trusted everyone else. They put up with the incompetent mechanic because he honestly tried to fix cars and never tried to cheat anyone. It was okay if the haircut did not look the greatest because the barber did the best that he could. Deputy Fife's antics were tolerated because he was "just being Barney."

Unfortunately, there are few places like Mayberry still in existence. There used to be a day when people did not worry about locking their cars or their homes—but those days are gone. People are fed up with crime. Politicians know that people are tired of living in fear. As a result, crime is now a central issue in almost every political race. You are probably fed up with the criminal activities in this place.

What does it do to us to live in a system that is filled with fear? Do you feel that the place where your wife and family live is safe, or do they have to live in fear? Do you feel that it is safe for your mother to drive by herself to this desolate place to visit you, or do you fear that something would happen to her if her car broke down during the trip?

Do you feel free from harm locked here in this prison? Even though there are correctional officers everywhere, many of you fear the wrath of fellow inmates. Fights break out frequently. Inmates are constantly getting hurt. Even with all of the problems here, the truth is that you are probably safer in here than you would be on the outside. The officers are not going to let things get but so far out of hand. And if this institution's officers can't handle the situation, reinforcements would be here quickly.

Yet even with all of this protection that completely surrounds you, you probably fear the actions of your fellow inmates. Stop for a moment and think about the various ways that you are different because of that fear. Not only are you different because of your fear of the actions of other inmates: Think about how much of your life here in this prison is controlled by the criminal activities that occur here.

Looking out for Number One

Each morning when you wake up you are again faced with the harsh reality of spending another day inside these four walls. And the longer you live here the more you realize that this prison could be a much nicer place to live if it were not for the criminal and selfish activities of the inmates who are living here now and that lived here long before you arrived.

You and every other inmate here earned his right to live here in this prison. In fact, the only people who are allowed to live here are those who have been convicted of a crime. You have been given a specific amount of time that you must spend here to pay the debt you created for the harm that you did to society through the commission of your crime. And you are going to be required to stay here until you have paid that debt or until a parole forgives you of part of that debt and you are released early. It is a harsh reality, but life here is as simple as that.

Another harsh reality about living in prison is the realization that this place is filled with people who look out only for themselves. This place is filled with people who have declared that they are Number One and can do anything that they want; say anything that they want, anytime that they want, anywhere that they want; and there is nothing that anyone can do about it, PERIOD!

People who look out only for Number One repeatedly show that they do not care about the feelings of others. Ivan Boszormenyi-Nagy, a noted family therapist, has discovered that people who are looking out only for Number One constantly try to make it seem like others are responsible for their actions. Listen to your fellow inmates and you will see what he is talking about. How many inmates are constantly making statements such as, "The guy had it coming to him" or "He owed me"? Others say, "The police [or society or whoever] gave me a bum rap, and when I get out I am going to make them pay for what they did to me."

As you continue to listen you will realize that these inmates honestly feel that since they got such a bum rap growing up; or that they got such a bum rap from the court; or that they got such a bum rap for whatever reason; that this gave them the right to do anything that they wanted; say anything

"Daddy, Why Did You Have To Go Away?"

that they wanted, anytime that they wanted, anywhere that they wanted; and then declared that there was nothing that anyone could do about it, PERIOD!

In describing "their cases," these inmates will try to figure out some way to convince you that they were entitled to do their crimes. As you listen, you will also realize that they also feel that if someone else got hurt while they were getting what they wanted, well that was just too bad. And besides that, since, for whatever reason, the victims had it coming to them, that makes these inmates innocent of the charges that put them in prison.

Listen carefully to how your fellow inmates talk about their crimes and watch their actions. Look at the attitudes that are being displayed. And while you are looking, ask yourself, "What attitude am I displaying, and what will others see in me when I talk about my crime?"

As you watch and listen, see if you don't start hearing the words, "I looked out for Number One" in almost everything they say. You will begin to hear yourself and your fellow inmates say things like, "I was more powerful than them; and besides, they had it coming; so I used my power and got what I wanted."

Here are some common excuses for criminal activity that illustrate this. One inmate may say, "I don't feel the least bit guilty about killing that man, he had it coming to him." A convicted thief says, "I don't feel the least bit guilty about robbing that business. That family got all of that money by sticking it to us poor folks, and they deserve to know what it feels like to have it taken from them." A variation of this same story is, "I was poor when I was growing up and we never had anything, so I deserved what I took to make up for the misery of being poor."

There's another variation of basically the same story that goes, "I didn't have a daddy [or mother, or both] when I was growing up, so I didn't have anyone to teach me to be productive, and stealing was the only way I knew to get what I needed. It's their fault because I was never taught any better."

Another inmate may say, "I don't feel the least bit guilty about raping that girl. I grabbed her as she was coming out of that bar. After all, everybody knows that women at bars are a bunch of sluts and on the make; you can't rape a 'bar hog.'" How about this version: "That girl walked by and wiggled her butt at me. She asked for it, so I gave it to her."

Did you notice some common threads running through each of these cases? Regardless of what their crime was, each of the inmates refused to admit that they did their crime to fulfill their own selfish needs. Instead, each inmate blamed his actions on society, or on his past, or even the victim

29

and then figured out a way to make it appear that the victims got what they deserved.

Each of these excuses are just that, excuses. Each of these statements try to make it look like the victim was to blame for the crime that was committed against them. If this is true and the victim is to blame, that means that the victim earned what they got. If you accept this line of reasoning, this also means that since the victim deserved what they got, the criminal does not need to feel guilty and is in fact being persecuted by being put in prison.

That's blowing smoke. The truth is that in each of these cases the offender was simply looking out for his own selfish needs. While looking out for Number One he abused his power and took something that he wanted. In each case, and in every other crime, the criminal saw something that he had no right to have, decided that society's laws did not apply to him, and abused his power and took it.

The killer declared that the victim owed him so much, for whatever reason, that he had to pay with his life, and killing the victim took care of his need to "settle the score." The killer declared that he had the power to overrule God and determined that it was time for this person to die. Actually, killing his victim was an abuse of power. The killer was looking out for Number One and did not care about his victim. The thief declared that because of the owner's—or someone else's—past actions the victim owed a debt to society and that the thief had the power to settle it. Actually, the thief was looking out for Number One and did not care about his victim. He saw something that he liked and declared that he had the power and authority to take it. And so he did.

The sex offender decided that because of the way his victim dressed or because "all bar hogs are nymphomaniacs," she owed him some sex and that he had the right to take it. In reality, not only this rapist but all sex offenders are looking out for their own personal needs at the time of the offense and do not care that their victims will be emotionally scarred for the rest of their lives. In committing the sexual offense, no consideration was given to the fact that when he forced his victim to submit to his own selfish needs he may have destroyed his victim's ability to give themselves sexually to the one they love or that the victim will probably have trouble trusting others for the rest of his or her life. All that was important to the sex offender at the time of each offense was that he needed or simply wanted some sex. Then he saw someone that could provide him with the sex that he wanted.

"Daddy, Why Did You Have To Go Away?"

He decided that he had the power to require the man, woman, or child to give it to him, so he abused his power and took it.

The only way that you can become involved in criminal activity is to abuse your power and violate the trust that society gives to you. Regardless of what the crime is, becoming involved in criminal activity takes three steps:

- seeing something that you want and don't have any right to have
- declaring that you have the power and authority to take it regardless of what society's rules say
- abusing your power and taking it without caring about the harm that your crime does to your victim or to society

In satisfying your own selfish needs you violated the trust that says people have the right for themselves, their family, and their property to be free from harm.

At the moment that you committed your crime you violated the trust that is the very foundation of the United States Constitution. Isn't it strange that people who violate the rights of others by committing criminal acts scream during their arrest and trial and while incarcerated about *their* rights being violated?

Think about the assignment in the last chapter. As you read what you wrote about your crime and you think about how you talk to others, what attitudes do you display? Are you like "Minority Sam" who says he did his crime because he was a member of a particular minority group? Are you like "Unfortunate Orphan Andy" who blames his behavior on the fact that he grew up with one or both of his parents missing? Are you like "Ira Wealthy" who blames his irresponsibility and his turning to drugs and/or crime to relieve his boredom on his family's wealth? Are you like "Ghetto Charlie" who says that he can't help the way that he is because he grew up in the tough part of town? And let's not forget "Forgotten John" whose parents were so busy that they forgot about his needs, and because of this he cannot help but do those awful things.

Or did you admit the truth in your letter? Did you admit that you did your crime because you chose to do it? Did you admit that you were looking out for Number One at the time you did it and that at the time you did it you did not care about what your crime did to your victim? Did you admit that you are now receiving what you earned at the moment that you did your crime?

Until you realize the mistakes you have made in the past, you will continue making those same mistakes. Once you can admit to yourself, and others, the mistakes you have made in the past, you will be less likely to make that same mistake again.

One big unhappy family

Even though you and all of the other inmates that are here earned your right to be here, living here is nothing like you imagined. It didn't take you long to discover that this place is like one big unhappy family. Just like all families, this family has its leaders. They are the ones with the seniority here who received their power long before you arrived. These self-proclaimed leaders use their self-proclaimed power to "rule" the family.

Then there are the inmates who have a special relationship to these self-proclaimed leaders. If they were female, and on the outside, they would be either the wives or the mistresses of the "family leaders." Notice that this group uses its special relationship with the self-proclaimed leaders to push others around. Notice also that this group will overrule and take over if given the chance.

The others could be compared to the children of the family. Unfortunately, most of these "children" have learned to look out only for Number One. Most inmates in the prison family consistently put their own needs above the needs of others, and because of this will tend to stay in conflict with everyone around them.

The root cause of all interpersonal conflict is the power struggle between two or more people to determine who is going to be the boss. The "boss" is the person who has the power to make things happen. The "boss" is the person who has the authority to decide who is going to do what and when it is going to be done. The "boss" is the person who makes the final decision.

Just as in all families, there are people within this prison who have the actual, and legitimate, power to make decisions. Your responsibility is to abide by those decisions. In this case, the decision has already been made as to who is actually the boss. But notice the number of inmates that constantly challenge the authority of those actually in power. The root cause of all interpersonal conflict is the power struggle between two or more people to determine who is going to be the boss; in this example, the inmate or the prison officials.

There are proper ways to appeal rules. But if you are looking out only for Number One and only for your own interests, which includes proving that you have the power to be the boss, you can't give in. This means that the fight must continue between the two until one overpowers the other and it is determined who is going to be the boss. One of the things that remains the same in every prison is the number of fights between the self-proclaimed leaders as each tries to overpower the other and take charge of the "family."

Watch their actions. Deciding which news program to watch becomes a major battle. It doesn't really matter which channel does the better job, the real battle is over who is going to be the boss and decide which channel to watch. Watch a man come up to a common table and tell another inmate to get up because "That's my seat." Watch two inmates meet in the hall and neither move over so the other can pass. What they are really saying is, "I'm the boss; you do what I say," then "No, you're not; I'm not going to be seen as a weakling and submit to you."

And on and on it goes. If only they could realize that real strength comes when you don't have to resort to force to convince people to follow you. This comes when people display an attitude that shows concern for the other's needs.

Prisonization and its effects on inmates

Just as it is with all families, the way you are treated and what you will become after you leave here will be determined, in part, by the behaviors and the legacy left by inmates who were part of this prison family years before you ever arrived. Because of the selfish, criminal, and improper actions of previous inmates across the years, there is a lack of trust that permeates this prison.

For example, you probably can't be trusted to eat with anything but a spoon because previous inmates have used knives and forks as weapons. If they do trust you with a knife and fork someone will be watching to see that you return them. You can't be trusted to have a plastic toilet seat because people in the past have used them as weapons. You can't even be trusted to sit on the toilet and have a bowel movement without being watched closely because body cavities are a popular way to transport drugs through the prison.

This prison must hire an officer simply to open your incoming mail. This is not because they want to read your letters, but because previous inmates have used the mail to send and receive drugs and other contraband.

Chapter 2

Previous inmates have proven themselves to be untrustworthy, and now you must suffer the consequences. You could probably name many more ways that a lack of trust permeates this place.

There seems to be an unwritten rule throughout all prisons that says inmates must be loyal to each other. This means that you must maintain a code of silence about the criminal activities that go on in this place. This also means that you must lie, if necessary, to protect the other inmates when they have violated the rules.

If you want to be a part of the prison family, you are also required to learn the prison language and accept the role assigned to you by the self-proclaimed prison family leaders. After all, if you want the self-proclaimed leader's protection you must pay his price for it. And his price is loyalty, no matter what it costs you. And since the self-proclaimed leaders keep the books, you will always be in debt to them, and you will always owe them favors. Unfortunately, as you focus so hard on doing what they require and try to mold your life to conform to their expectations, you will begin to act just like them because you want to be part of the family.

Accepting the language, relationships, roles, and career goals of the prison family is called prisonization. When this happens you start to identify yourself as a criminal. You will forget that being a convicted criminal says something about your past and nothing about your future. You start accepting the group's ideas that you are the victim of society's ills.

As you listen to the others talk, you will begin to feel that you were actually entitled to commit your crime because of the harm that members of society had done to you. You will start accepting the idea that by doing your crime you were attempting to balance the books and will blame others for what you did. You will actually start believing that it was society's fault that you did your crime. Since you have been convinced that it was society's fault or that someone else was to blame you will start feeling that your rights have been violated and you are being unfairly punished.

A part of becoming prisonized is becoming convinced that you were not at fault for your crime and feeling that there is no need for you to change. The longer you stay here and the longer you listen to fellow inmates talk about how unfair their sentence is compared to what someone else got and how messed up everyone else is but them, the more convinced you will become that there is no reason for you to change anything about yourself.

There is an easy way for you to tell when this has happened. It's when you hear yourself say, "I know the mistakes I have made, just let me out and everything will be okay; you'll see." You say that, but then can't identify a single mistake that you have made or any specific plans of how you will do things differently in the future.

You have become prisonized when you are willing to play the role of the punk, sissy, or queen or the role of the "man" simply because that is what the group is telling you that you must do to be accepted. Once you have reached that point, you have lost part of your own identity. Once you have yielded your own sexual identity to the group's desires, allowed the group to convince you to choose a sexual preference based on what the system wants and not on your own personal sexual preference, you have become prisonized.

You have become prisonized when you refuse to tell the prison officials who assaulted a fellow inmate simply because the perpetrator of the assault demands that you remain loyal to him and not squeal. You have become prisonized when you feel that informing on a fellow inmate would be a violation of the prison family's trust and feel that to violate the trust of the other inmates is the worst thing that you can do. You have become prisonized when you have decided that it is more important to be loyal to your fellow inmates than to be labeled a snitch.

The truth is that the self-proclaimed leaders who require such improper loyalty and trust are simply looking out for Number One. These people are making sure that you will help *them* do anything that they want, to anyone that they want, anytime that they want, and then require you to make sure that there is nothing anyone else can do about what they have done, PERIOD!

When this happens, you have allowed someone else within this prison to require you to help them overpower the prison system itself to help him get what he wants regardless of how much trouble it causes you.

When you allow yourself to become prisonized you might as well forget any ideas that you have about leaving this place and becoming a part of society again. Yes, your sentence will end as scheduled. But you will not have changed. You will walk out of the front door of this prison still looking out for Number One. You will think like a criminal because you will in fact have become one, and you will likely be one who returns to prison within one year after his release.

Think about this: What if the "rules" of the prison family were like the rules of a healthy family? In a healthy family, things that harm others are not tolerated. If the prison were a healthy system, the inmates would help the authorities enforce the rules by forming a "neighborhood watch" within the prison. If this happened, how long would it be before much of the illegal activity would cease? If there were no illegal activities in this prison it would be a much nicer place to live in.

How to prevent prisonization from happening to you

There is a way to keep prisonization from happening to you, and it will require some hard work on your part. Inmates who keep their families alive and close while they are incarcerated usually stay out once they are released. In fact, focusing your thoughts and dreams on becoming a part of your family back home instead of how to become part of the "prison family" is one of the best ways to prevent prisonization.

Having a healthy family life while you are here is extremely important to your future success when you get out. E. L. Homer reports that research studies in the last 50 years have proven repeatedly the relationship between strength of family ties and parole success. In a 1979 study, Homer discovered that only 2 percent of inmates with three or more regular visitors while incarcerated had to be sent back to prison while on parole.

What this means is that you need to keep your focus on becoming part of a family again. You need to start dreaming of ways that you can be part of family life and society again. You need to change your focus from yourself to others. You need to stop thinking about how many of your "rights" were violated and begin thinking about the changes you need to make before your release date that will enable you to get out and stay out.

Unless you enjoy prison life and want to keep bouncing in and out for the rest of your life, you have to keep your family alive while you are here. You must learn how to help your family over the trauma of your crime and imprisonment. Try the suggestions that you will find throughout this book and see if they work for you as well as they have for others.

If you can keep your family relationships alive and healthy while you are here, then you will have a family to welcome you home. Then you will have someone who you can settle down with, someone you can become part of your community with, and someone who will help to keep you from ever returning to prison again.

Imagine two inmates walking out of the front gate, each beginning their new life of freedom. One inmate is all alone. There is no one to greet him. He has all of his belongings in his sack and the money for a bus ticket. He looks lost. Unless he has someplace to call home, his chances of staying out are slim.

Contrast this with the inmate walking out the gate the following week. His father and brother have driven halfway across the state and wait patiently for him to be released. They have brought him some new clothes to wear, including new underwear, so that he won't have to wear prison-issued clothes home. His chances are good because he has a loving family that is willing to help him get a fresh start.

Every inmate dreams that the time will come when they can get this time of their lives behind them and successfully reenter family life and society. However, there is something in your past that prevents this from happening.

Have you ever stopped to realize the damage that your criminal conviction has done to your family relationship? Do you also realize that since your old way of doing things has not worked that something has to change before your family relationship can improve? That something is YOU!

To accomplish this task, you will need to change the way you think about yourself and your family. PLUS, you need to learn an entirely new way of doing things. Are you willing to do this? Unless you want to bounce in and out of prison for the rest of your life, you *must!*

How families work

This chapter has examined two types of families. The first was Sheriff Taylor's family. His healthy home situation helped to create a healthy community. Then there was the unhealthy prison family.

These families, as well as your family at home, have many things in common. As you begin to understand how families operate, you will also be able to understand why your family is the way it is and the things that you can do to make your family better.

Changes must be made by the rules, or they won't work. Every group, whether it be a family, prison, or work, has rules that apply throughout the group. Drawing from the McMaster Model of Family Functioning, the following are four rules that apply to all families:

Rule Number 1: The way each person acts affects all the other members of the family. The actions, good or bad, of any one person in a family have a powerful effect on the entire family.

Chapter 2

This rule is the most powerful of the rules. It goes back to the law of the harvest: you will reap what you sow. One person can change an entire system, either by making it better or by making it worse. This rule means that any time that you change, the rest of the family will also change. If you change for the worse, your family relationship will worsen. On the other hand, positive changes will have a positive effect on the family relationship. For example, if a fellow inmate grabbed a CO and held a handmade knife to his neck, think about how his actions would have an immediate effect on the entire prison family. All prison activities would be immediately cancelled because of his improper actions, and everyone would be quickly locked into their cells or dorms. Prison officials would become nervous and wonder how far the violence would spread. This is an example of how one person's improper actions hurt the entire family.

All it takes to end a marriage is for one partner to call it quits, say good-bye, and leave. When this happens the other partner might be able to delay the divorce, but can't stop it from happening. That one person has changed the entire family. Think about how your criminal actions affected your entire family. Not only did they lose you, but your crime caused your children to be teased and your wife to lose some friends. Ask your children what it's like when other children taunt them with "Your daddy is a jailbird, your daddy is a jailbird." Your wife may find it harder to find a good job because she's "the criminal's wife." Ask her what it's like to be known as the rapist's wife, or the thief's wife, or the killer's wife. You might not like her answer.

Earlier the question was asked, "What would it be like if the 'prison family' rules said that the inmates would help the authorities enforce the prison's rules?" This would mean that illegal drugs or stealing from another inmate would not be tolerated. Inmates would be willing to report crimes and testify if necessary to ensure that the rules were enforced. Needless to say, with things like they are now in this prison, any inmate who started to live up to that rule would get a lot of grief from other inmates who still wanted to live by their own rules. But if one brave inmate kept the commitment, others would find it easier to follow the new rule. Soon it would spread, and life in this prison would become much better.

Using this rule in your own family means that if your family can begin to see that you are changing and taking their needs into consideration, they will respond to the new you. This means using the material you will find in this book and others like it to discover what areas of your life need improvement. This means taking every rehabilitation course that this prison

"Daddy, Why Did You Have To Go Away?"

offers. This means finding a worship group that will help you to grow spiritually. This also means taking care of your body so you will be healthy.

At first, your family will be suspicious and wonder if these changes are real. After all, in the past, when you were nice to them wasn't it frequently because you wanted something in return? They are going to find it hard to believe that you are actually becoming a nicer person. They may even resist your changes because, by nature, people don't like change.

The law of the harvest promises that sowing seeds of trust will grow trustworthy relationships. It takes time for a crop to grow. You need to allow at least as much time as it took to damage the relationship. As you allow yourself to become a more loving and kinder person who responds to their needs instead of focusing on your own needs, you will start to see your family relationships improve.

In other words, family relationships do not start improving until someone leads the way. That someone can be you, if you are willing to be strong enough to be loving and kind even when others are not. Families respond to men who can put the family's needs above their own.

People who can remain nice to others regardless of their circumstances can turn a hell into a pleasant place to live. Ugly, bitter, and nasty people can turn heaven itself into a living hell.

Rule Number 2: The way the family functions affects each member of the family. You can see this rule in operation right here in this prison. Each dorm and each work station are their own "families." Some of the dorms and some of the work places are nicer than others. That's not because the beds are nicer or the work better, it's because the people in those groups are nicer to each other.

Notice what happens when a bitter, quarrelsome, hateful person is assigned to a work assignment or dorm where everyone seems to get along. Soon, either his attitude will begin to improve, or he will begin to feel so out of place that he will ask for a transfer, or the group will do the asking for him. The group knows that if they tolerate his kind of behavior that it will rub off on them, and the entire group will become bitter, quarrelsome, and hateful, just like him.

On the other hand, notice what happens to a man with a happy, friendly personality when he arrives in a dorm of unhappy, grumbling inmates. Soon you will hear him start complaining and grumbling. He is beginning to adopt the ways of the entire "family." It's his way of saying, "I want to be part of your family, and I'm willing to change my ways of doing things to show you that I am part of the group."

Think about your family back home. Which kind are they? Are they basically loving and kind people who will tell its members, "I love you too much to allow you to continue to act that way" when someone does improper things, or do the improper actions of the group have a negative effect on each member? How that family functions will be continued for generations, unless someone steps in and changes it.

Rule Number 3: Families have rules that govern how people are to act within the family. Some of these rules are obvious. Don't run out in the street without looking. Don't eat from the dog's dish, and so forth. These rules aren't written down but are followed just the same. How much profanity is allowed before someone says something about it? Is dad allowed to come home drunk, but nobody else? Are the boys allowed to stay out late on dates, but not the girls? How much clothing is required as you walk around the house? How much affection is given to each member of the family?

There are some that apply at your house, to this prison, and all families. When the one in authority tells you something to do, is it done or is there automatic backtalk and rebellion? Who decides what television channel will be watched? What are the rules about picking up your stuff off the floor? Who empties the trash? Can you think of others?

Rule Number 4: The way children are treated by their parents is usually the way the children will treat their children. This is another rule that applies to both prisons and at home. It is actually a continuation of Rule Number Two. Within all families, patterns are established. Attitudes, values, and behavior patterns become blended. As new people become part of the group they are expected to adopt the standards of the family.

This means that the way new inmates are treated is usually the same way inmates were treated here at this prison last year, and the year before, and the year before that. This also means that, although each dorm is different, the way that particular dorm treats people stays about the same year after year.

Because of the loyalty family members feel for each other, children tend to copy attitudes, actions, and behavior patterns, repeating them when they are grown. Their children do the same, and their children, and in turn, their children. This loyalty to the family's traditional way of doing things forms invisible chains that link and bind people to their past. This invisible chain shows itself when people repeat behavior patterns of generations past; behavior of people who they have never even met.

Underlying each of these rules is a basic premise that each member in the family will be loyal to each other and that each member will be able to trust the others. Families and groups get into trouble when their members continue to demand loyalty when their actions prove that they cannot be trusted.

Your criminal record proves that somewhere in your past you picked up a tendency to look out for Number One and could not be trusted to consider the needs of others when you make your decisions about what to do. The fact that you committed your crime or crimes proves that you, at times, think of yourself as a person who can do anything you want; say anything you want anytime that you want, to anyone that you want; and there is nothing anyone can do about it, PERIOD!

You did not wake up one morning and decide, "Today, I am going to become a criminal." Somewhere in your past you learned to put your own feelings above the feelings of others. You were taught to abuse your power and break the trust of respectability. You must have learned your lesson very well, because here you are. You probably learned how to abuse your power from your family or from others that were part of your "system" while you were growing up.

As the twig is bent, so grows the tree

Back in 1939, L. B. Hohman wrote a book titled *As The Twig Is Bent*. From that title has come this saying: "As the twig is bent, so grows the tree." It has some real applications as you look at your life.

Over the years, you have seen trees growing in some very interesting ways. Regardless of the type of tree, it starts as a young sapling, just a little twig growing out of the ground. Little by little it grows, until it finally becomes a fully mature tree.

Have you ever noticed that the way that trees grow is affected by their surroundings? The next time that you see a picture of trees along the oceanfront, notice that the limbs have grown twisted and turned because of the many storms along the coast. Notice also that the trees seem to have a mind of their own and grow in such a way that they lean toward the ocean. It's almost as if the tree knows that if it wants to survive, it must lean *against* the prevailing wind.

Chapter 2

Have you ever noticed the difference between the trees on a mountain and the ones in the middle of a pasture? A single tree in the middle of a pasture grows tall and wide. That's because there's nothing in its way to stop it, and its branches are free to grow where they want. But there is a problem if you are a big, fat, tree standing all alone in the middle of the pasture. They tend to get blown over when the storms come through. They have spread out so far that a sudden wind from a powerful thunderstorm can catch the leaves like the sail on a ship and pull it out of the ground.

The trees on a mountain are different. You won't find many branches along the bottom because there is no room for them to stretch out. Instead, they grow tall and straight. The wind can't pull them out of the ground because the individual trees have interlocked their branches and their roots. The wind can blow with all of its might, but they will still be standing long after the storm has lost its power. These trees support each other and become stronger than the storm.

Notice too that the way that an individual tree grows depends on the influence of the older trees that surround it. As a younger tree grows under the limb of an older tree, it will simply bend itself around that limb and continue its reach toward the sky. In fact, when a tree is very young, you can bend that young sapling at an angle and then tie it so that it will stay at that angle. That tree will continue to grow, but not at the angle you tied it. The tip of the tree will turn and start growing toward the sky again. If, after a period of time, you cut the rope and release the tree from its bondage, you would discover that the bend you put in the tree when it was young will remain a part of that tree for the rest of its life.

Every tree in the world is unique. If you could plant one million identical maple saplings across the United States and then examine them fifty years later, each one of them would be different. Each one of them would still be a maple tree. Some would have died and been reduced to a rotten stump. Some would be straight and tall, because they grew up with the support of other trees, and they have hooked their roots and their limbs together to keep the wind from blowing them over. Others would be short and fat, or twisted and ugly, because of the way they have been shaped by their environment.

Like the tree, your family and the others that surrounded you as you were growing up helped to mold you into the person that you are today. Your parents, or whoever reared you, taught you what to think about yourself, and you listened to them and you learned your lessons. You were taught how to act by watching how others acted.

You were taught how to love by watching others love. You were taught what it meant to be a part of the human race, and you watched how they treated others. You were taught how to act when the "storms of life" came along. You learned your lessons well. Even today, you can identify ways that you act "just like (mom, dad, uncle so-and-so, or whoever)."

But you are different from a tree; you can choose to act differently than the way you were taught. Your parents, family, or friends did not *make* you what you are today. The person you are today is what you chose to be. If you are like other members of your family, it is because you chose to copy their attitudes, actions, and behavior patterns. You have become like you are today because you accepted their ways and made them part of your life.

Your parents were taught by your grandparents. But your parents then chose which attitudes, actions, and behavior patterns they would use in their lives. From these early foundations, your parents chose the things they would teach you that you must do in order for you to be accepted as part of the family. This has been going on for generations and links you to people that you have never even met.

This chain continues. You were taught certain things as a child. From the things that you were taught as a child, you will choose what you will teach your children. Then from these attitudes, each individual child decides what their own actions and behavior patterns are going to be. The attitude can be the same, but it can display itself in many different ways.

Each generation gives the next generation a legacy, or inheritance, of how things are supposed to be within the family and in their community. Unless you change and begin doing things differently, you will pass the same set of attitudes that you received while you were growing up along to your children, and they will grow up to be just like you.

Boszormenyi-Nagy showed repeatedly that this transmission of attitudes, actions, and behavior patterns from one generation to the next creates invisible chains of loyalty that bind you to your past and will bind your children to their past. That is unless someone steps in and breaks those chains.

What this means is that people who were beaten when they were children have a tendency to beat their children. Children who were molested as children have a tendency to molest their children. Paul H. Van Wyk, a clinical psychologist and sex researcher, has discovered that child molesters who were molested at the age of six are frequently attracted to six-year-olds. Those molested at the age of twelve are frequently attracted to twelve-year-olds.

Your invisible chains of loyalty that bind you to your past also mean that you probably have a marriage that is quite similar to the marriage that your parents had. You probably don't get along with your wife any better than your parents got along with each other. If your parents are divorced, you are more likely to be involved in a divorce, and your children are more likely to be involved in a divorce. This also means that your children may wind up with the same kind of relationship with their spouses as you have with yours. That is unless someone can find a way to break those invisible chains. Chains are strong and hard to break.

All parents have the responsibility to train their children when they are young. All parents have the responsibility to see to it that their children, like the trees on the side of the mountain, are surrounded by relationships that can be trusted so that they don't become uprooted when the storms of life strike. Children should be able to trust their parents not to twist their minds and bodies while they are young so they can grow up strong and straight.

You can't blame your parents for your actions

Before you can break the chains that bind you to your past, you must realize that even though your parents made every conceivable mistake in the world while rearing you, you cannot blame them for your actions.

At this point, you may be thinking that I just don't understand the circumstances at your home while you were growing up. "After all," you say, "my mom and/or dad _____." (Fill in the blank with the appropriate phrase.)

- was constantly drunk or abused drugs
- was physically, sexually, or mentally abusive
- gave me away, and I was reared by someone else
- continually told me that I was no good
- made me help them do illegal things
- never had time for me
- did things too terrible to mention
- did all of the above and more

Are you trying to convince yourself that because of the mistakes that

"Daddy, Why Did You Have To Go Away?"

your parents or the other people around you made while you were growing up, you can't help being the way that you are? HOGWASH! Using your parent's actions as an excuse for the way that you act will not work. In fact, people have been using that same excuse for centuries.

Approximately 2,600 years ago, Jeremiah reported that Israel had become an awful place to live. Crime was rampant. Family life had deteriorated. Divorce had reached epidemic proportions. Parents did not care about their children and in fact were routinely killing them. It seemed that everyone in the entire kingdom was involved in illicit sex.

The religious leaders of the day tried to warn the people of the consequences of their actions. The people responded that the reason that they were acting that way was because their fathers had eaten sour grapes. The people were claiming that their improper actions were the result of what their parents did in years past. Since their actions were their parent's fault, they were not responsible for their own actions or for how society had become.

"Not so," the people were told. "You can't blame your parents for what you have done. You alone are responsible for your own actions and for the damage that you have done to society."

Approximately fifty years later the grandchildren were acting in the same improper ways. When confronted by Ezekiel, they used the same excuse that their grandparents had used. Again they claimed, "The way I am acting is not my fault, my parents made me this way, and I can't act any other way. Besides, it's not my fault for the way this country has gotten."

Again the people were told, "You can't blame your parents for what you have done. You alone are responsible for your own actions and for the damage that you have done to society."

This is an example of how invisible chains of improper attitudes, values, and behavior patterns can be passed from the grandparents to the parents and then to the children. Each of these three generations acted in the same improper ways and then gave the same excuses for their own improper actions. Each of these generations also tried to claim that things their parents did caused them to act in criminal and immoral ways. Each of these generations also tried to claim that their parents were responsible for their own improper actions and for how messed up society was instead of themselves. Each of these generations found a reason to blame someone else for the harm that they had done to society.

The words that the leaders spoke to those ancient families are just as true today as they were 2,600 years ago. Although your parents had a huge influence on you, your parents, family, and others you grew up with are not responsible for your behavior; you are. Even though those you model yourself after may have been involved in immoral, unethical, or even illegal living, you are like them because you have chosen to adopt their unethical and immoral lifestyle, and because you chose to copy their values, attitudes, and behavior patterns, you are in prison.

You did not become a criminal because you had improper parents or because you came from a troubled family or had evil friends. Yes, you can still feel the influence they had on your life. They taught you their moral and ethical values. But you had to decide what you would do with their instruction, and just as it has been all throughout history: you and only you are responsible for your own actions, and you must reap what you have sown.

If you plant corn seeds in the ground, you will grow corn. If you plant flower seeds, you will get flowers. If you plant hatred and violence, your life will be full of hatred and violence, and your children will be full of hatred and violence.

On the other hand, if you plant seeds of trust and responsibility, you will reap trust and responsibility, and your children will learn trust and responsibility.

Here is a statement that you will find proven again and again: *History does not repeat itself, people repeat history.*

Look at the legacy you are leaving your children

As you look back at the wrong attitudes that you picked up from your parents and your grandparents, look at the legacy you are leaving to your children. Just as your parents showed you improper attitudes, your criminal actions showed your children improper attitudes.

Criminal behavior teaches children things such as: society's rules aren't important; society owes them a living; they are entitled to take what isn't theirs; it's okay to hurt others; it's okay to make money by selling drugs because you are entitled to it; it's okay to force someone to have sex with you; it's okay to neglect your family and your responsibilities; it's okay to cheat on your wife; etc., etc., etc.

Your actions are teaching your children that the most important thing in the world is to look out only for Number One and be a person who can

"Daddy, Why Did You Have To Go Away?"

do anything he wants, anytime he wants, anywhere he wants, to anyone he wants, and there is nothing anyone can do about it, period!

Regardless of what your crime is, your actions told your children that getting what you want is more important that obeying the rules of society. Your actions tell your children that it is okay to do things without thinking about the long-term consequences of those actions or of the harm it does to others.

Just as you were loyal to your parents and/or family by copying their improper attitudes and values, your children will be loyal to you. They will copy your improper attitudes and values and be just like you. And they, like you, will wind up in prison, or worse. Your children trust you not to steer them in the wrong direction. You have violated that trust by requiring them to be loyal to you when you should not have.

What you have done is proven to your children that if you are more powerful you can make people do things. If you are more powerful, you can make people have sex with you. You can make people give you their property. You can make people hold still while they are being beaten. You can make people come crawling to you for the drugs that they need, etc.

Even while you are sitting here in this prison you are giving your children the same legacy that you received from your parents, one that says, "I am a powerful person who has the power to do anything that I want; say anything that I want, anytime I want, anywhere I want, to whomever I want, including my family; and there is nothing anyone can do about it, period!"

Is that the legacy that you want to leave your children? Do you want them to grow up and abuse their children? Do you want them to grow up and be in trouble with the law? Wouldn't it be better if you taught them that if you abuse your power you also get the consequences that go with it? The things that you teach your children while they are young will stay with them their entire lives.

What are you teaching them? They saw you abuse your power. To them, the reward you received for your abuse of power is to be sent to a place that looks a lot like the summer camp that they may go to each year, or wish they could. It's clean. It has a place to do crafts. It has a basketball court and/or other recreational facilities. It has a nice-looking chow hall, maybe even nicer than the one at their school. So they think, "Why not do just like daddy did? Prison's not so bad."

You can help to change that legacy by telling your children the truth when they ask, "Daddy, why did you have to go away?" You need to admit to them the mistakes that you made and what those mistakes cost you. Tell them:

1. "I am here because I accepted the wrong attitudes from my parents, family, or friends when I was growing up."
2. "I made some wrong decisions," and tell them the specific wrong decisions that you made. Tell them, "I am responsible for those decisions."
3. "I am here because I am reaping what I sowed."

Your children need to hear you say that your prison sentence is the wage that you earned when you committed your crime and that if they follow in your footsteps, they will earn the same wage that you did by walking the path that you walked.

Your children have learned a lot from you and have probably already adopted many of your attitudes. Instead of fussing at them when they act in certain ways, admit that they are copying one of your improper attiudes. Show them how hard you are working to correct those attitudes. Tell them about how you got hurt while you were growing up because you used your improper attitudes, values, or behavior patterns. Then when you see them copying those same behaviors, instead of fussing at them, gently tell them what happened to you and how it affected your life when you did it. Don't be afraid to share any part of your life with your children if it will help them not to make the mistakes that you made.

A letter to your child(ren)

Sit down and write a letter to your children. If you don't have any now, write a letter to the children that you will have when you get out of here. In this letter, answer the question, "Daddy, why did you have to go away?"

In this letter, you need to identify the specific wrong attitudes that you adopted from your parents, family, or friends that influenced you while you were growing up and how these improper attitudes affected your decision making. Tell them about the specific mistakes that you made and what the mistakes cost you. Identify the ways that you have treated them in the same way that your family treated you.

You may not want to mail this letter, and then again you might. The purpose of this assignment is to teach you how to share your true feelings.

"Daddy, Why Did You Have To Go Away?"

As you write, remember that this letter might start your children thinking and may help prevent them from becoming involved in criminal activity. It may help them from becoming "just like daddy."

Inmates say that writing this letter is the hardest part of the book. They also say that it gives the highest returns. It may start a big improvement in the relationship you have with your children. What do you have to lose?

Here is an example of how you might write this letter if you were in prison for breaking into a house to get enough money to buy drugs:

Dear Son,

This is a very hard letter for me to write to you, but it is time for me to tell you the truth about why I am here. I know that my being in prison is hard for you. It's hard growing up without a daddy there to help you. And I realize that my being in prison has caused you some hard times, especially at school. Nobody likes to be teased, and I know that it hurts when they say ugly things about your dad.

Son, as you know, I got hooked on drugs. I thought that I needed them so badly that I was willing to steal to get the money to pay for them. I thought that since I needed the drugs so badly, this made it okay for me to break into that house and take their things. "After all," I thought, "they are rich, and their insurance company will pay them back." I was so wrong. What I actually did was earn a prison sentence the minute that I broke their window. It's not the judge's fault, he just gave me what I earned.

Son, what I worry about most is how much you are like me in so many ways. I know that it seems like your mom and I pick on you a lot about some of your ways. I wish now that I had told you why instead of just fussing at you. Son, the reason that I am so hard on you about certain things is because I did some of those same types of things when I was your age, and I don't want you to get hurt and have to face the same consequences.

You didn't know my daddy that much, and he was pretty nice to you before he died. But I used to watch my daddy come home late from work every Friday night. As usual, he had spent most of his pay down at the local bar, and he'd be drunk. My mother used to fuss at him, but he would tell her "Shut up" and slap her around until she did. He would scream at her that he had been out working all week and he deserved to go out and drink a "couple of beers" before he came home. Then he would pass out on the couch and spend the night there. I used to think that it was neat how he stood up to my mother like that, and I wanted to be tough, just like my dad.

I used to watch my mother wipe the tears, then wait until he was asleep and slip his wallet out of his pocket and take a few dollars out, hoping that it wouldn't be missed. She would hide this money away and use it later if we ran out of milk or if she needed something. We would tease her about it, and she would get some out and take us down to the ice cream parlor to bribe us into promising not to tell "our little secret" about where the money came from. Every so often, when the money got really tight, mom would get us kids to help her stretch the food budget by having a contest to see who could help her sneak the most food out of the store without being caught. I used to think that was exciting.

I kept promising myself that I wasn't ever going to get drunk like my daddy did, and I didn't want to ever make my wife sneak around and steal money from me or steal groceries just so she could have the things she wanted and needed. And I kept that promise, or so I thought.

Instead of drinking, I began to use drugs. At first I experimented with marijuana, then harder drugs. Soon they became more expensive than I realized. I didn't realize that I was copying my dad's attitude, but I was. When I started stealing to get the money to pay for the drugs, I convinced myself that it was okay because I thought I was just keeping my promise not to ever make my wife steal to have what she needed. What I realize now is that I copied my mom's attitude that it was okay to steal if the reason was good enough and used it to justify my own actions.

I was so wrong. Yes, I watched my dad get drunk, become abusive, and neglect his wife and children. I helped my mother steal. But there comes a time when a man has to be responsible for his own actions. I knew that having the drugs that I used was illegal, and I knew that stealing was wrong. But I did it anyway. What I was doing was saying to the whole world, "You don't have any right to tell me what to do. Your laws don't apply to me. It's my body. I have the right to put anything in it that I want."

Well, because I insisted on abusing my power and doing it my way, I earned the right to live here in this penitentiary, and my family is now in much the same shape as the one I grew up in. And you want to know something? You are worse off than I ever was. Your daddy doesn't come home at all because of his addiction, and I'm not able to bring home a paycheck at all. And worst of all, I have set an even worse example for you than my parents set for me. All of this because I chose the wrong set of attitudes to copy.

Son, I see a lot of me in you. I see how you talk about how cool you think it is that your friend stole some beer and got drunk last weekend. Your mom told me that she found some marijuana in your room last week. Son, it hurts me so much to live here in this prison each day. It hurts me so much not to be able to live with you. It hurts me to think about how stupid I was to ever listen to my "friend" at school who told me that smoking pot was different from drinking. But son, what hurts me even more is to see you act just like I did when I was your age because I know where that road goes. It ends here in this prison, or worse.

I can't make your decisions for you. I can't stop you from drinking or doing drugs. I just hope that you will learn from my mistake instead of repeating it. I don't want you to be "just like daddy." I don't want you to ever find out that alcohol and drugs will help you to do things that you never thought possible. They are a dead-end street.

Son, you are young, and you are sowing seeds that will grow for the rest of your life. But the day to reap what you are sowing is coming soon. I wish I could go back and make different decisions about what I sowed. It would not have included drugs, and it would not have included stealing. I love you, and I would like to be able to sit down with you and have a long talk about the choices I made when I was growing up.

Your dad,

Chapter 3
"Quick, Throw Me A Lifesaver!"

D o not read this paragraph! Skip down to next section immediately! If you read it, you'll be sorry because this paragraph is magical. It's too late, you've already gone too far. Because you didn't stop before the last sentence a huge chain has just magically wrapped itself around your neck. However, if you look in a mirror, you won't see the chain because it's invisible. In fact, at this very moment, you can feel that invisible chain becoming heavier and heavier, cutting into your shoulders and pushing you down onto the floor.

Even though the magical chain that you are wearing is invisible, it is very real. And right now you couldn't take it off even if you tried because you don't have the power. It's stuck there. If you quit reading this book that invisible chain will probably be there for the rest of your life. That would be unfortunate because that chain binds you to your past and is what caused you to do the things that put you in prison.

"Quick, Throw Me A Lifesaver!"

Actually, this entire chapter is magical. Not only does it have the power to put an invisible chain around your neck, hidden in this chapter are the keys to remove those chains. If you can find those keys and use them to remove the invisible chain, your life will suddenly be changed. They are filled with such powerful magic that as long as you keep the keys, once you get out you will never have to spend another day in prison for as long as you live.

You are probably thinking that the writer of this book is a mental patient writing from his padded cell at the "crazy house." First I tell you that this chapter is magic. Then I tell you that just because you read one sentence too many you now have an invisible chain wrapped around your neck that is so heavy that it is pushing you down onto the ground. Magical keys? That sounds crazy. Besides, even the title of this chapter, "Quick, Throw Me A Lifesaver," sounds stupid. How could a lifesaver help to save an inmate's family relationship? How indeed?

This bit of "craziness" makes a point and shows you one of the main causes of communication problems. Whenever people read or hear something, they automatically assign their own definition to the words that are used. Unfortunately, their definition may be different from the one intended. Then, instead of trying to find out what the writer or speaker meant, you'll hear the listener say something like, "That's crazy; that's the dumbest thing I have ever heard in my life." This applies here. Before you can decide if this chapter has any value at all, you must first discover what is meant by the words invisible chains, lifesaver, and keys. As you discover the definition to these words, you may also discover that this chapter has some information that, if used, may save your life. It may also teach you how to be one of the ones that leave this prison and remain as free as an eagle for the rest of your life.

What's a lifesaver?

One lifesaver looks like an innertube and is designed to be thrown to a person who is in danger of drowning. Another lifesaver is someone or something that shows up at just the right moment to give support or assistance in a time of need. It could be a soft drink, a stick of gum, or a piece of candy that says, "I care!" It could be words of comfort or encouragement spoken at just the right moment, a hug, or something as simple as a smile.

Chapter 3

The story is told of a young boy who was standing on the pitcher's mound during his little league championship game. It was the bottom of the ninth inning, there were two outs, and the bases were loaded. The count was three and two, and his team was ahead by just one run.

Talk about pressure! As he stood there this young pitcher knew that one more strike would not only win the game, but also the championship. He was also keenly aware that one more ball would tie the score and that a hit might let the other team win the game, and the championship. Echoing in his ears were the taunts of half of the crowd and the screams of encouragement from the other half.

The crowd became suddenly silent as the young boy began staring straight into the catcher's mit. With the sweat running down across his face, he began his windup, then threw the ball as fast and as straight as his little arm could throw it.

Suddenly, the air was charged by the unmistakable cracking sound of a bat connecting with the ball. Horrorstruck, the young pitcher followed the ball as it sailed across the fence. Painfully, he stood frozen to the mound as he watched not one, but two, then three, and then four players cross home plate. With his eyes filling with tears and glued to the dirt, he remained frozen on the mound as his teammates walked jeeringly past him and off the field, leaving him there—all by himself. A soft hug from his mother made him realize that he wasn't alone anymore. Then his father knelt down in front of him on one knee. With tears running down his cheeks, the father looked his son straight in the eye and said, "Son, you're still a winner in our book! You led your team to win second place; let's go celebrate!"

Both the hug and quiet "celebration" after the game were lifesavers. They were a way for those loving parents to say, "Even though you lost, we still believe in you, and we still love you."

By now, your mind is probably screaming, "Quick, I need a lifesaver!" You may feel like you're drowning, and you could probably use some comforting. This place is starting to get to you. Life is so slow here. Days drag into weeks, and it seems like your sentence is getting longer instead of shorter. You constantly worry about being "set up" or doing something wrong that might mess up your chances of getting parole. Worse yet, the longer that you stay here the more pressure you feel to accept the values and norms of your fellow inmates.

The worst part about living here is the realization that your wife and/or family seem to be drifting away. You may not be able to admit it, but the truth is that when you feel like you are losing your family's love you also feel like you're all alone in this seemingly Godforsaken place.

You may feel that if you could just get out and go back home everything would get better. You would be free again, to come and go as you liked. You just know that the moment that you are able to put your arms around your wife and kids and give them a great big hug and a kiss everything will be alright. Then you will live happily ever after, just like they do in the fairy tales.

Your invisible chain

But there is a problem. You have an invisible chain around your neck; a chain of improper loyalties, the improper use of power, the violation of trust, and looking out for Number One. That chain is the attitudes, values, and behavior patterns that you accepted from the people who were a significant part of your life while you were growing up.

No, that chain was not put there by magic. You have been wearing that chain all along but didn't realize it. You were wearing it when you committed your crime. You were wearing it when you were tried. You were wearing it when you were escorted into this prison. You wear it to sleep at night, in the shower, and everywhere you go, and if you're still wearing it when you leave this prison you will probably be back within a year.

You are the only one who can't see your chain. Everyone else knows that it is there. It is the invisible chain that binds you to your past and controls the way that you think and behave. It was given to you by your family and the people who were a significant part of your life while you were growing up. You accepted their chain and made it your own because you wanted to be part of their family. Each link was formed as you copied behaviors that put you in a lot of trouble. Nobody forced you to accept that chain, you chose to accept it and then used your chain to convince yourself that it was okay to do what you did.

You did not get involved in criminal activities because you were unlucky. You got involved in criminal activity because you chose to. Your criminal activities made the chain stronger, and it now binds you to your past improper actions. It is the chain that caused you to commit your crime and earn your prison sentence.

That invisible chain does feel awfully heavy around your neck, doesn't it? There is hope! By the time you reach the end of this chapter you will know about a new and ethical way of living that will allow you to remove that chain forever. This is important to you because the only inmates who get out and stay out are the ones that leave prison without their chains.

The lifesaver you want is one called End of Sentence or Parole. But if you are about to drown, a lifesaver can't hold both you and the chain up. If you grab hold of a lifesaver while you have a heavy chain wrapped around your neck both you and the lifesaver are going to the bottom.

If you're still wearing that chain when the warden shakes your hand and sends you out the front door to freedom, your freedom will not last very long. You will be right back in here or in another prison before you even know what happened. You know that because you have seen too many of your friends leave here with high hopes, only to be back in what seems like days. That's because they left here with their invisible chain still wrapped around their necks.

As long as that invisible chain is around your neck, you have not changed. Unless you change your old ways of doing things, your chain will drag you back into doing the same types of things that put you in prison in the first place. Many of you feel like that young pitcher: you blew it. You threw your pitch, the ball was hit, and you lost. Your whole team lost the game because of your pitch, and the guilt is killing you. And you should feel guilty because your whole family is suffering because of what you did.

Because of what you did, you can't watch your child's little league ballgame. You aren't there to comfort your children when they skin their knees or to cry with them about a lost date, or any other time that your family needs you.

For this reason, an inmate's family is frequently called "the second victim of crime." No one read them their rights at the time of your arrest. They did not have a lawyer to represent them at the trial, and they have no way to appeal their sentence. But they are paying a very real, and a very dear price for what you have done. Did you realize that your family—your team—is hurting just as badly as you are? They did not ask to become a victim of your crime, you forced them into that position.

People do some strange things when they are hurting. Some family members are hurting so badly that they can't look at you or speak to you because of what you have done. They walk away and act like you don't exist anymore. Some scream and torment you with ugly words. Others lie and pretend that you have joined the military or make up other excuses for your disappearance that sound socially acceptable. And like that young pitcher, all you can do is hang your head and look at the dirt as your team walks by, leaving you all alone.

You could lash out at them or make a bunch of excuses for the lousy pitch, but it wouldn't change anything. The game is over, and you lost.

Are you like that young pitcher? Do you need someone to rescue you from drowning by saying, "Even though you blew it, I love you, and I still believe in you"?

Well, even though you blew it and hurt your entire family, and society, I love you, and I believe in you. In fact, this is why I invested over 2,500 hours and a year and a half to write this book and the education courses that go with it and continue to teach the courses to inmates and their families.

Did that make that chain feel any lighter? Maybe a little bit, but not much, because your chain is still there. You put it on, and only you can take it off. But right now you couldn't even if you tried because, as everyone knows, you can't remove invisible chains. Or can you?

Every generation is linked by chains of loyalty

Let's look at those invisible chains that bind you to your past. Let's explore each link of that chain and see how it locked you into a behavioral pattern that led you to this prison and can kill your family relationship while you are here. Unless you learn how to remove your chain it will be passed to your children, then your grandchildren, and will assure that future generations are full of unhappiness and trouble. This will happen unless you can find a way of breaking the invisible chain of loyalty to your past that is wrapped around your neck at this moment.

Everyone has a history. You and everyone else in the world have a mother and father. Your mother and father both had a mother and father. All of your grandparents had mothers and fathers. You probably have brothers and sisters, aunts and uncles, and a bunch of cousins. In this day of divorce, remarriage, live-in relationships, or whatever, your family tree may be even larger because of stepparents, half-brothers and sisters, in-laws, out-laws, and whatever else is perched on the limbs.

Each of these people are part of your family tree. They created the history that surrounds you and helped to mold you into what you are today. Your family had its own attitudes, values, and behavior patterns. One of the

Chapter 3

ways that family members prove their loyalty to each other is by copying family attitudes and making them their own. These invisible chains of loyalty then lock people into repeating the family's attitudes, values, and patterns of behavior generation after generation.

You are your own person. There's nobody else in this world exactly like you. You make your own decisions and are responsible for each of those decisions. However, an examination of your family tree will show you where you got your attitudes, values, and behavior patterns. Once you realize that, you can then break the invisible chains that bind you to your past. Then, you can begin a new life of ethical living.

As you think about your family, think about the invisible chains that loop around you and around other members of your family. Think about the ways the various family members act alike. Think about how you would answer this question: "Which are you more like, your mother or your father?" How about your brothers and sisters, who are they more like? Isn't it odd, you knew the answer to that immediately.

Think about the family traditions that took place in your family as you were growing up. These traditions are part of the invisible chains of loyalty that bind you to your past. For example, you usually knew what chair to sit in when you ate your meals, which toothbrush to use, and which bed to sleep in. Because of your family's traditional way of doing things, you knew what to expect on your birthday, at Christmas, and other special times of the year. For some the holidays were special because that was when the family got together and shared pleasant, quality time together. For others, the holidays were a time of terror because they became a time when family members got drunk and mean.

These traditions become part of the links of the chain and are copied by future generations. But sometimes, the similar attitudes show up looking totally different. Here's an example of how an improper attitude can be passed from generation to generation, but with totally different behavior patterns.

Little Jimmy talks back to his dad, and his dad decides to teach little Jimmy to show proper respect. So he grabs little Jimmy by the ear, hauls him out to the woodshed, takes off his belt, and proceeds to beat him "within an inch of his life."

Jimmy grows up, gets married, and has a little boy named Johnny. He swears that he will never treat Johnny like his dad treated him. So instead, when little Johnny misbehaves or does something that displeases him, Jimmy gives him a stern lecture. He sits Johnny down in a chair and screams,

"Quick, Throw Me A Lifesaver!"

"Johnny, you are a dumb, stupid idiot. You don't have the brains that God gave a crabapple. Our dog knows how to act better than you do. You are disgusting and make me want to puke. Now go to your room so that I won't have to look at your face."

Each of these scenes are different. Jimmy's body was abused with a belt. Johnny's mind was abused with ugly, hateful words. Which would hurt more, the beating or the tongue-lashing? To a child, there is little difference between being beaten with words and being beaten with a belt. In fact, many say being beaten with words hurts more.

Both forms of abuse display the same attitude. Both actions say that parents can force their children to be still while they vent their anger, abuse their power, and injure their children. Both forms of abuse teach children that they have no value and destroy their self-image.

Let's carry this illustration one more step. One day at school, someone cuts in front of little Johnny while he is waiting in line to use the water fountain. Johnny gets angry, grabs the child by the ear, pushes him to the ground, then starts pounding on the child's head. Jim is called to the principal's office. After hearing about the incident he exclaims, "I can't understand why my little Johnny would ever act that way; he never sees any violence at home." Little Johnny was simply showing his loyalty to his family by copying their family chain. All three generations now have an identical chain, an identical attitude, which says that it is okay to abuse your power when you are angry and injure others over minor infractions.

Here is another example provided by a child molester. Whenever the molester's father became angry with him he was forced to remove his clothing and lay down on the bed while his father beat his bottom with the broad side of a meat cleaver. This child molester realized that although he hated his father, he had adopted his same attitude. Both men, when angry, abused their power by requiring their children to remove their clothing and lay on the bed while their bottoms were hurt with a hard object.

Another inmate, incarcerated for selling drugs and breaking into homes, said that nobody in his family had any influence on him in his decision to do his crimes. An examination of his family tree revealed that one of his grandfathers was a bootlegger during the prohibition days, and his grandmother used to steal Social Security checks whenever she needed some money, though she was never caught. He had never realized that selling illegal drugs displayed the same attitude as selling bootleg moonshine during prohibition or that breaking into a house displayed the same attitude as opening a mailbox and stealing a check.

Chapter 3

Unfortunately, most inmates can tell stories like these and worse. Family scientists such as S. K. Steinmetz have discovered that most inmates come from family relationships filled with violence and trouble. This probably means that your being in prison is simply the reward that you are receiving for accepting and repeating improper attitudes formed during a long-standing chain of history that connects you to family members who may have died before you were even born.

How to draw a family tree

By drawing your family tree and studying it, you will begin to see how many of your family members are linked by invisible chains of loyalty and display many of the same attitudes, values, and behavior patterns. You will also see chains that need to be broken and replaced. Your goal is to replace the defective chains with proper attitudes, correct moral values, and ethical living patterns.

Drawing a family tree requires following a few simple rules. Circles are females, squares are the males. Solid lines connect family members. Put slash marks (—/ /—) through the lines if there has been a separation or divorce. Put an "X" through those who have died. Beside each person, list their occupations, any trouble with the law, substance abuse problems, etc. Then draw lines around the members connected by chains and describe what that chain is.

Drawing a family tree is simple and can be quite fun. Most people have to call their parents or other family members to learn the names of aunts and uncles and sometimes even brothers and sisters. As you talk to them, listen to the stories that are told about the individual people. Because of numerous divorces, you may need a wide sheet of paper to show all of the husbands and wives.

To help you see how chains link family members I am going to draw my family tree and show you some of the chains in my family.

My paternal grandfather (my father's father) was a bi-vocational minister, meaning that he worked a regular job during the week and preached on the weekends. During the week he worked as a laborer in a tannery changing cattle hides into leather. On the weekends he became an evangelist, driving across the mountains that surrounded Roanoke, Virginia, to one of the many churches that he served. He was a big, stout, hard-working, self-made man who was dedicated to the "Lord's work." His big, booming

60

"Quick, Throw Me A Lifesaver!"

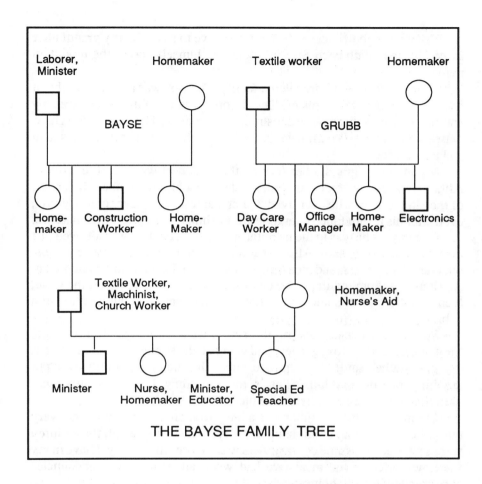

THE BAYSE FAMILY TREE

voice was well-adapted to the hellfire and brimstone-type of sermon that he delivered. His ministry began when his pastor asked him to preach for him at the local jail.

Grandfather drove like he preached—wide open and full of fury. There isn't a roller coaster in the world that could match what went on inside of his big Packard as it hurled itself over and around those mountain roads (and this was before guardrails). His driving was so bad that it took a whole host of guardian angels to keep him safe.

My paternal grandmother stayed at home and took care of the children. She was a kindly woman who always thought of herself as frail and sickly, right up until the day she died at the ripe old age of 84. Some felt that her

Chapter 3

"spells" were a good excuse for her not to have to ride with my grandfather as he cheated death each Sunday rocketing himself across the mountain roads.

There were four children in the family. The first was a daughter who m rried a bi-vocational minister. The second was my father, followed by another son who became a construction foreman. The last, a daughter, married a bi-vocational minister and became a homemaker to her husband and ten children.

My maternal grandfather (my mother's father) was a textile worker. Although he died when I was in elementary school, I remember him as one of the kindest men who ever lived. Quiet and reserved, never complaining, even after his health failed everyone around him felt the warmth of his love.

One day, as he was in the hospital and nearing death, I was allowed just a few minutes to see him. After speaking to him, I sat down on a bench just outside of his room and positioned myself so I could still watch him. Anxiously, I thumbed through one of the tattered magazines on the table, then laid it on top of some books, not realizing that I had put it on top of a Bible.

Suddenly, I became aware of a small, weak voice calling my name. From underneath his oxygen tent and using all the strength he could muster, my grandfather said, "Dan, please move the magazine; don't ever put anything on top of God." That's the last thing I can remember my grandfather saying to me before he died.

My maternal grandmother was a busy woman, always on the go, very outspoken, having an opinion about everything. Even though the children were scattered across the country, hers was a close-knit family. I have many fond memories of the meals we had when all of my aunts and uncles converged on the old homestead.

Five children were born into the family. The first, a daughter, married a mechanic and cared for children in a day-care center. The second was my mother. The third daughter married a mechanic and became an office manager. The fourth married a factory supervisor and became a homemaker. The last, a son, helped develop this nation's radar defense system during his career in the Air Force. The German woman that he married became a housewife.

My mother and father met in high school. Shortly after graduation my father was drafted into the Navy during World War II. After his discharge he worked in a textile plant running the machines that produced women's hosiery. After it closed, he became a milkman, and then a machinist for

"Quick, Throw Me A Lifesaver!"

General Electric. Our family was poor, and my dad worked many long hours, frequently at two jobs and in our garden to provide for his family. On the weekends, he taught Sunday school classes and served his church on a volunteer basis as their treasurer.

My father taught us to always rely on God during difficult times. His actions taught us to never give up. Recently, because of a sudden attack of glaucoma, he became blind overnight. That forced him to retire, but not quit. On a recent visit to my home he spent several hours on his hands and knees digging a trench beside my house so I could do a repair. Even though he is basically blind, he did a better job than I would have done. He was giving of himself to make my life easier.

My mother is a kind, loving, outspoken, somewhat bossy woman who has an opinion about everything. On my first day in the second grade, she arrived at school carrying a quart of milk and some sandwiches because she knew some parents thought that school was going to be out before lunch. There were no free lunches then and she didn't want any of the children to be hungry because they didn't bring a lunch.

Over the years our home was opened to foster children, visiting ministers, an elderly blind woman with no family to care for her, my paternal grandmother during her last years, and anyone else she could help. When her children, husband, or grandchildren had illnesses, mother was always there to help—even if it meant driving or flying halfway across the country. Mother did not enter the work force until after her children were out of school, then became a nurse's aide working on a mental ward at a Veteran's Administration hospital. As each of us married, it became clear that the new spouses were considered part of the family. Mother let me know that she approved of my choice by giving me her engagement ring to give to my future bride.

There were four children in the family. My oldest brother obtained a degree in electrical engineering, changed vocations, went to seminary and became a pastor. My oldest sister is a kind, outspoken, somewhat bossy woman who has an opinion about everything. She has always been an encourager to me and others and was never afraid to tell me to "go for it." She worked as a registered nurse in a sanitorium for tuberculosis patients, then in a newborn intensive care unit for several years. She left that profession to become the wife of an engineer and later mother to three children.

My younger sister became a special education teacher and married an engineer. After the birth of her first child, she temporarily left full-time teaching to be a homemaker.

The third of four children, I began dating the woman who would become my wife in high school. After graduation, I served for seven years as a Navy photographer and camera repairman. Following that, I became a Virginia State Trooper. During those ten years I taught in their academy and was one of their pilots. My wife is a nurse and the daughter of a construction foreman. In 1983, I left the state police to begin my preparation for the ministry by enrolling in Florida Baptist Theological College. From there we moved to Auburn University, where I earned a Master of Science degree in Family and Child Development. During my years in the Navy and with the state police, I served several churches as a bi-vocational minister of music and youth or by providing for their publicity needs. I am presently an evangelist who specializes in family and prison ministry.

As you read this you can already see some of our chains. One chain ties us to church activities. Dad held a church office until his health forced him to retire; Mom served in the mission societies and provided a home away from home to all of the visiting ministers. Like our grandfather, my brother and I are both ministers. My sister and her husband are the volunteer ministers of music at their church. My other sister helps with the education program at her church. All of the Bayse children are involved in helping others. In doing so, we have accepted and continued the chain that links us to both sets of grandparents.

Both my father and I met our wives in high school, then spent time in the military, as did three uncles. I have been heavily involved in the construction industry, just like my uncle and my wife's father. I am handy with tools, just like my uncle. My ministry has its roots in evangelism and prison work, just like my grandfather.

I have continued the chain given to me by my maternal grandfather in that hospital room and try to never allow anything to come between myself and my God. When I failed a course in graduate school and it looked like I wouldn't be able to finish, I followed my Dad's example and hung in there while trusting God to guide me. Because I copied my Dad's chain and did not quit, I earned my degree, wrote Alabama's first three family life education programs for inmates, and wrote the book that you are now reading.

Even my decision to become a state trooper is part of the chain that binds me to my past. Remember my grandfather's driving? I used to ride with him on those trips. A constant topic around our house was the wish for the power to make grandfather change his driving habits. For a while, I had that power, and I was good at helping the state remove drivers like my grandfather from the highways. And like my grandfather, when I chased them, I drove wide open and full of fury.

All of the Bayse men and women have been hard workers and unafraid to work many long hours. Some might call us workaholics. My thirteen-year-old son says he wants to be a brain surgeon. If he does, he will be accepting a chain linking him to his past; one with links to the medical field, long hours of work, and giving of himself to make others' lives better. Like his dad, he wants to change what goes on inside of people's heads. His dream is to be the first doctor to perform a brain transplant.

These are just a few of the chains that bind me to my past. Everyone has them. Unfortunately, not everyone's family was as loving as the one that I grew up in. Most inmates grow up in families that are full of conflict and violence.

Where did the chains come from?

As mentioned in the last chapter, the root cause of all interpersonal conflict is the power struggle between two or more people to determine who is going to be the boss and make the final decision, and it has been this way since the beginning of time.

Think back to the biblical story about the first couple on earth, Adam and Eve. Even if you don't believe that these people actually existed, the story demonstrates several things: (1) how a family should function in today's world; (2) how the invisible chain that is presently around your neck was created; (3) how improper attitudes, value systems, and behavior patterns are passed from one generation to the next; and (4) what happens to people's lives when they adopt an attitude that says, "I'm Number One."

At the beginning of their relationship, Adam and Eve had the most perfect marriage that this world has ever known. They were literally made for each other. Adam and Eve got along perfectly with their family. They realized that society's rules were created to keep them and their family safe and free from harm. It was a whole new world out there, and it was a jungle—a jungle that they were free to explore. Frequently, they ran into situations that they had never faced before. When this happened they would ask their parents for advice. Like you, they then had to decide what to do with their parents' advice and were responsible for the decisions that they made.

Adam and Eve realized that only the leaders had the right to make the rules, which included setting the penalty for breaking those rules. They also knew that their continued freedom depended on their respect for the rules and taking responsibility for their own actions.

The family worked together as a team with the goal of meeting each other's needs. They were not afraid to ask each other for help. They listened to their children because they realized that their opinions were important and because they wanted to teach the children that they were persons of value with something to offer their family and society.

Adam and Eve understood their four main responsibilities as parents: (1) to provide their children proper spiritual training; (2) to give them a good self-image; (3) to teach them how to be good marriage partners, including what to look for in a mate; and (4) know their children so well that they could provide the necessary training that would change their natural interests into skills that would enable them to enter adulthood as productive members of society. These first parents would have recognized that Cain enjoyed working in the soil while Abel enjoyed being around animals.

Adam and Eve enjoyed being together and dreaming up things that they could do as a family and with each other. But Adam and Eve also recognized that each of them needed time to be alone—time to do things by themselves just for their own individual growth. Both of them realized that the foundation of an intimate relationship is the ability to trust each other. Because they understood this, neither of them felt rejected when the other said, "I need some time to myself." And why should they? Neither of them had ever done anything that indicated that they could not be trusted.

They knew who the leaders were in the family. Since neither had the desire to overpower the other, the leadership roles could change if necessary, especially if one was better at a particular task. Adam did not try to boss Eve around, and Eve did not try to boss Adam around. In this perfect family, Adam wanted to be Eve's partner, and Eve wanted to be his partner. So they constantly worked together to make this happen.

Adam never told Eve that he wasn't going to do something simply because it was "woman's work." Adam didn't mind changing his children's diapers, washing the dishes, or cleaning up the house because his goal was to help make Eve's life easier.

Adam and Eve knew all about each other—there were no secrets between them. They talked to each other and shared their innermost thoughts and feelings without fear of being attacked. Both knew and supplied what the other needed spiritually, emotionally, and sexually. Their goal was to respect the other's needs and to give of themselves to provide for the other's well-being.

Like their parents, Adam and Eve set the family rules and the penalty for the violation of those rules, then explained them to the children before any enforcement took place. The children would have known that mom and dad would listen to them if they requested that the rules be changed, but also knew that mom and dad would always make the final decision. As discipline was needed, Adam or Eve would choose something that would say to their children, "I love you too much to allow you to continue acting that way."

The problems in this family did not start until each individual decided that they had the power to disobey the rules and began looking out for their own selfish wants and desires. Eve developed an improper attitude and decided that she was more powerful than her father and did not have to obey the rules of society. To demonstrate that she was more powerful, she listened to a suggestion and deliberately chose to disobey the rules.

Adam copied Eve's new attitude and made it his own when he followed her example and also chose to deliberately disobey the rules of society. When confronted, Adam quickly developed an improper attitude of his own. Instead of admitting that he himself, of his own free will, with full knowledge of the consequences of his act, chose to violate the rules of the family and of society, Adam blamed his wife and said that she made him do the improper act. Then, Eve quickly copied Adam's attitude and blamed someone else for her decision to violate the rules.

By now both Adam and Eve had decided that society no longer had any right to require them to control their urges. Both saw something that they wanted, but had no right to have. So they abused their power and took it. Then, instead of accepting the responsibility for their own actions, each began to blame others for causing their problem. This new attitude caused Adam and Eve to change for the worse, and as they did, their entire world changed with them.

Suddenly, instead of their goal being to respect the other's needs, they became locked into a power struggle to determine who was going to be the boss. The feeling of mutual trust had been replaced with anger, and now they fought constantly. Mutual caring was replaced by trying to find ways to override or overpower the other.

Sometimes they would try physical violence or yelling and screaming at each other to force the other into compliance with their demands. Other

Chapter 3

times they would bury themselves in their work and neglect the other's needs.

Before they changed, their sexual life had been the closest thing on earth to heaven itself, but now their bedroom had become a battleground. First one and then the other learned that if you withhold sex and/or affection long enough the other gives in to demands faster. It became more important to be in control than to provide for the other's sexual needs. Sex had become a weapon and something to argue about.

This continuing power struggle became a chain around their necks, locking them into a routine that grew increasingly tense and unhappy. As the chain became stronger, they added a new link, an attitude that said that yielding was a sign of weakness. Adam and Eve soon forgot that the only time that they had been happy together was when they were yielding to each other's needs.

Their children watched this power struggle and accepted their parents' way of doing things. By accepting their parents' improper methods of resolving conflict, they placed a set of chains around their own necks—chains that would lock them into a lifestyle of conflict and pain.

Abel lived by the rules of society and was accepted by the leaders. Cain accepted the chain from his parents. He copied his parent's attitudes by deciding on his own that he did not have to obey the rules of society and that he could live by his own rules.

Cain was caught disobeying the rules of society. Like his parents, instead of admitting his mistake, accepting the responsibility for his own improper actions, then changing his life to conform to the rules of society, Cain added his own improper attitude to the chain. He used violence to prove he was the one in power and murdered his brother simply because he was angry at the system. Cain then had to pay the penalty for his abuse of power.

Cain had children, and those children accepted the chain of improper actions, attitudes, and values that started with their grandparents; a chain called "Looking out for Number One." Cain's son had a disagreement with a man who wounded him and a boy who struck him. So to prove that he was more powerful, he used the same method that his father did. Cain's son killed the man and the boy, then dared anyone to do anything about it.

And on it goes. Even today that same chain that began with Adam and Eve is still being passed down from generation to generation. People who commit violent crimes tend to come from homes that use brutal childrearing techniques. People who abuse their power by requiring children to have sex with them were frequently abused themselves. Children who watch their parents abuse alcohol or drugs also learn to abuse alcohol or drugs. Even if the children do not copy the exact behavior patterns of the parents, the parent's attitudes and value systems will appear in different forms.

The invisible chain of loyalty means that you probably found a wife who is really quite similar to your mother, and you are probably similar to how your wife views her father. And on and on and on the chain is passed, from one generation to the next.

You accepted the chain that binds you to your past

Long before you can even remember, the people in your life were influencing you. They were molding your life by showing you their attitudes and values. You liked or didn't like what you saw. As you grew, you started copying what you saw in others until you found a set of norms, values, and behavior patterns that you could call your own. These form the invisible chains that bind you to your past.

Most inmates wear an invisible chain called alcohol or drug abuse. Anytime that anyone puts something in their body that would harm them it is an abuse of power. It's saying, just like Adam and Eve did, "I can make my own rules, and society does not have any right to tell me what I can put into my body." Anyone who requires others to tolerate cursing, screaming, yelling, hitting, throwing things, breaking things, or changing their plans because of one individual's level of sobriety is abusing their power. Anyone who spends the money needed to supply the family with food, clothing, and shelter for one's own selfish needs is abusing their power. Substance abusers do this and more, and then blame the substance for their behavior.

It is an abuse of power when a parent's life demonstrates to their children that it is okay to use alcohol or drugs to solve one's problems. The ultimate abuse of power comes when parents encourage their children to begin using alcohol or drugs. The children then show their loyalty by copying those attitudes.

Most inmates also have an invisible chain of child abuse that binds them to their past. Here's how it happens: Everyone, including children, has a need for power and to feel in control over their own lives. Everyone also has times when they feel depressed and powerless. One way to meet the emotional need for power is by using physical threats or violence.

Unfortunately, this power play, like a drug fix, soon goes away, and the parent becomes depressed because of what they have done. Afterwards, when the reality of the abuse sets in, the abuser begins to feel depressed because of what happened. Feeling powerless again, they abuse again. This power play/depression cycle creates a circle and a chain that will be passed from generation to generation.

Here's how it works. You become angry at your family situation, at your child, at your job, or whatever and feel powerless to deal with or change the situation. So you require your child to submit to a beating, to being insulted and screamed at, to have sex with you, or whatever else you want them to do. As part of the abuse you tell your child that they deserved it or that this is your "special way of showing them your love." And for a moment, this satisfies your need for power and to be in control.

Later, you realize what you've done and that you have, again, failed to control yourself. Then, you feel powerless and depressed. So you find a reason to make the child submit to the abuse again.

Even though your child hates what you are doing, your attitude is teaching them that when you feel powerless, angry, or depressed, the ability to intimidate or overpower others gives a temporary sense of power and control. As they begin to copy your improper attitude, each time they feel powerless and depressed they will start picking on people smaller than them. For a moment, this satisfies their need for power and control. But down inside, they know that what they did was wrong. This makes them feel bad, powerless, and depressed. So they start looking for someone to abuse. By now, your child has copied your chain of abuse and is wearing it proudly for the whole world to see.

Your children grow up with this chain around their necks. They may have children. Then as parents, your now grown-up children use that same chain and follow the same pattern that they were taught as children: they abuse their power as parents by abusing their children. And 'round and 'round it goes; where it stops nobody knows.

In this age of divorce and unstable relationships, parents frequently abuse their power by abandoning their children. In doing so, they declare that it is okay to leave dependent children that need a parent. Their attitude says, "So what if I created that child's life and am responsible for its well-being. Let the welfare department, a family member, or someone else take care of my children."

If this happened to you, this means that you may have never seen your parent(s) while you were growing up. As a result, you were reared by only one parent who may have been too busy to care, grandparents or other family members, a series of foster homes, or basically reared yourself and had no one to watch after your welfare.

Not being able to get along with one's wife or being sent to prison does not relieve you from your responsibilities as a father. In fact, by earning your prison sentence, just like any parent who abandons their children, you are forcing them to live without your presence in the home.

Every man who uses his power to create life is also entrusted with the responsibility to parent that child. Parents who abandon their children violate their trust and abuse their power. They also teach their children that it is okay to avoid one's responsibility and duty. There are many, many different ways that this attitude can be copied.

Research has shown that any time that a parent leaves the home, *if* the couple are able to put aside their hostilities, *if* they do not try to make the children decide which parent to be loyal to, and *if* the absent parent maintains contact with his children, *then* the children are better able to adjust to the new situation. This means, if at all possible, it is extremely important for you to maintain contact with your children while you are in prison and that they know that you still love them and are not going to abandon them.

The family bank account

What is it that makes those invisible chains so hard to remove? Why is it so hard to change habit patterns? Three reasons: trust, loyalty, and the "family bank account."

Trust is the foundation on which families are formed. Trust means that no matter what, you and your needs are important to the other members of the family, just as their needs are important to you.

For example, a man begins his marriage relationship when he and his bride stand in front of a minister, judge, or other official and repeat words similar to these:

I take this woman to be my lawful wife. I promise to love her, comfort her, honor and keep her in sickness and in health, and forsaking all others keep her only unto me so long as we both shall live.

Look at the words. The very basis of a marriage contract is a promise that you can be trusted to take care of her needs even when she and/or the relationship becomes sick and that she could trust you never to do anything that would allow someone or something else to come between her and the relationship. In other words, you promised to continually fill the "family bank account" with trust so that when hard times hit you would have a reserve to keep things going.

The family bank account holds a balance of trust. If you are building trust, you are putting deposits in your bank account. If you are abusing that trust, you are creating a debt that must be paid. If your bank account becomes empty, the relationship will likely die.

In any relationship, everything that is said and done will have one of two effects: (1) it will build trust and make the relationship grow or (2) it will destroy trust and damage the relationship. There is no middle ground. No matter what you do, it makes the relationship stronger, or it makes it weaker. Children enter this world with a full supply of basic trust and loyalty toward their family. They also enter this world with two things in common: (1) they did not ask to be born and (2) they are totally dependent on others for their care. When you are totally dependent on others, you quickly learn who you can trust and who you can't.

Children need to be able to trust their parents to provide for their physical needs of food, clothing, and shelter. Children need to know that there was a reason for them to be born. Children also need to be able to trust their parents to provide for their emotional needs of love and acceptance. If, during their childhood years, your children learn to trust and be trustworthy and that they are loved and are someone special, they will grow up with a good self-image, strong in character, and ready for anything. This trust can grow only in an atmosphere where the parents show mutual trust for each other.

Parents are sometimes cruel. No matter how damaging the relationship becomes, children have a deep desire to keep the family bank account of trust going. A child will show that trust by being loyal and coming back to the parents no matter how mean they have been. If an abused child falls down and skins its knee, it will run to its abusive parent hoping to be comforted.

But if a child's basic trust is ever destroyed, that child will be emotionally damaged for the rest of its life. That child will have a hard time ever trusting others. It will have a hard time forming intimate relationships, and it will enter adulthood with a low self-image.

If you have ever violated the trust that your children had in you by abusing them emotionally, physically, or sexually, you have put a heavy chain around their necks that may take years of therapy to remove. You can help your child survive the severe injury that you did to their spirit by admitting your mistake and asking forgiveness. Let your children know that they did not do anything to deserve what you did to them. Admit that you violated your position of power in the family. Admit that you were wrong to do what you did. You owe your children that.

Loyalty is the invisible bond that binds families together across the generations no matter what. It is what keeps those chains in place. Everyone is born with a basic loyalty toward their parents and their family. They show that loyalty by copying the attitudes, values, and behavior patterns of other family members.

A child complained to the school counselor that his mother was a monster and was constantly beating the children. Later that day, this child was sent to the office for beating up another student. When asked the reason the child said, "He said something bad about my mother."

How many fights have you seen started after somebody was called a son of a bitch? This makes a lot of men angry because it says that their mother is no better than a dog. The anger is their loyalty to their mothers.

Another example of loyalties can be found after parents divorce, remarry, and then attempt to blend their individual children into this new relationship. The new husband frequently hears, "I don't have to obey you because you are not my *REAL* father." What they are really saying, in rebellious terms is, "I am still loyal to my father and not to you."

Families demand loyalty, but sometimes it is not deserved. For relationships to grow there must be a balance between trust and loyalty. The proper way to gain loyalty is to show the other family members that you can be trusted to be concerned about their needs. They, in turn, will respond with greater loyalty.

Problems start in families when one person starts looking out for Number One and at the same time demands that the others remain loyal to him. They have forgotten that any time you do something that proves you to be untrustworthy you have damaged the relationship and have created a debt in the family bank account.

If you require other family members to be improperly loyal to you when you are continually proving yourself to be untrustworthy, you will soon find that the family bank account of trust is bankrupt. You may also find that the other family members will terminate the relationship rather than allow you to run up any more debts.

It is being improperly loyal to your family if you abuse alcohol and drugs just like they did, abuse your children just like you were abused, or abandon your children just like you were abandoned.

If your parents told you that you would never amount to anything, you have been improperly loyal to them by doing something that would earn you a prison sentence, which proves your parents right.

Nobody can make you do anything. Everything that you do involves making a decision and then doing it. As you make your decisions about how to behave, you are also making a decision about your family bank account. Every time that you decide to do something that proves you to be trustworthy, you have added to your family bank account. On the other hand, the untrustworthy things you have done have subtracted from your bank account.

As long as the account is growing, your family is growing stronger. But any time that you start doing untrustworthy things, that account dwindles, and when there is nothing left and a debt is created, the relationship is likely to die.

Your crime, and the imprisonment that you requested by doing the crime, not only emptied your account, they created such a debt that you no longer have any right to ask your family to be loyal to you. You forfeited that privilege when you chose to do your crime.

Right now, legally and morally, your wife would be justified to divorce you and remove herself from your life. If she does, she would not be abandoning you. When you committed your crime you asked the state to remove you from your family. You abandoned her and are forcing her and the children to live without you. Part of earning a prison sentence is asking the state to remove you from your family.

And because you abandoned her, she now has every right to say, "You wanted out; okay good-bye!" If she decides to divorce you, she will only be making permanent what you have already done. She will simply be giving you what you asked for the moment that you did your crime.

Stan Sack, noted legal expert and author, says that imprisonment for over a specified time gives an inmate's wife the legal grounds necessary to obtain a divorce in every state. Divorce courts have been known to remove an inmate's right to have any contact with their children while they are in prison and after they get out. Although each state's laws are different, most states allow a judge to consider your debt to your family to be so great that he or she *could* give your wife (1) freedom from the marriage, (2) sole custody of the children, (3) removal of any rights that you have to ever see your children again, and (4) possession of all of your property.

"Quick, Throw Me A Lifesaver!"

As a practical matter, if the judge did those things there would be nothing that you could do about it. Your criminal activity violated the trust that your family had in you. Because of your violation of trust, you have created a huge debt, not only to society, which you are presently paying off, but also to your family. If the divorce court judge did all or part of the things mentioned above, he or she would simply be settling the debt that you created with your family when you chose to do your criminal act.

Your wife is under no obligation to stand by you while you are here. If she does, it will be because she loves you and is choosing to remain loyal to you. Her loyalty is based on her hope that while you are in prison you will change and that after you are released you will be the husband that she has always wanted. This is probably the only reason that she is willing to wait for you.

You know how changeable people can be. Your wife could change her mind at any moment and give you the divorce that you asked for. If she does, there will be nothing you can do about it. If you don't want this to happen you must start showing her the specific things you have already changed about yourself that make you worth waiting for.

You can begin rebuilding the trust in your family by admitting to your wife and/or family what they already know. Admit that you realize they have no obligation to stand by you and are choosing to do so simply to show you that they love you and care about you. Tell them how much you appreciate their loyalty. Then, start showing that you can always be trusted to be considerate of their feelings.

Removing the chain that binds you to your past

Before throwing you a lifesaver would do any good, you need to learn how to remove your invisible chain. It won't do you any good to throw you a lifesaver if the chain will pull you under the water anyway. The chain will cause you to drown.

The way to remove the invisible chain that binds you to your past is by making, and keeping, a commitment to practice ethical living. This commitment means that from now on, in everything that you will do and say, you will no longer look out only for Number One, but instead will always consider the interests and needs of everyone concerned *before* you make any final decisions.

Before you can remove those chains you *MUST* break the ties that bind you to your past ways of doing things. You must first acknowledge that your roots gave you an identity and a way of life. Then you must acknowledge that you accepted improper attitudes, values, and behavior patterns from your family and made them your own.

You must also acknowledge that even though you may not have had good examples to follow, you are the one that created your own improper attitude that said, "I'm going to look out only for Number One. I'm going to do anything that I want; say anything that I want, anytime I want, anywhere I want; and there is nothing that anyone can do about it, PERIOD!"

Then you must make, and keep, a commitment to practice ethical living. This means deciding that you will never again abuse your power and will always be considerate of others by treating them fairly. It also means that you will treat people like you want to be treated.

Your commitment must include a promise that starting today, this very minute, you will begin to rebuild your family bank account so that it is full of trustworthiness. This means becoming a loving husband and father.

Will you make that commitment to ethical living? If so, here are the keys that will unlock the chain and allow you to remove it from your neck. They are the keys to freedom: respecting the rules of society and taking responsibility for your own actions. It takes both keys to open the door to freedom, then keeping your commitment to ethical living to remain free.

Respect means that from now on you will always respect the rules of society. This includes respect for moral laws, the laws and rules of society, the rules and regulations of this prison, and being respectful to the needs of others—including those in your family.

True freedom always starts with respect. If you want to drive with freedom you must respect the traffic laws, otherwise you will soon lose your freedom to drive. If you want to be a concert pianist you must respect your instructor's guidance through years of piano lessons. Only then can you be free to play the piano professionally. It only takes a short time for people to know if you are the type that is willing to respect the rules of society.

If you want to have a healthy family life, you must respect the rules of ethical family living. You will learn how to accomplish this through the rest of this book.

The second key is accepting the responsibility for all your actions. This means that you will stop blaming others for your actions and begin admitting to yourself and others that you and only you are responsible for them. Being a responsible person means that you think about the consequences that will follow before you make the decision about what to say or how to act.

Accepting the consequences of your decisions is part of being responsible for your own actions. Among other things, this means that you will admit that you earned your prison sentence and that you earned your right to be here. Being a responsible person includes the realization that any time you abuse your power new debts are created that will need to be paid.

Part of your responsibility is teaching your children what will happen if they follow in your footsteps and copy your improper attitudes, values, and behavior patterns.

Finally, responsible people are those who, anytime they realize that their improper actions have harmed others, will go to them and say the two most important sentences known to mankind: "I was wrong; will you forgive me?" followed by, "What can I do to make it right?"

You have been thrown a lifesaver. It's now up to you to take it and use it to save your life. The decision can't be made for you. Your only chance to become truly free is to use your keys to freedom to unlock the invisible chain that is part of your life. Then you must grab hold of your personal lifesaver by keeping your commitment to practice ethical living. Do these things, and once you get out, you will never have to spend another day in prison for as long as you live.

An exercise

Write a letter to your wife, children, or other family member and tell them what you have learned about yourself by reading this chapter. Thank them for the lifesavers they have thrown you—the things that they have done to help keep you from drowning. Then, tell them about your commitment to practice ethical living and the specific things that you are going to do differently in the future that will show them that you can be trusted to keep this commitment.

Remember, at first your family will be skeptical. In the past, you have proven repeatedly that you can't be trusted. If you want to keep your family relationship alive, you're going to have to prove to them that you have changed into a person who can be trusted. This can begin when you can show them specific things in your life that you know need to be changed and the specific steps that you are now taking to make that change.

Here is a sample letter that you might write to your wife. This letter comes from a husband incarcerated for breaking into a house so he could get the money to buy drugs.

> *My dearest wife,*
>
> *I hope that by now you can see that I am changing. My goal is to become the husband that you have always wanted and needed. I have failed so miserably in the past.*
>
> *This book that I am reading and the other programs that I am taking have convinced me that I owe you such a huge debt that I don't know if I will ever be able to repay it. I also realize now that your continued loyalty to me is a gift and not an obligation. Your continued love has been a real lifesaver. I appreciate your accepting my collect phone calls, the trouble you go through to come visit when you can, and the little things like the little drawings that you put on the outside of your envelopes. Thank you for putting your trust in me, even though I don't deserve it.*
>
> *I'm writing you this letter to show you that I am learning new things. I also want to see how you like some new ideas that I have come up with that will demonstrate to you that I have changed and that I can be trusted in the future.*
>
> *I'm learning that you need a man who can be trusted not to abuse his power. I'm learning that you need a man who will always consider your needs and the needs of our family before he makes any decisions. I've already tried to show you that I am changing by the new attitude that I have shown you in the last letter.*
>
> *One of the things that has really stuck with me is the realization that everything I do will do one of two things: either make our relationship stronger or make it weaker. I have learned that the only way that I can build our relationship is by constantly demonstrating trustworthy actions.*
>
> *I have to admit that because of my background and because of the improper habits that I learned while I was growing up, I will always have a desire for alcohol or drugs and be tempted to take things that don't belong to me. The Alcoholics Anonymous meetings have helped, as has the substance abuse program. But even more than that, I want to be known as a person who can be trusted. I now realize, for the first*

time, that the only way that this will ever happen will be if I NEVER AGAIN touch any alcoholic beverage, illegal drugs, or do anything else that I know is morally wrong.

I'm sorry for the grief that my crime has caused you and the children. I wish that I could go back and change all of that, but I can't. What I can do is to teach our children why I made these mistakes, show them how they are copying my improper attitudes, and what it will cost them if they continue to follow in my footsteps. I also realize that showing them these things will not do any good unless I give them new footsteps to follow; footsteps of trust and respectability. In other words, I now realize that I must give them a better example to follow than I have in the past.

I still have a lot of attitudes that need to be straightened out. I am learning how to control my temper and to think about the consequences before acting rather than acting impulsively based on my feelings at the moment. I know its hard for you to believe, but I'm even learning how to make rational decisions based on proper ethical and moral values. More importantly, I have learned that the keys to freedom are respecting the rules of society and taking responsibility for my own actions.

I'm looking forward to learning how to love, how to communicate my true feelings without blaming others, and proper methods of disciplining children. I will be learning problem-solving skills, how to forgive myself and others, and how to rebuild my own and my family's self-esteem. As I learn these things I will share them with you.

Dear, I need your help. I want you to help me start dreaming of ways that we can make our home better when I get out. Help me to start dreaming about being a family man again. Teach me how to be the kind of man that you need and the changes that you are expecting me to make while I am here. Help me to start dreaming about going to work, to church, and to community and school activities.

Thank you for loving me. Thank you for showing me what it is like to love someone who doesn't deserve it. Thank you for being my wife. Thank you for being my personal lifesaver. Your love keeps me from drowning here in prison. Thank you!

Your loving husband,

Chapter 4
CPR For A Dying Relationship

Today, it is possible to bring a dead person back to life. You don't have to be a prophet or some type of god to accomplish this marvelous miracle. Instead, you have to be fast and know the techniques of cardiopulmonary resuscitation—otherwise known as CPR.

While it is true that some people can be "raised from the dead" through the use of CPR, there are also times that it just will not work. There is a point of no return, and once an individual passes that point it is impossible to bring them back to life.

Relationships can also reach a point of no return. Sometimes there has been so much damage done that all of the prayer, all of the marriage and family therapy, all of the begging and pleading in the world will not bring that relationship back to life.

Not all relationships need to be kept alive. When people find that their relationship has deteriorated to the point that simply being together creates a violent atmosphere, either there need to be some changes made or they need to get out. People are not designed to continually stay in conflict to determine who is going to be the boss. People are not designed to continually give love to people who give nothing in return. People are not built to be continually abused or to put up with those who repeatedly prove that they cannot be trusted.

For example, if your family members are actively involved in criminal activities and encourage you to participate, you need to back away from them. If, in the past, they have led you into temptation and are unwilling to change, maybe you would be better off without them. This also works the other way. Unless you are willing to change your way of doing things and start proving to your family that you can be trusted, maybe they would be better off without you.

With the exception of involuntary actions such as breathing, everything that you think, do, and say involves the process of decision making. Each decision begins as a thought, followed by a time of deciding what to do with that thought, then putting your decision into practice. Since everything that you do involves a decision, you become responsible for your words, thoughts, and actions.

People make some decisions so quickly that it almost seems automatic. Someone may decide to strike someone else before the victim could finish saying "You son-of-a-bit.. (BAM! WHAP!)." Instead of hitting, that person could have also chosen to ignore the statement. One inmate tells of "automatically" hitting a man in a bar with a beer bottle after being insulted and pushed. He now wishes that he had run away while screaming, "You're right, I'm chicken!" His decision to handle it just like his dad cost him 15 years of his life for attempted murder.

How many marriages have you seen end because someone blew their temper and said or did things that were later regretted? Instead of controlling their temper, these people made decisions to allow their tempers to control them. Those decisions cost them their marriages.

Every time you make a decision about what to say, how to act, what attitude you display, or how quickly you act, you are also deciding about the kind of relationship that you want. Your actions affect others around you, and as a result, have consequences. Everything that you say or do will have one of two effects on a relationship. It will either build the relationship up and make it stronger, or it will cause damage to the relationship, making it weaker. There is no middle ground.

Part of every decision that you make is accepting the consequences of your actions, good or bad. As your family looks at how you treat them, what kind of relationship are your actions telling them that you want?

Many relationships appear to be dead or dying

If you're like most inmates, you probably have a gnawing feeling that tells you that your marriage and/or family relationships are dying and may soon be dead. It seems that every day another inmate receives a "Dear John" letter or divorce papers or complains of family members who have stopped accepting his phone calls. If this hasn't already happened to you, you fear that you'll be the next victim and you'll be stuck here, all alone.

This does not have to happen to you! Even though most inmates have troubled family relationships, neither your marriage nor your family relationships have to die simply because you have been put in prison. If you can learn to identify the mistakes that you have made in the past, do the work to correct them, and begin rebuilding your bank account of trust, there is a possibility that the relationships can be revived. In fact, it can become even stronger while you are here.

You may have a second chance with your wife. Sometimes "absence makes the heart grow fonder." Your trial is over, and you are gone. As a result of your imprisonment many of your neighbors and former friends are treating your wife and children like social outcasts because of the crime you committed. When you abandoned her by earning a prison sentence, you also forced her to make a decision about what to do with you. Sometimes she hates you for that; other times she is lonely and misses you. When she has warm feelings about you, she will tend to focus on your good side and ignore the crime that you did. You might be able to take advantage of those feelings by starting to show her that you are worth waiting for. She may not decide to call it quits if you begin demonstrating that you are using this time to straighten out your improper attitudes and provide evidence that you are trying to rebuild your family's trust.

Unfortunately, because of your particular background, you have a tendency to act in certain ways, ways that got you in a lot of trouble. The invisible chains of loyalty to your parents, family, and others provided you with improper attitudes. Since you never tried to learn how to do things differently, you are stuck with only one way of doing things that obviously does not work. It will be hard to undo your years of training and learn how to live a completely new and ethical lifestyle. But you've got to do it if you want your family relationship to grow stronger.

Repeating improper attitudes, values, and behavior patterns from previous generations displays an improper loyalty to your past. It is an improper chain of loyalty if it requires you to live in a way that proves you untrustworthy or if it requires you to do things that are harmful. It is an improper chain of loyalty if you require your family to be loyal to you when you are not being trustworthy. These improper chains of loyalty need to be broken.

If your son copies your behavior and you both wind up in prison at the same time, will they allow you to live in the same dorm or cell? Is that what you want for your children? If not, you had better start showing them another way of living before it is too late.

How can you tell when a relationship is dead?

Some possible responses are, "whenever the feeling is gone"; "whenever one or both start having affairs"; "whenever communication is broken off"; "whenever people stop trying to see each other"; "whenever you can't stand to be around each other anymore." Each of these are symptoms of a dying relationship but don't necessarily mean that the relationship is dead.

A couple's relationship is dead when one of the partners declares it dead. All it takes is for one partner to say "Good-bye," and the relationship is over.

Even though one partner may be totally surprised when it happens, a close examination of the facts would probably show that the relationship began to die long before the actual decision was made to obtain the divorce. Relationships usually die slowly and in five recognizable stages.

Stage One begins when one person starts becoming unhappy with the relationship. Instead of confronting the other about the specific things that are causing the unhappiness, he or she will start showing signs of depression. As things get worse, each starts blaming the other for the problems instead of admitting their own part and taking responsibility for their own improper actions.

As this stage progresses and the conflicts become more frequent, it becomes more important to "win" arguments than to respect the other's needs. Both seem to forget that, in a relationship, when one person wins an argument, both lose. Finally, someone brings up the subject of divorce.

Stage Two comes when parents and friends are told that there are problems in the marriage. You begin picking on each other in public. Things that would normally remain private matters are openly discussed with family and friends. Without realizing it, you are building a support group for yourself so that if the split comes you won't have to go through it alone.

A common characteristic of this stage is when one or both partners begin experiencing mood swings. There is a feeling of sadness because the relationship is dying and at the same time joy at the thought of the conflict finally ending. As the people involved realize that they are drifting apart, sometimes they will cling to each other and act very loving. At other times they experience hostility, bitterness, anger, and hatred.

As this stage continues, the children are told that mom and dad may not be living together anymore. In response, the children will begin to pull back from their parents and begin to look for friends who have been through divorce. In doing so, they are looking for a support group so that if the split comes they won't have to go through it alone. Also, by pulling back and cutting off contact now, the children feel that maybe it won't hurt so much if one of their parents leaves.

Stage Three begins when someone announces that the marriage is over, and an attorney is contacted. Plans are made about how they want their new life to be. Frequently, the one ending the relationship begins an affair so they will have someone special in their lives to make the transition easier. When this happens, the "dumped" partner usually blames the affair for ending the marriage, but that's not the case. Although the affair may have provided the fatal blow, it would again prove the old saying, "People don't go out looking for what they have at home." Most relationships are sick long before affairs start.

As this stage continues, one of the partners moves out and the relationship is split. The transition between Stage Three and Four can be one of the most painful times in one's life. Even in the worst of marriages, and even if there is someone waiting to take the "dumped" spouse's place, divorce hurts. Even in marriages where both want out, divorce hurts. Part of your life is being torn from your very soul. Each will probably feel rejected. Both started the relationship with high hopes of a lifetime of happiness. They didn't make it, and now both feel like failures.

Stage Four begins when the judge signs the divorce papers and both begin to rebuild their two separate lives. It only takes one partner to force this to happen. Divorces are frequently granted over the objections of the other spouse.

Stage Five is reached when all emotional bonds are broken between the two. This doesn't mean that the couple must never see or talk to each other again. It simply means that the wound has healed and each can then go on with their own individual lives. The couple may decide to remain in touch for the sake of the children, or remain acquaintances, or to never see each other again.

Some people never reach Stage Five and continually grieve at their loss. People who remarry before reaching this stage usually have marriages doomed to failure. Marriages will not work if you are emotionally tied to someone else. One way to tell when a person reaches this stage is their ability to hear that their ex-spouse is seeing someone else without getting jealous.

You have made it extremely easy for your wife to obtain a divorce. As was discussed in Chapter 3, when you committed your crime you asked the state to remove you from your family. In doing so, you abandoned her and forced her and the children to live without you. This violated both your marriage contract and promise to live with her and provide for her needs "for better or worse, in sickness and health, until death do you part." This entitles your wife to a divorce if she wants one. If your wife decides to divorce you, she will not be abandoning you. She will only be asking the court to make permanent what you have already done to the family.

Frequently, many people "suddenly" find themselves involved in a divorce that they never saw coming. They thought that everything was fine only to discover that their spouse is in Stage Four. In fact, after reading this, you may suddenly realize that you are closer to a divorce than you ever thought possible.

If you see yourself in one of the later stages, remember these words: "It ain't over 'til it's over." The rules of family relationships say that whenever one person changes, the entire family will change. Because of this, it is sometimes possible for you to save your marriage even when your partner is uncooperative.

CPR is used only when a person is near death. If your family relationship appears to be dead, and if you want to give your family relationship the CPR it needs to bring it back to life, you are going to have to act quickly by making the changes in your life that will make you attractive to your family again.

Chapter 4

How your family relationship got sick to begin with

Let's again look at what causes family relationships to get sick. As you will recall, the root cause of all interpersonal conflict is the power struggle between two or more people to determine who is going to be the boss and have the final say. This means that the conflict in homes begins when one or more people begin saying, "I'm Number One! Because I'm Number One, I can do anything I want; say anything that I want, anytime that I want, to anyone that I want; and there is nothing that anyone can do about it, period!"

Looking out for your own needs does not allow you to consider the desires of the other members of the family. As a result, anytime there is a decision to be made, the family members must first have a fight to determine who is going to be the boss. Yielding becomes a sign of weakness; thus, the conflict must continue until someone becomes "the winner" and gets to have his or her own way.

This starts a cycle that unfortunately becomes a part of many American homes. Whenever there is a disagreement, instead of using problem-solving skills, each becomes angry and tries to force the other into compliance. Voices are raised, temper tantrums are displayed, sex is withheld, physical force is used, or whatever else each can think of until one gives in to the other's demands.

Unfortunately, many people feel that these methods are proper ways of resolving conflict in the home. The problem with this type of lifestyle is that it makes matters worse instead of better. It also teaches the children that these are appropriate ways of resolving conflict. As a result, the children grow up and become "just like mom and dad." As adults, whenever they don't get their own way, they raise their voices, throw a temper tantrum, withhold sex, use physical force, or whatever until they get their way. When this happens, the invisible chain has been passed to yet another generation.

It becomes obvious to everyone when children begin to accept their parents' invisible chain that says it is permissible to abuse one's power in order to get your own way. Children start using hateful words and threats to get their own way, just like their parents. Or the abused child starts abusing other children. Another sign is when the children, after listening to their parents curse each other, start cursing their friends, their parents, other children, and even their teachers.

Failing to discipline children is an abuse of power

Parents frequently reinforce their children's abuse of power. An example of this is when a child throws a temper tantrum in the supermarket until the parent caves in and gives the child its way.

Children are naturally rebellious and will push their self-proclaimed power to the limit. When children misbehave, the parents have a choice: to discipline them in a way that says "I love you too much to allow you to act that way" or to abuse their power. If you fail to provide discipline to your children it proves that you don't care about them.

Picture a lovely summer day. You and your family have driven into the mountains for a picnic. You find a perfect spot overlooking the valley. Next to the picnic table is a large field that would make a perfect place for the children to play. There is a tall chainlink fence at the edge of the field, and you notice that on the other side of the fence is a sheer drop of at least a mile. After walking along the fence and shaking it in several places you discover that it is secure and tight. Only then do you feel safe in allowing your children to play in the field or walk to the edge and look out over the valley. Having the fence there provides security and allows your family to enjoy the field without any fear of falling off the edge to a certain death. But if you found a hole in the fence or if the fence was loose, you would not allow your children near it.

Discipline is the fence that keeps children from doing things that would allow them to hurt themselves and others. It is the parents' responsibility to build the fence by creating and enforcing appropriate rules of behavior.

Children will "test" their family's fence. If parents prove, by providing consistent and appropriate discipline, that the fence will not give, the children will feel secure and be happier. Children want the fence to hold. Undisciplined children will be unhappy because there is no fence, and they are afraid they will get hurt because the fence isn't strong enough. In homes where there is a constant power struggle between the family members, the children are simply "testing the fence" and parents overreact to the child's improper behavior. Instead of providing loving discipline, the parents chose to abuse their power, violate their position of trust, and abuse their children physically, sexually, or emotionally.

Failing to provide proper discipline is also an abuse of power. In fact, any parent who fails to properly discipline their children displays the same attitude as the parent who physically or sexually abuses their children. Physical or sexual abuse says to the child, "It's okay for parents to do things that would cause their children physical, sexual, or emotional harm." Failing to provide loving discipline says to the child, "It's okay with me if you to do things that would cause yourself physical, sexual, or emotional harm."

Both failing to discipline children and being physically abusive are forms of emotional abuse. Either way the child grows up with an insecure feeling, knowing that the parents didn't care if they got harmed or killed. Parents who fail to provide proper discipline to their children prove to their children that they are not loved. These children will enter adulthood having learned from their parents that when you are an adult it is okay to abuse your power and avoid your responsibility; it is okay to hurt others or to allow them to get hurt because of your actions and to hate those whom you are supposed to love.

Instead of teaching the children that their parent's love for them prohibited them from allowing the children to continue misbehaving, the parents improper actions will teach them that it's okay to abuse your power and force people to comply with your rules. Unfortunately, if you are guilty of either of these, your children will grow up just like you and think that this is the way things are supposed to be.

Understanding what you owe your family

Before you can begin to clear your family debt, you must understand exactly what you owe your family. Your family does not owe you anything; you owe them. Your trial probably left your wife physically, emotionally, and financially bankrupt. If she attended the trial, it was because of her loyalty to you.

Because of her love for you, she was willing to spend everything the family had to provide you with good clothes to wear to your trial and the best lawyer that money could buy. Because of her loyalty to you, she was willing to take time away from her household duties or from her job just to give you emotional support by being at your trial. Because of her loyalty to you (even though you do not deserve it) she sends you money that she cannot afford and goes to great lengths to visit you in this remote place, just to show you her loyalty and love.

Don't forget that deep down inside, she is keeping track of these sacrifices in the family bank account. Your wife may have some resentment

CPR For A Dying Relationship

because your living conditions are better than hers. You have three hot meals cooked for you each day. Does she? You have a clean place to sleep. Does she? You can take classes to improve yourself. Does she have the time to do that? You have access to a complete team of physical and mental health professionals that are available to you without charge. Does she have the money to get similar help if she or the children need it? You don't even have to wash your clothes.

Mary Schwartz and Judith Weintraub found that once a husband is sent to prison, the wife's parents frequently encourage her to "dump the bum." Your parents may still be showing loyalty to you by blaming her, saying that if she had been a better wife you would not have had to turn to a life of crime. If this happens, every time your wife takes the children to see their grandparents, she has to face their anger over and over again. As a result, your children may not see their grandparents as often. Because of your crime, not only have they lost you, but also their grandparents.

Your wife must decide what to tell your children about where you have gone and why. Some lie and say that you have joined the military and been stationed overseas, are sick, or whatever. Again, she is trying to prove her loyalty to you by making your disappearance appear to be something that is socially acceptable. Unfortunately, when the children find out the truth (and they almost always do) they will lose their ability to trust their mothers.

Because of your crime and imprisonment, your wife has to deal with increased problems with the children. When you committed your crime you abused your power. You told society that it did not have any right to tell you how to live your life and that the rules did not apply to you. Then, you probably blamed your crime on someone or something else.

Now that you are gone your children are copying your attitudes. They are misbehaving more and refusing to obey the rules at home and at school. And instead of taking responsibility for their own actions, they are blaming it on the situation that you created.

If your family relationship is dying it is because you did everything to kill it by committing your crime. If your wife is still standing by you, she is hoping that when you get out, you will be ready to settle down, exchange your criminal career for a respectable job, and be the husband that she has always wanted. That hope is the *only* reason that your wife is being loyal to you and is willing to wait for you.

Although serving this time in prison pays your debt to society, it actually increases your debt in the family bank account. One way that you can begin rebuilding trust in your family bank account is to show your family that you are using this time to learn how to be a good family man and how to repay them for the harm that you have done to the family.

The remainder of this book will provide you with specific ways to practice ethical living. Learning how to practice ethical living is the only way that you can begin repaying your debt in the family bank account and replace it with a balance of trust. If your family relationship is dying, keeping your commitment to practice ethical living is the CPR that might give your family relationship life again.

Giving yourself and your family good self-esteem

In order to pay a debt, you must give the person holding the bill something of value. You can make yourself something of value by giving yourself the gift of a good self-image and then passing that gift on to your wife and/or children. Good self-esteem and a feeling of completeness require four things: (1) to feel loved, (2) to feel accepted, (3) to feel competent, and (4) ethical living.

You will feel loved when you know that the others within your group will treat you with respect and will never intentionally do anything that would harm you. You can get that loving feeling by doing three things: (1) by loving others even when they are acting unlovable, (2) by treating others with respect even when they are not treating you with respect, and (3) by treating others the way you want to be treated.

Do each of your family members know that you will always treat them with respect? Do they know that you will love them even when they are acting unlovable? Do your children know that you will discipline them in a way that says, "I love you too much to allow you to act that way" when they misbehave? If not, you are robbing them of their self-esteem.

Sometimes, you will never feel loved while you are in certain groups. For example, a cat will never feel loved in a dog pound. If you find yourself in such a group, you had better change groups quickly—or learn how to bark!

To feel accepted means that you can convince others to follow your suggestions without having to resort to using threats or violence. This will happen when others around you know that you always consider their feelings when offering suggestions. This also means that you will listen to their suggestions and are willing to yield if it is best for the entire group.

You have given this gift to your family when they know that you always consider their feelings before making suggestions and that you are willing to yield to their needs. Do your children know that you accept them just the way they are? Can they trust you to provide them with the necessary training—including discipline—that will enable them to enter an adult world when they are grown?

You will feel competent when there is a job that you know that you can do well; something that you and everyone else knows is your job. It doesn't have to be a big job or even something that you are being paid for. It may be something as simple as being trusted to empty the trash each morning. If you can be trusted to do little, seemingly unimportant jobs, soon you will be trusted to do more important jobs. Being competent is another way to describe people who can be trusted to do what needs to be done.

You can give this gift to your family by acknowledging the areas that they can do well. Praise your children for their work instead of criticizing them. Encourage them to develop their talents. Praise your wife for the things she has done right instead of criticizing her for her faults. Praise her for her leadership abilities.

Ethical living is a lifestyle and involves a commitment to live according to the keys to freedom: respect for the rules of society and taking responsibility for your own actions. Ethical living means always treating others with respect no matter how they treat you. It means treating others in the same way that you want to be treated.

Ethical living means living in such a way that you have nothing to hide. You won't care who watches you or worry about being seen in the "wrong place." As you practice ethical living you will never fear sudden inspections or when the correctional officer says "fill the cup" and he doesn't mean with coffee. Ethical living means doing what is right simply because it is the right thing to do.

You can't teach your children ethical living, but they will learn it from you. They learn it by watching how you act and seeing if you practice what you preach. Telling your children to "do as I say and not as I do" won't work because actions speak louder than words. Take a good hard look at yourself: Is the way you act the way you want your children to act?

Practicing ethical living is the way to keep your children from accepting your invisible chains of improper attitudes, improper values, and improper behavior patterns. Ethical living means admitting to your children the mistakes that you have made. This also means giving them a proper example to follow.

If you do these things, you will have begun to pay your debt and given your children a better chance to grow up and become healthy, happy, and productive adults. Your wife and family will begin seeing that you really mean to keep your commitment to practice ethical living.

What is love?

Once you realize that you are in fact someone of value, then you are ready to start truly loving your family and others. What is love? Love is not something that you feel, love is something that you do. This means that love is a decision and not something that just happens.

Love is giving a part of yourself that is the best you have to offer, expecting nothing in return except that the gift be accepted. A true gift of love asks only that it be accepted. It never harms, and it is never given for selfish reasons. For example, illegal drugs can never be a true gift of love because they make you dependent on the giver and are harmful.

A true gift of love asks only that it be accepted. It will have no strings attached that say how the gift is to be used or not used. If you reject a gift of love, you have rejected the giver of that gift and not the gift itself.

Here's an illustration: suppose you spend hours in the craft shop creating a leather belt for the chaplain. You carefully carve marijuana leaves all the way around it. Finally, after it is complete, you proudly present it to him. Considering his position in the prison and the fact that he is a minister, would it be appropriate for him to wear a belt with marijuana leaves carved in it? How would you feel if he gave it back to you and told you that it is no good? You would feel rotten, and rightfully so.

Rejecting a true gift of love is rejecting the giver of the gift and not the gift itself. By giving the belt back to you, the chaplain would be rejecting more than just a belt that he could not use, he would be rejecting you. If he accepts the belt and compliments you on the workmanship, he would be accepting you and your relationship would grow.

If it were a true gift of love you would be asking only that he accept it and would allow him to use or not use it according to his wishes. This also means that it would be okay with you if he gave it to someone else or even exchanged it for something else.

If he wanted your relationship to continue to grow, he would offer you a gift of love in return. But if your gift and his gift were true gifts of love, neither would have been given with the hopes of receiving something in return, because a true gift of love never asks for anything in return except that the gift be accepted.

That's how true love works. As you exchange little gifts of love, each of you will learn to give the other gifts that say, "I know what you need, and I am responding to that need." Each exchange of a gift of love will cause the relationship to grow stronger.

You can start the process by offering someone, even an enemy, a gift of love. If they accept the gift, that's a start. If you wait for them to start the process, it may never happen.

You may ask, "What can an inmate give to someone as a gift of love or in return for the gifts of love that are given to him? We can't run down to the local gift shop."

Letters like the ones at the end of the first three chapters are gifts of love. Sometimes all you have to give in return for a gift is a heartfelt "thank you." How long has it been since you sat down and wrote a long letter to each family member, including your children, spelling out the exact things you appreciate about them? Do you need to write any letters of apology? Those letters would be gifts of love.

How to communicate your true feelings to others

Ethical living includes learning to communicate your true feelings to others. You cannot not communicate. For example, during next week's visiting hours, suppose a good-looking woman walks into the prison to see her husband. Let's also suppose that another inmate continually runs his eyes up and down her body while licking his lips and panting like a dog. Although this inmate never said a word, would there be any question what he is thinking?

Now suppose that this woman's husband sees this inmate and starts to walk toward him with his teeth clenched and his hand in a fist. Would anyone have any trouble understanding the message being conveyed? If a correctional officer simply walked over and stood in the vicinity of the two men, would there be any question about what he was "saying"?

Walking out of a room and slamming the door lets people know that the person is angry. A tear in an eye communicates pain. Sometimes a warm smile can convey a message that will melt the hardest heart.

One of the best gifts of love that you can give your family is the ability to share each other's true feelings without fear. Virginia Satir said that this is the only way that you can have any chance to heal relationships, to break down walls between you, or to build bridges between two opposing sides. The ability to communicate your true feelings is one of the keys to building close relationships.

Unless you can communicate your true feelings, the other family members can't know how to respond to you. No one in your family knows how to read your mind. In fact, you have no right to be angry with anyone unless they know exactly what you are angry about. You can accomplish this task—without starting a fight—if you share your feelings without blaming them or telling them how they should be feeling.

For example: "I felt angry when you didn't call like you promised" simply states a fact and does not blame. The statement, "Right now I feel so angry that I feel like a bomb ready to explode," shares a personal feeling. So does, "I don't like what I am hearing, so I'm leaving," or "I like that, tell me more."

The way to build the relationship is by being open and honest with your feelings. Feelings are neither right nor wrong, they are simply the truth about how you feel about a particular thing at that particular time. Feelings are your "gut-level" reaction to the things that happen in your life.

In other words, if you want to become closer to someone, you have to start leveling with them. Leveling with someone simply states your feelings at the moment and never places blame. Here is a simple rule that you can follow. If you can substitute the words "I think" in any sentence that starts with "I feel," you are not sharing feelings. Instead you are placing blame or passing judgement. For example: "I think you were wrong to do that" can be said, "I feel you were wrong to do that." When you tell someone that they are wrong, they will tend to get defensive, and that tends to start arguments.

You can even criticize someone without placing blame. To accomplish this, you simply share your feelings. For example:

Honey, I felt rotten last night after our fight. I didn't like it when you cursed at me. I felt hostile and cold. Fighting like this is not helping our relationship. We need to stop, take a look, and use our problem-solving skills to determine what is wrong and how we can correct it.

A proper apology always shares feelings without casting blame. For example: "I'm sorry for the way that I treated you. What I did was wrong, and I shouldn't have done it." Think about how much better that sounds than "Yeah, I'm sorry, but if you hadn't opened your big mouth it wouldn't have happened." The first statement shares honest feelings, the second casts blame.

Learn the difference between a "why" question and a "what" question. Only someone who has authority over another person has the right to ask "why" questions. For example, it is proper for a parent to ask a child why they did what they did. It is also proper for prison officials or your boss to ask you why you did what you did.

Your wife is your partner and your equal. Being a leader in your family does not give you the right to boss her around. If you ask her why she did a particular thing, she may think that you are trying to be her boss. Do you remember the cause of interpersonal conflict? It is the power struggle to determine who is going to be the boss. So she comes back with, "Why do you need to know?" and the fight is on.

"What" questions show concern for the other person's needs. For example, "What can I do to help?" instead of "Why do *I* need to help?" "What can I do to make things right?" instead of "Why do *I* need to apologize?" "Can you tell me what you are feeling right now?" instead of "Why are *you* acting like that?"

When you truly love someone you will be willing to risk sharing your most intimate thoughts with them, expecting nothing in return except that they be accepted for what they are: feelings. This means that you can admit to feeling afraid, vulnerable, foolish, happy, sad, peaceful, angry, or anything else you are feeling.

The flip side of the same coin says that when you truly love someone you will be willing to *listen* to their most intimate thoughts and accept them for what they are: feelings.

This means that, if for example, your children came up to you and said, "Daddy, we're so mad at you that we hope you drop dead," that you thank them for sharing their feelings with you. If you love them you will accept their statement and realize that you have an opportunity to find out what is bothering them and what you could do to change their minds. So instead of being defensive and giving them an ugly answer, you could reply, "What have I done that makes you feel that way?" or "What can I do to change that feeling?"

Forgiveness is not forgetting

The next step up your ladder of ethical living is the ability to forgive. Forgiveness is not forgetting; you don't have the ability to do that. *Forgiveness is a decision to treat them like it never happened while still holding them accountable for their actions.*

Forgiveness means that you have decided that the person who harmed you will not have to pay you personally for the harm they have done. Instead you have decided to leave the punishment up to God and/or society.

Whenever someone unjustly harms you, their improper actions have created a debt with you and with society. You can release them from the debt they owe you by deciding that they do not have to pay you personally for what they did. After you have made this decision, you can then treat them like it never happened.

This, however, *will not* release them from the debt they owe society for the harm they have done. If, for example, they have violated the law, you *do not* have the authority to forgive them for that. Society will still require them to pay for the damage they did, according to society's rules. If you hang onto the evil and think, "I'll never forget what you have done, and someday I will make you pay!" that incident will gnaw on you until the day you die, and you will get more bitter as time goes on.

In other words, forgiveness will do you more good than it will the person who harmed you because you will be free of it. But they will still have to answer to society and/or to God, and they can do a lot better job of holding people accountable for their improper actions than you can. What forgiveness does is turn you loose from the incident. Forgive them and suddenly it will no longer be your problem.

Forgiveness is saying that even though what the person did was wrong they still have value. Your wife or girlfriend could look you right in the eye and say, "I love you and I care for you" and mean it. That's because even though you are in prison because of the crime that you committed, she values you as an individual. Your crime makes you responsible to the state and to God, but *not* to her. Because of this, she can treat you as if it never happened.

How about forgiving yourself for mistakes that you have made? Here's how. You do what is required to repay your "debts" to your family, to your victim, and to society by doing your time and making any restitution that is required. You may ask God's forgiveness. Once that is done, accept the fact that you now have a clean slate and that your debt is paid. Then, quit punishing yourself and start living the rest of your life as if your moral failures never happened.

This will be hard for you to do. You are going to have to face unforgiving people for the rest of your life who will delight in reminding you of your failures. When this happens, you have a choice: you can get angry and defensive, or you can give them love and allow them the freedom to express their feelings about you.

For example, suppose you have done the steps to forgiving yourself for your crime. After you get out, someone comes up to you and says, "I remember you; you're the guy that broke into that house and stole all that stuff just so you can buy drugs [or whatever else you might have done wrong]." Instead of getting angry and defensive, you could reply:

You're right, that's me. I was wrong to do that, and I earned the sentence that I got. I've paid my debt, and I certainly don't want to do anything that would create a new debt and put me back in prison.

That would sound a whole lot better than, "So what, I've done my time, so get off my back, you (expletive deleted)!"

Learn from your mistakes. Since you won't be able to forget about your moral failures, admit them. When you do, be sure that you include the penalty that you earned because of your failure.

Some day, the warden is going to tell you to pack your bag and then escort you to the front door of this prison and slam the door behind you. When this happens, you will have a clean slate. Even if you have 100 years of probation hanging over your head, the state will not let you back into this or any other prison unless you decide to do something that violates the rules.

If you want to keep your slate clean, realize that once you have repaid your debts that it takes ethical living to keep from creating new debts.

How to develop and use problem-solving skills

Ethical living includes learning how to use proper problem-solving skills and teaching this to your family. Here is a simple five-step problem-solving formula that will work for most problems you will encounter in your life.

Chapter 4

Step One: Identify the problem—the real problem. Frequently the reason that problems aren't solved is because people don't realize what the real problem is. For example, if you have the shakes because you are used to abusing alcohol or drugs, the real problem is your substance abuse, not a lack of alcohol and drugs. If you are constantly losing fistfights, the real problem is not your inability to fight. The real problem is that you don't know how to control your temper.

Step Two: Brainstorm possible solutions. Brainstorming solutions is not something that you do all by yourself. Part of ethical living is always talking it over with all of the people involved in the problem. This includes the children, if necessary.

As you brainstorm solutions, come up with as many ideas as you can. Put down everything that you or anyone else thinks of—even the wild ones that sound completely stupid. You should be able to think of at least four possible solutions to each problem, but it's better if you could come up with at least ten. For example, possible solutions to a substance abuse problem could include the following:

1. Buying some drugs from one of the local prison pushers.
2. Getting your thrills by taking off your clothes and standing on your head all day. (Remember, include the silly ones. Sometimes they turn out to be the best solution.)
3. Deciding to quit on your own and then doing it.
4. Attending the Alcoholic Anonymous or Narcotics Anonymous meetings here in the prison.
5. Voluntarily entering the substance abuse program.
6. Staying to yourself and refusing to talk to anyone.
7. Spending all of your time studying.
8. Ignoring the problem until it goes away.
9. Deciding that using a small amount won't hurt you or anyone else and then only using that amount.
10. Asking God to remove the problem from you.

Step Three: Consider the long-term consequences for each possible solution. Everything that you do has consequences: some good and some bad. These consequences are the logical conclusion of each action. As you decide which solution to use, remember that you are also asking for the consequences that go along with that action.

Let's look at some long-term consequences to the suggested solutions.

CPR For A Dying Relationship

1. Buying drugs or booze from a prison pusher helps an inmate become prisonized, which means that when they get out they'll probably be right back. Besides, getting caught with drugs might give an inmate more time or mess up his chances for parole.

2. Even though taking off your clothes and standing on your head sounds silly, it might just work. After all, being put in solitary confinement long enough for a psychological workup might give an inmate's body enough time to get the substance out of his system. But then what would that do to that person's chances when they meet with the parole board?

3. There are many advantages to a person quitting on their own. You don't have to admit to anyone that you have a problem. There are also many disadvantages. Trying to hide a substance abuse problem is like trying to hide an elephant. It is such a big problem that everyone around already knows that it's there. Admitting one's addiction is the first step to recovery, and recovery becomes more effective if it is done in front of a loving individual or group who is willing to help. Anyone who considers this option by trying to quit on their own should also consider how many times they have tried this before and how many times it has not worked in the past.

4. The first step in finding out about the prison's Alcoholics or Narcotics Anonymous groups is to find out if there are any openings and what their admission policies are. Generally, both inside of prisons and in the free world, the only admission requirement is a sincere desire to kick the habit. Ask questions; see if there is any evidence that this particular group really works and helps people kick their habits. Some groups are better than others. And remember, just because that group didn't work for one person doesn't mean that it won't work for you. The only way that you can find out if it will work for you is to try it.

5. Going to the prison officials and asking for help with a drug addiction is a big step and is hard to do. Being strong enough to risk admitting that you have a problem is the first step to recovery.

    If your prison has a substance abuse program it will be

professionally run. The leaders will have specialized training and experience. More importantly, your progress will become part of your prison record. Knowing that "flunking out" would go on one's record can be a powerful incentive to keep trying when tempted to quit. Usually this program is a popular one because so many inmates have substance abuse addictions and know that recovery is vital to their parole chances. Unfortunately, treatment programs must be limited in size. This means that frequently inmates have to spend some time on a waiting list.

6. Think about it: Is staying to yourself and refusing to talk to anyone really a workable solution? Drugs and alcohol are frequently used to combat loneliness. Staying to yourself forces loneliness and would provide plenty of time to think about how some drugs or booze might eliminate some of the pain of living here. Man was not designed to live alone and handle his problems by himself.

7. If you try to end a substance abuse problem by studying all of the time, pretty soon you would be studying about how to find some drugs or some booze.

8. Many people, instead of quitting, decide to cut back and use the substance in moderation. This will not work. People who try this usually find that within a short time they are back at their old level of use or even higher. An addiction to alcohol or drugs is never satisfied. It always wants more.

9. If you ignore a substance abuse problem it will only get worse.

10. Asking God to remove a substance abuse addiction is probably one of the most popular methods used. A few people testify that after a religious experience God immediately removed their habit and desire for alcohol or drugs. Well, God is still in the miracle business and that does happen sometimes, but most of the time it doesn't. God is a loving father, and loving fathers allow their children to reap the consequences of their own actions.

It takes 21 days without the substance for the human body to dry out, months and even years to get over a psychological addiction, and the potential for relapse will remain for the rest of that individual's life. Simply stated, *there is no permanent cure for addiction.*

If you are trying to recover from an addiction, God will, if allowed, provide you with enough strength to do without whatever it is that you are addicted to for one day at a time—for the rest of your life.

Step Four: Pick the best-looking solution and try it. Of the ones listed above, the most logical choice would be either going to the Alcoholics or Narcotics Anonymous meetings or to sign up for the substance abuse program.

Step Five: If that solution did not work, go back to step one and start over. But before you do, be sure that you have given it enough time to work. For example, it would be foolish to go to one Alcoholics Anonymous meeting and declare that it would not work for you.

Before you try a different solution, make sure that you identified the real problem. For example, using all of the techniques in this book will not solve your family problems if the real problem is that you are still looking out for Number One. In this case, before the family problems can be cured, you must change.

If in fact you did identify the real problem properly, then select a *different* solution than you tried the first time. Believe it or not, the reason that many people never get their problems solved is that they will continue to use the same solution, even though they have proved over and over that it does not work.

Sometimes it takes a combination of solutions to solve the problem. For example, it might take a combination of the substance abuse program, Narcotics Anonymous, and asking God for strength to solve a drug addiction.

Start dreaming about getting out

Ethical living includes the ability to dream. Even if you are just beginning a long prison sentence, you need to start dreaming about what you are going to do when you get out. Most inmates feel that someway, somehow, everything is going to be okay once they leave the front gate to freedom. It doesn't work that way.

Everything that you will ever accomplish in your life begins with a dream; a dream that says, "I wonder what it would be like to (fill in the blank)."

Charles Lindbergh dreamed of being the first man to fly solo across the Atlantic Ocean. He followed that dream and found ways to make it happen.

George Bush dreamed of what it would be like to be President of the United States. He followed that dream and found ways to make it happen.

Martin Luther King, Jr. had a dream of teaching all people to learn to live together in peace and harmony. He followed that dream and found ways to make it happen.

The time to start dreaming about what you want to be and what you want to do after you get out is NOW! Get together with other inmates and talk about the dreams you have about what you want to accomplish while you are in prison and after you get out. Find inmates who returned, and if they will be honest, find out from them where they went wrong so that you won't make the same mistakes. Once you have developed your dreams, you can treat those dreams like any other problem.

First, identify the problem. In this case, the problem here is how to accomplish your dreams.

Next, brainstorm possible solutions. This includes finding and talking with people who can help you achieve your dreams. Talk to the counselors here in this prison. Tell your family about the things that you hope to achieve and the specific steps that you might be able to take that would make that dream a reality. Ask their opinion. Find out what they are willing to help you accomplish. For example, your wife might be happy to continue working if it meant that you could finish school and then get a better job.

Consider the long-term consequences of achieving your dream. Many questions need to be answered. For example, will fulfilling your dream make you a better person? Will your family and community be better if your dream comes true?

If so, then go for it. Give it your best shot. Try to make your dream come true. As you do, remember this old saying: "You'll never know how much you can do until you have bitten off more than you can chew."

Suppose that things didn't work out like you planned and your dream did not come true. In fact, suppose that things turned out so badly that your dream is now a nightmare. Then you have a problem. And when you have a problem you use your newly developed problem-solving skills.

Start by finding out what the problem really is. Maybe your dream was impossible to achieve. You can't build a ladder to the moon no matter how hard you try.

As you think about your failure, you might realize that the dream can be accomplished if you can find another way to get there. Or maybe you need to try another dream.

Differences between growing and dying family relationships

In 1989, while conducting a research project among a randomly selected group of inmates, I discovered that 33 percent of the men were less than happy with their family relationships. In fact, 17 percent were very unhappy with them, while only 9 percent were very happy with their present family relationships.

Why the differences? Many times the way the inmate decides to treat his family is the determining factor. Over the years, research has discovered that there are several differences between the inmates who have growing family relationships and those with dying family relationships.

Inmates with unhappy relationships seem to have several common characteristics. If they write at all, they write short letters full of requests for things that they need. Many times these letters are used to fuss at the family members for not visiting, calling, or writing. These men don't share their feelings and seldom ask about the welfare of other family members.

When their families come to visit, men who have relationships that are dying spend the first few minutes of the time saying things like:

"What did you find out about my appeal?"

"Did you get the rest of the money to the attorney so he will do some more work for me?"

"How much money can you leave for me today?"

"Kids, you shut up or I'll really smack you or give you a good shaking."

To say all of this takes only a few minutes. After that, these inmates and their families will spend the rest of their time either sitting and staring at the walls in stony silence or making small talk. If you could listen in on what they were saying you would probably hear them exchanging a constant barrage of complaints about the rotten living conditions, their lack of money, their own troubles, and how rotten the "system" is.

These men seem to always seem to be acting harshly toward their children. Their children will retreat from the insults by falling asleep or by copying their parent's aggression toward them by bothering the other visitors.

These inmates are the ones who are still looking out for Number One and do not seem to care about the needs of their families. Their entire attitude seems to revolve around their own needs. Their favorite saying is probably, "What's in it for me?"

Inmates with improving family relationships also have many similar characteristics. These men write long and intimate letters to their wives and family members. They're not afraid to say things like, "I love you"; or "I'm sorry"; or "Will you forgive me?"

These men want their family members back home to feel like they are a part of their everyday lives. So their letters talk to their families as if they were sitting right there with them. These guys even describe the events of the day so that the family always knows exactly what the inmate is doing. In these letters, they will talk about the happy things, the sad things, their successes and failures. They will talk about the little things that really don't seem important. These men might even describe the meals for the day, just like they might do if they were sitting around the table at home. Their letter might go like this:

> *I thought about you at breakfast this morning. The biscuits were good, and the sausage was excellent, but the cook burned the eggs. You know, I like them like you fix them, over easy and without so much grease. I'll be glad when I can eat your cooking again. I miss you.*
>
> *I got in sort of a disagreement with a correctional officer today. I didn't like something that she said, and I lost my temper. I know I promised not to do that again, and I am doing better. Even though I was wrong to lose my temper, I am kind of proud of myself. This time I caught myself and stopped before I said or did anything that I would regret later.*

Men who write letters like the one above have found a secret benefit comes with them. If you make a commitment to not have any secrets between you and your spouse or other family member, you will be less likely to do something that would hurt your relationship.

Inmates with growing relationships level with their families. They realize that by sharing their true feelings they are sharing a part of themselves that is the best they have to offer, asking nothing in return but that the letter be accepted.

These men share their dreams with their families because they *want* their families to know what they have to look forward to when they get out. These men *want* their families to be part of their dreams and are not afraid to say so. The letter continues:

> *Dear, sitting here in prison gives me a lot of time to think. I try to spend that time dreaming about what my life will be like when we are together again. I'm looking forward to painting the house for you and even helping you with the dishes.*
>
> *It's going to be hard for me to get used to keeping a schedule at work. I'm not used to working eight hours a day anymore. Will you help me? I've been thinking about trying to learn how to be a brick mason. What do you think about that?*

When their families visit, the inmates with growing family relationships begin each visit by reassuring each individual member of their family that they are loved. Wives, children, parents, and friends need to hear over and over that you love them and appreciate the sacrifices that they are making for you. And you need to be specific about what you appreciate.

These inmates notice the little things that their family does on visiting day to make it a special day; for example, if his wife wears his favorite dress. These guys would beam with pride if, like J. E. Hughes saw during his study, one of their children arrived at the prison wearing a T-shirt with "My Daddy's Number is C-92760" printed on the front.

Next, they listen to their families' concerns. These inmates ask for forgiveness when necessary and are willing to forgive. They don't mind it when their wives ask questions like, "Why did you get in the fight last week?" or when the children ask, "Daddy, why did you have to go away?" Inmates who want their family relationships to grow answer questions like this truthfully instead of getting angry and defensive.

The inmates with growing family relationships realize that they owe a great deal to their families. They also understand that the only way to begin repaying that debt is to give their families love and by demonstrating that they can be trusted to live an ethical life.

How to keep your family alive while in prison

"But," you say, "I'm locked up here in prison. I can't put my arms around my family and hug them; I can't even sit down and have a private conversation with them. How can I put these things into practice? How can I keep my family alive while I'm serving a prison sentence?"

First, you need to break the invisible chains of improper loyalties that bind you to your past and keep you from trying new ways of doing things. Start by admitting to yourself and others the fact that you are a convicted criminal. Remember, this says something about your past and nothing about your future. You, and only you, must decide if you are ever going to be a criminal again. Keeping your commitment to practice ethical living will prevent you from ever being a criminal again.

Recognize that your family and friends influenced you as you were growing up. Everyone has memories of unloving and uncaring adults who gave us physical or emotional scars while we were growing up that still hurt. You can't change these memories or these people. You are not responsible for their actions—they are.

Recognize that you copied the improper attitudes of those around you while you were growing up and made them your own. In fact, not only did you copy their attitudes, you probably added a few improper attitudes of your own. No one forced you to act in improper ways, it was your decision. This makes you responsible for your own thoughts, actions, and words.

Realize that the only person that you can change is you. However, when you change, those around you will also change. As you make those decisions about how to act, realize that you are also making the decision about how you want to be treated. If you begin to practice ethical living, those around you will begin to respond to the new you. People who always treat others with respect tend to be treated with respect.

If you focus only on the other inmates, become more prisonized, and continue to look out only for Number One, you will be treated just like what you are becoming—a career criminal.

Second, if you want to keep your family alive while you are here you must begin repaying your debt in the family bank account. This starts when you begin respecting the needs of your family instead of looking out only for Number One. This also means spending the rest of your life finding out what your family needs from you and trying to fill those needs. Repaying your debt in the family bank account requires that you practice ethical living.

Ethical living means that you will no longer look out only for Number One and will never again abuse your power. Since your goal is to always consider your family's needs when you are making decisions, you will not try to be a dictator. Whenever a problem involves the other members of the family, you will discuss the problem with the members involved. Ethical living includes using your problem-solving skills instead of forcing your will on others.

To keep from creating new debts in the family bank account you must keep your promise to live in such a way that you will never have to keep anything a secret from them. You know the difference between right and wrong. You also know that doing anything that proves you to be untrustworthy will hurt your family relationship.

Everyone, including your family, should realize from your actions that your primary desire is to treat others like you want to be treated yourself. This also means that when you slip up and act improperly you will immediately admit your mistake, ask for forgiveness, and then make any restitution that is needed.

This means that you must learn the two hardest sentences known to man (1) "I was wrong, can you forgive me?" and (2) "What can I do to make things right again?"

And last but not least, it is important that you begin to truly love your family. Remember, love is something that you do and not something that you feel. Love is giving a part of yourself that is the best you have to offer, expecting nothing in return except that the gift be accepted.

If you want to keep your family alive while you are here in prison, think about the individual needs of your family each and every day. Then ask yourself: "What can I give each member of my family that is a part of myself, that is the best that I have to offer, that would help fill that need?" Then, as you begin exchanging little gifts of love you will be able to watch the relationship grow.

There is no guarantee that you can keep your family alive while you are in prison and then after you get out. This book can show you a new way of doing things that is probably different than anything that you have ever tried before. Like all ideas that are presented to you, you must now make a decision. Do you throw these ideas away and do things like you always have? Or, even though they are different, are you willing to try them and see if they work as well for you as they have for other inmates across the years?

As you make that decision, remember that fifty years of research has shown that people who stay out once they walk out of the front door to freedom are those who go home to their families, settle down, and practice ethical living.

The choice is now yours and the consequences very real, and you alone are responsible for the decision that you make about what to do with this material.

If you feel that you need additional information about how to save your marriage, I highly recommend the book *Love Life For Every Married Couple* by Ed Wheat (Zondervan, 1980).

Chapter 5
So You Want To Get Out, Or Do You?

C ould anyone interest you in reenlisting and serving some additional time here in this prison? After all, there are so many advantages to prison life. Here in the penitentiary you have no bills to pay. When you leave you will have to start buying things. A loaf of bread and a pack of cigarettes now cost over $1 each. Today, it is not unusual for utility bills to average over $100 a month.

Inmates have some special privileges that ordinary people don't have. An inmate doesn't have to worry about going hungry or having to fix meals. A fast food restaurant meal for two of one large cheeseburger, one small cheeseburger, one large order of french fries, and two medium soft drinks comes to over $5 today.

Here in the penitentiary it doesn't cost you $30 for five minutes of a doctor's time just to get a prescription for $20 worth of medicine. That's a real advantage today because many doctors require payment before you even see them, and the drugstore won't give you the medicine unless you pay for it on the spot.

While you are in prison, you don't have to worry about getting into a fight with your wife or listening to her nag, except maybe on visiting day. Even if you do get into a squabble while she is visiting you, it will be over as soon as visiting hours end. If it gets too bad the COs will end it immediately. On the outside, you won't have a friendly correctional officer to supervise your time with your wife, and no one will stop your arguments unless they get so violent that a neighbor calls the police. While you are an inmate you will definitely never have to worry about your wife turning you down, for the fifth night in a row, when you ask her to make love to you.

While you are incarcerated, you usually don't have to worry about what clothes to wear. The state is usually kind enough to furnish them for you, and they never go out of style. Once your sentence is up, you are going to have to start buying clothes. You're going to have to buy work clothes, dress clothes, and several different pairs of shoes. Clothes are expensive. If you are lucky, you might find a pair of blue jeans on sale and possibly a shirt for $20 each. Tennis shoes are $20 and up. Dress shoes can run over $70. A simple pair of underwear can be $3. If you stayed here you wouldn't have to worry about it.

In here the state is also kind enough to furnish you with free laundry service. Out there, you are going to be responsible for keeping your clothes cleaned and pressed. A washer and dryer can easily cost $800 or more. The 25-cent laundromats are now 75 cents or more for a single load. Then there is the cost of detergent, bleach, fabric softener, and spot remover.

If you are interested in remaining in prison all you have to do is write a letter to the warden and ask him to tell the parole board that you're not interested. If that doesn't work, maybe if you wrote a letter to the judge who pronounced your sentence he would be kind enough to add some time to your sentence. You're not convinced, are you? In fact, you're probably saying, "This guy's gone nuts; nobody in their right mind would want to live in here."

Inmates dislike prison, yet return

Prisons are not nice places to live. One of the most frequent complaints that inmates have about prison life is the feeling throughout the place that no one can be trusted. It doesn't take an inmate long to find out that this

So You Want To Get Out, Or Do You?

place is full of snitches who will act friendly just so they can find out things about other inmates then tell prison officials the other inmate's secrets if they think it will be beneficial to them. As a result, many inmates are afraid to make friends. Even as you read this you probably fear that, at this very moment, someone, somewhere, is setting you up for a fall and that it may cost you your chances for an early release or parole.

Because previous inmates have proven themselves untrustworthy, you can't even be trusted to go to the toilet in private. Do you enjoy sitting on the "john" with one of the correctional officers watching you? How does it feel to sit on that stainless steel bowl knowing the reason you can't have a plastic one is because prison officials fear that you might take it off and use it as a weapon? Wouldn't it be nice, just once, to sit on a "regular" toilet and be able to close the door?

By now you have discovered that your sexuality didn't stop when you began living here, and that causes you a lot of pain. You never realized just how much you would miss making love to your wife or girlfriend. You've probably discovered that masturbation is a poor substitute for the sexual relationship that you left behind. Besides, it's embarrassing if you're caught. Then there's the problem of homosexuality. "How can I handle the disgust, the anger, or the dirtiness I feel deep inside because of the homosexual advances of other inmates?" ask many.

Yet in spite of the fact that inmates hate living in prison and long for the day of their release, many return. According to the Bureau of Justice Statistics, the national average recidivism rate in 1988 was about 35 percent. Research by James Boudouris indicates that 62 percent of those who abuse alcohol or drugs after their release will return within one year. R. J. Homant followed a group of ex-offenders for ten years after their release. This study found that 86 percent of the former inmates who lasted less than one month on their first job were arrested again. However, none of the former inmates who stayed on their first job for one year after their release got arrested for the next ten years.

The most consistent finding among researchers revolves around inmates and their families. Inmates with unhealthy family relationships return to prison; inmates who maintain their relationships while incarcerated and return to healthy family relationships stay out once released.

Inmates who become prisonized consistently return. As you learned in Chapter 2, prisonization occurs when an inmate begins to develop a prison mentality. This happens when they stop thinking about their life and their friends on the outside and begin looking only at other inmates. By following their strong desire to be accepted by their fellow inmates—and an equally strong desire to become part of the prison group—inmates frequently accept the group's attitudes, values, and behavior patterns. As inmates become more prisonized, they become part of the criminal subculture that is part of every prison.

Prisonized inmates begin to think of themselves and identify themselves as criminals. Once you start thinking of yourself as a criminal, you will become a criminal. That's because what you think about yourself is what you will become. If you leave this place still thinking like a criminal it won't be long before you do something that will earn you more time in prison.

This does not have to happen to you! You don't have to accept the prison mentality that says, "Once a criminal, always a criminal." Frequently, inmates forget that being a convicted criminal does not make one a criminal. Admitting that you are a convicted criminal says something about your past and nothing about what you are now or what you will be in the future. Instead, you can choose which you are going to be. Are you a criminal, or someone who used to be a criminal but has now retired from criminal activities? It's your decision.

The only way that any inmate can return to prison once released is to choose to do something that would earn him more time. Returning to one's old hard-living lifestyle is why so many inmates return to prison.

Common stresses of reentry into family life and society

Prison life is slow. Life on the outside is fast. Recently released inmates are consistently amazed at how nervous they get simply walking down the street. It has been months, and even years, since they have had to deal with crowded shopping centers or city traffic. They discover that simply crossing the street without getting run over can be a major accomplishment. In prison, if people started rushing around too much, a correctional officer would slow them down. Out there, people are always in a hurry, and you will get run over you if you get in their way.

For a while, if you are like most recently released inmates, you will have to deal with the uneasy feeling of being someplace that you aren't supposed to be. Just a few days before, if you had been seen on the city street, you

So You Want To Get Out, Or Do You?

would have been picked up and charged with escape. Now you may find yourself questioning the fact that you really are free.

As strange as it may seem, you may miss the security of the prison. In here, if another inmate jumps you, a CO will immediately stop the fight. Out there, if you get in a fight you are on your own. You may find it stressful simply being in an unlocked room or walking through an area that's not surrounded by fences. Dogs may suddenly seem more ferocious than you remembered.

You will find that many things have changed since you entered prison. For example, your children will be different. They will have grown and matured so much that you will hardly recognize them. Your wife will be different. She will be glad to see you home, but while you were in prison she learned how to be independent and knows that she can live without you if necessary. You have a bad reputation because of your crime. No matter how long you have been in here there will be unforgiving people on the outside who will remember your crime and hold it against you. Because of this, you may find it harder to find work. Then, after you have found a job, you will discover that it is easier to find a job than to keep it.

Here in the prison you are used to being told what to do and when you are going to do it. You get up when you are told to get up. You wear what you are told to wear. You work when and where they tell you to work. You eat when they tell you that you are hungry. You eat what they tell you to eat. Do they even tell you when to go to the bathroom?

When you leave this prison, you will be responsible for creating your own schedule. You are the one that must remember to set your alarm clock and get up on time. That is hard to do; in fact, many report that this is their hardest adjustment when returning to the free world. Former inmates who can't accomplish this task are consistently late for work, frequently wind up being fired, and are likely to return to prison within one year.

No one will tell you where to work when you leave this prison. You will have to find a place to work and hope that the hours fit your needs and that it will be a job that you can enjoy. You may have to take a job that pays less than you wanted to make or is less satisfying than you had hoped. And even in the best of jobs, there will always be days when you will get so frustrated that you will want to quit.

You're also going to find that going to work is stressful. How long has it been since you have done eight hours of work each day for a week, a month, or a year? Your new employer will need to make a profit from your labor in order to pay your salary. He or she is not going to allow any goofing

113

Chapter 5

off. There is a good possibility that he or she will be more demanding and have more "chicken" regulations than this prison does. In here, if you break the rules all that will happen is that you will lose some privileges for a while; out there on the job you will get fired. Living by the "company's rules" may be hard, but if you can do it for the first year, you will have a much better chance of staying out.

You must decide what to wear and if it is appropriate for the job, and it will be your responsibility to see that the clothes you wear are clean and pressed. You will be responsible for obtaining your own meals and will discover that a 30-minute lunch break can be very short.

One of the most important things that has changed since your incarceration is you. You are not the same person who entered this prison. When your sentence is up and you walk out the front door, you will leave this place either bitter or better because of your experiences here. The only difference between the two words is the letter "I." If "I" must be in everything you think, say, or do, you will have become bitter instead of better.

Learning how to live as free as an eagle

All transitions and changes are stressful. In fact, making transitions and changes is one of the hardest things that people have to do. Even if they are stuck in a rut, people simply do not like to change. This is because it takes time to get used to the new patterns, and people fear that either they will make mistakes and look foolish or that the new way will not work.

One of the ways that you could handle the transition back into family life and society would be to go back to your old ways of doing things and live your life just like you did before you arrived here. Unfortunately, if you do and go back to those old ways you will probably wind up right back in prison. You will simply be repeating history.

A better way to handle the transition would be to learn how to live as free as an eagle. From now on, every time you face one of life's transitions, think of how an eagle learns to fly.

One day, as that young eagle is sitting securely in its nest high above the canyon, the mother eagle decides that it is time for that baby eagle to be on its own. Notice that this change is forced on the baby eagle. If that baby eagle had its way, it would remain in that comfortable nest and allow the parents to bring its meals while he sat there enjoying the view. But that isn't what happens.

114

So You Want To Get Out, Or Do You?

Instead, the mother eagle picks up her baby and places it on her back. Then she spreads her wings and flies out over the canyon until she finds a nice, strong updraft. Higher and higher she soars; riding the updrafts until she reaches the top of the sky—sometimes as high as 15,000 feet.

Suddenly, and without warning, she reaches back with her powerful beak and grabs her baby and flings it out into the air. Instantly, that baby eagle finds itself falling from the sky. The baby starts squawking and wildly flapping its wings as it continues to plummet toward the ground, hoping that his mother will rescue him from a certain death.

You can almost picture that baby eagle looking up, with tears in its eyes (if that's possible), screaming, "Mama, don't you love me anymore? Don't you care that I am about to die?" But he gets no answer. All he can hear is the wind rushing by his head. All he can see is his mother calmly circling overhead as the ground gets closer and closer.

Then, just before the baby eagle hits the ground, the mother eagle folds her wings tight against her body and dives under her falling child. The baby eagle grabs hold of her back and hangs on for dear life. For a while, the baby eagle feels safe and secure as it rides around on its mother's back as she circles quietly.

What that young eagle doesn't know is that whenever that mother eagle is circling she is looking for more updrafts and that she is slowly climbing higher and higher. She reaches out and throws the young eagle out again, and she will keep on throwing the baby eagle out until it learns to stretch out its wings and start flying on his own.

What would happen if that baby eagle kept on doing it his way and refused to climb on his mother's back when she dove under him? He would crash instead of becoming a mature bird with the freedom to fly. What if he continued to try to fly his way instead of simply stretching out his wings like his mother has been trying to show him by circling overhead? He would die. Only after that young eagle learns to respect the laws of nature does he gain the freedom to live as free as an eagle.

Think of the terror that the baby eagle feels as it is falling through space. Think of how terrified you would be if you found yourself falling from a height of 15,000 feet with no parachute. Making transitions can seem that scary sometimes.

The same thing is going to happen to you someday. This prison is your eagle's nest, and one day you are going to be thrown out of it. When this happens you are either going to learn to fly on your own, or by refusing to

Chapter 5

change and going back to your old way of doing things, you are going to crash.

"Hard living" will cause you to return to prison

What are these old ways that make inmates crash? L. T. Fishman calls them "hard living." Former inmates who travel along the hard-living road almost always crash.

An inmate who follows the hard-living lifestyle will typically leave the penitentiary and then quickly get tired of looking for work. Instead of going out and pounding the pavement until he finds a job, he will start lying around the house. His wife doesn't like this because she expected him to find a job and help support the family once he got out.

She's disappointed and angry. After standing by him for all that time and hoping that prison life would teach him his lesson and transform him into the loving and caring husband that she had always wanted, he's gone back to his old ways. He's determined that everything is going to be just like he left it. She's already been down that hard-living road once and knows what's coming. So she decides to go back to her old way of doing things and starts to nag.

The children react to the increasing tension around the house by copying their parent's attitudes that say, "You can't tell me what to do; I'm the boss," or "If I nag and complain enough maybe you'll quit." As their behavior worsens they will nag and complain more, and fights with each other and with their parents become more frequent.

About this time, the hard-living ex-inmate will "just happen" to discover that his old friends down at the bar do not nag and may even offer to buy him a drink. So instead of listening to a nagging wife and chirping kids, he spends more time with his "friends" at the local bar. His wife soon gets tired of his hard-living lifestyle and starts to withdraw.

For a while, the booze and drugs flow freely. Then the money runs out. His "friends" desert him, his wife is angry with him because he failed to keep his promise, the kids are constantly fighting, and it seems that everyone in the world has ganged up on him. Our ex-inmate then discovers that his wife will not have sex with him after he has spent the evening at the local bar.

Then one day, while sitting at the bar feeling sorry for himself, he starts thinking, "Why should I work all day in the hot sun for $35 when Mr. Smith & Wesson and I can make more money than that in five minutes at the local convenience store? Why should I cook hamburgers at the fast food place when I can make more money from one sale of drugs than I would make all week there? Why should I carry another two-by-four to build a house when I can break into one and make a lot more money with a lot less work?"

He has no job, no money, and no place to go. His mind is clouded by the alcohol or drugs that he has been taking, and he is angry. Then, because of his anger, and because he has returned to his old way of thinking, he takes that anger out on a new victim. Either he breaks into a house, or robs a store, or rapes someone, molests one of his children, or whatever. No matter how you say it, our ex-inmate is on his way back to jail. He has just earned more time in prison. He has crashed.

Alcohol or drug dependency contributes to hard living

Inmates have a chance to dry out while they are in prison. Did you know that if you have ever had a drinking or drug dependency problem that it will be there for the rest of your life? If you have attended Alcoholics Anonymous meetings you learned that it takes 21 days to get over a physical addiction. You also learned that the potential risk for readdiction will be with you for the rest of your life.

Here's why. Your brain produces hormones called endorphins. These are your body's natural painkillers. Exercise stimulates the production of these endorphins, which are more potent than heroin. These painkillers are what give you your second wind when you have worked or exercised so hard that you have "hit the wall." The endorphins kill the pain, and your body stops hurting for a while so you can keep on going. This is why you feel so good after a long walk or after jogging. Your body has given you a "natural high."

Your body was not designed to absorb alcohol or drugs. If you continue absorbing alcohol or drugs your brain will stop the production of endorphins and start producing a substitute chemical known as THIQ. When this happens, your body has no natural pain relievers, and the only way to get the synthetic pain reliever, THIQ, is by having alcohol or drugs in your system.

To get over a physical addiction, you must go 21 days without having anything in your body that would cause the production of THIQ. This will mean days of misery as your body goes without any pain relief until the brain starts the production of endorphins again. Unfortunately, this is not a cure for addiction. There is no such thing.

You will always be able to remember how good the "high" felt while you were under the influence of the substance. You will forget, or minimize, the pain associated with the hangover or coming down. This produces a psychological addiction that will remain with you for the rest of your life. Whenever you are in a situation similar to when you previously used alcohol or drugs, you will find it easy to try it "just this once."

If you do try it "just this once," you're going to have the physical addiction to contend with again. Picture a garden hose that has burst and is spraying water all over. The faucet is quickly turned off, and water is no longer spewing through the leak. But what will happen if someone turns the faucet back on? The hose would immediately start spraying water again, and the hole might become even bigger this time.

The production of THIQ in the brain is similar to the hole in the garden hose. Staying off the substance for the required amount of time is like turning off the faucet, but the hole is still there.

If you have ever been dependent on alcohol or drugs, all it may take is one drink, one snort of cocaine, one hit of heroin, one toke of marijuana to start a cycle in your body. As the substance hits your brain, it will stop producing endorphins and start producing THIQ again. You've "turned the faucet back on" and water is gushing out of the hole in the garden hose. When this happens, you are suddenly dependent again, and it will take the same amount or more of the substance to satisfy your craving as it did before you quit.

It is not the alcohol or the drugs that you are dependent on. It is the THIQ. Unfortunately, the only way you can get THIQ is by drinking and drugging. In plain terms, what this means is that if you have ever been addicted to alcohol or drugs and decide to take one drink, or one snort, or one toke, or one hit of any drug, you will start a process that has a good chance of landing you back in prison. If you ever decide to try drinking or drugging again you have also decided that you want to return to prison. That's a mighty big price for one "high."

So You Want To Get Out, Or Do You?

THIQ dependency affects all four areas of your life: your spiritual side, your mental side, your emotional side, and your physical side.

Your spiritual side is your value system that tells you right from wrong. It's where your conscience is housed.

Consider this scene. Suppose you are sitting on a park bench reading a book and someone walks up to you and says, "May I borrow this book?" Before you have a chance to answer, he takes the book from your hands and says "Thank you" as he walks away. Is what he just did morally right? Of course not. Even though he asked and said "thank you" after he took it from you, he would be guilty of stealing your book because he did not wait for you to give permission to take it.

Consider the same scene again. Suppose he asks to borrow the book and waits for you to say "Yes." Would this be wrong? Of course not. The difference between the two scenes is that in the second one he waited for you to give permission before he took it.

Would it be okay for someone to have an affair with your wife while you are in here? Almost every inmate would agree that it would be morally wrong for anyone to have an affair with your wife, and it wouldn't matter if you are in the penitentiary or if you were out. Fooling around with another man's wife is morally wrong. If you were asked if it were morally wrong to drive when you've had too much to drink, to steal, to slack off on the job, to hit your wife, etc., you would reply, "Of course it is."

You know the difference between things that are morally right and things that are morally wrong. You have a spiritual side and it is working properly.

The emotional part of your body is how you feel about things and how you feel about yourself. Remember, feelings are neither right nor wrong, they are simply the truth about how you feel about a specific thing at that particular time. Feelings are your "gut-level" reaction to the things that happen in your life.

Your mental side is where you make all of your decisions about the attitudes you will display, your values, and the way you will act. It is the process you use to make decisions, and you control that. Whenever you have a decision to make, you will make it in one of two ways (1) by listening to your spiritual side and doing what you know to be morally right or (2) by listening to your emotional side and doing what your feelings are telling you to do. A mature person is one who can do what they know to be morally right even when they don't feel like it. Emotionally immature people—like children—make their decisions based solely on how they feel at the moment, regardless of what their spiritual side is telling them.

People who are dependent on alcohol or drugs do some crazy things to get high. Frequently they complain that they feel like they're going crazy. Here's why.

Because of their dependency, and because their brain is not producing endorphins, the brain is constantly screaming for THIQ. So they go drinking or drugging and get a new supply. Then, whenever they stop the intake of alcohol or drugs, their blood will begin to return to normal, and their brain stops producing THIQ.

When this happens, their brain sends a message to their emotions saying, "I need more THIQ." Their emotions translate that message into, "You either put more drugs or alcohol in this body or some very bad things will happen!" They will either experience a slow and painful death or at the very least, a withdrawal period that will be worse than the biblical version of hell.

This puts addicts in a bind. On one hand their personal values tell them not to do things that they know are morally wrong. On the other hand, their emotions are telling them that they must have some alcohol or drugs to survive. By now, they are afraid not to listen to what their emotions are telling them. They make mental decisions to do whatever is necessary to satisfy their body's longing for THIQ and will even do things that they know are morally wrong to buy the drugs or alcohol that their body craves.

Whenever people reach this point there will be a complete breakdown of their moral values. They will lie, cheat, steal, or do anything else necessary to get the alcohol or drugs into their systems so that their brain will produce more THIQ. Even if they are shown the obvious evidence of their alcohol or drug dependency, they will deny that they have a problem. Instead, they may start blowing up. After all, screaming at the top of one's lungs is a good way to keep from having to talk about their emotions. It is also an effective way to say, "Leave me alone" to the people who care about you. That's crazy, isn't it?

It doesn't have to be that way. With help, the alcoholic or drug addict can learn to listen to their spiritual side and go to a treatment center or program and ask for help instead of listening to their emotions cry out for THIQ. They can decide to use these people to show them how to live one day at a time without whatever they are addicted to for the rest of their lives.

Your physical side is your body. If you constantly allow your emotions to control your life, you will feel depressed because you are not in control

So You Want To Get Out, Or Do You?

of your own life. If you fail to listen to your spiritual side, you will feel guilty. Both will make the physical side feel perfectly awful. Alcohol and drug addiction affects a person's entire body. As the addiction continues, people get to the point where they would rather have alcohol or drugs than sex. This usually has a negative affect on their marital and family relationships. Living in a rotten marriage can seem like a living hell. More booze or more drugs becomes a way to try to relieve the pain.

As people continue drinking and drugging, their health will begin to fail. They will start feeling too bad to go to work because they feel sick all the time. People who continually lay off of the job because they "feel sick" get fired. Their boss knows that the real reason that they are sick is because of their alcohol or drug habit.

Is this section talking about you? Can you imagine this scene? One day, after you've shown up late for work again, the boss calls you into his office and says, "I knew you were a jailbird, but you promised me that you had changed. I should never have trusted you. You're fired!"

Not only has he fired you, but has destroyed your self-esteem in the process. When you get home, that wife that stood by you for all of your years in the penitentiary is going to be angry. This is because she can see that you are going right back to the way you were before you went to prison the last time. You've let her down—again!

You will notice that your wife will start to withdraw from you. There will be less emotional support; less sexual intimacy; and she will stop giving you money. She's been through it before, and she knows you are acting just like you did before you went to prison the last time. She's preparing herself emotionally for your departure that she knows is coming.

Then the fights start, and they become more violent. You will begin to blame her because she just does not understand that you "just have to have" those drugs or alcohol. All that you can see is that she is trying to prevent you from getting them. By now, your chemical dependency has completely clouded your spiritual, emotional, and mental sides, and you are convinced that all of your problems are her fault because she will not give you the money for more alcohol or drugs. You will also feel that none of your family's problems are your fault at all.

Are you starting to see how ridiculous this type of thinking is?

Chapter 5

The road back to prison

If you begin living this way you will have just moved into the fast lane of the Hard-living Highway. As you continue around the loop, instead of looking for the cause of the problem, you will start looking for ways to get away from your "nagging wife" and "impossible" family who "just don't understand" your need for alcohol or drugs.

You'll start finding new "friends" who won't get on your nerves by nagging you about your drinking and drugging. And since "birds of a feather flock together," you will start hanging out with others who will lie, cheat, steal, or whatever else is necessary to satisfy their body's craving for THIQ. Unfortunately, the only way to satisfy that craving is to somehow get enough money to buy more booze or dope to put in your system so that your brain will produce some more THIQ.

Drugs and booze are expensive. You have no income because the boss just fired you, and your wife will have started hiding her money. By now your chemical dependency will have completely distorted your moral reasoning. You will begin to allow your physical addiction and emotional "need" for THIQ to rule your life.

As your mind becomes focused on finding some way to get enough money to buy something that will make your brain produce THIQ, you will fall back on your old ways of doing things. Once again, you start thinking like a criminal: "Why should I sweat all day at a hamburger joint for minimum wage or clean floors for $40 a day [$5 an hour] or lay bricks for $80 a day [$10 an hour] when I could make more than that selling a line of coke or six nickel bags of grass, or robbing a convenience store, or breaking into a house, or whatever else to get the stuff I need to keep from dying?"

You will see something that you want but have no right to have. You will declare that society has no right to require you to control your urges. Then you will abuse your power and take it and earn a new prison sentence the moment you violate the rules of society.

If you follow this route you will soon discover that the "system" still works. It may be something as simple as finding yourself behind bars for a parole violation after your probation officer collects some "dirty" urine. Or you get caught committing a new crime while trying to support your habit. Just like before, at the time that you are doing your new crime, you won't even consider that you are creating a new debt to society that will need to be paid.

So You Want To Get Out, Or Do You?

Later, at your trial, you will suddenly remember the illustration about the "Fly-by-Night Auto Repair" mentioned in Chapter 1 and realize that you forgot to find out what it would cost before you decided how to act. At sentencing, you will discover that judges have a tendency to add something called recidivism time to your sentence.

Many states have a habitual offender law, but you didn't stop to think if your new crime would qualify you for its special conditions. In Alabama, it's life without parole.

If you were on probation at the time, you now have two sentences to serve; the rest of the first one plus the second one. Even if the new charges are dismissed you may still have to face the revocation of your parole.

Because you returned to hard living and your old way of doing things, you will join the large percentage of inmates who return to prison. But something will be different this time. Last time, your wife stood by you. This time she probably won't back you up. She stayed with you once, but now you have once again let her down. There is a good chance that she will let you face your problems alone this time.

The way to keep from returning to prison

There is a way to keep yourself from returning to hard living and to keep from returning to prison. It involves a bold new way of living. It involves looking at life's everyday problems in a way that you probably have never even considered before. It is a way to keep your life balanced.

The diagram on page 124 represents how life should be: balanced. That's a nice dream, but it rarely happens. Everyday problems, stresses, and transitions can become crises and threaten to tip the balance. Notice in the diagram that the way to keep the stressors and problems from tipping the scale is by having enough resources on the other side to keep your life balanced. To accomplish this, you must use problem-solving skills.

The creation of a crisis follows a set pattern. First comes a stressor or a problem; something in your life that requires you to change. It may be something big, like getting out of prison and reentering family life and society, or it may be something as small as deciding which clothes to wear to your first job interview.

Whenever you face a stressor or a problem, it is natural for you to immediately start thinking about the hardships that the change will make. For example, when you leave here there will be an endless stream of

123

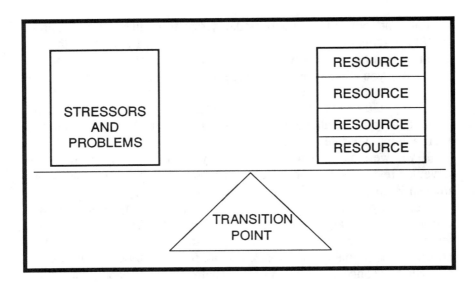

problems that will bombard you and pull you down. You will need to decide on the type of job you want, how to find it, how to make love to your wife for the first time; the list is endless. You will feel the weight of the stressor or problem pulling you down, and you won't see any way to stop it.

One of the reasons that you will be afraid to try new things is because you can remember the other times that you tried to change but failed. That fear of failure can keep you from trying anything new, and that fear causes you to feel bad.

Then, as you think more and more about the changes that you will have to make, the burden will become heavier. The weight of that burden will begin to give you a sinking feeling, similar to the panic that the baby eagle feels as it plummets through space while learning how to fly. You will realize the truth of the old saying, "There is no heavier burden than a great opportunity."

Fear quickly turns to panic as you realize that if you don't do something quickly to balance the beam, that see-saw called life is going to drop you on the ground, and you won't be able to get up. All of this is being determined by how heavy *you feel* that the problem is and not by how heavy the problem actually is.

Making changes is scary. Even if your old way of doing things kept you in a rut, you knew what to expect. If you try something new or make a permanent change in your life, everything will become suddenly different.

So You Want To Get Out, Or Do You?

You won't know what to expect. Doing things differently will be like trying to walk through the woods at night without a flashlight. Because you're afraid to go through that period of time when you feel lost, instead of trying something new, you will simply try the same old thing again, and you wind up in the same old rut again, and again, and again, and again.

Frequently the time of feeling lost is extremely short. Usually the new path is not hard to learn. It just takes the courage to try it and to find enough resources to keep you balanced while you try.

Using problem-solving skills to balance your life

As long as you are living, you are going to have problems that will weigh you down and throw your life out of balance. When this happens you will feel rotten. Bad feelings do not tell you what the problem is or how to solve it; bad feelings only tell you that you have a problem. Good feelings generally mean that everything is going okay and that your life is balanced.

Whenever there are bad feelings, use the problem-solving formula to find the resources that would bring balance back to your life. Let's look at how this formula works and help you find resources for some common stressors that you will find on the outside.

First, you identify the problem. But you have to make sure that it is the real problem. In the previous section we saw how you can be fooled by your mind. If you are dependent on alcohol or drugs, your mind is saying, "I need some THIQ, and if you don't put some booze or drugs in me I will die." However, the real problem is your dependency on the alcohol or drugs. If you don't correct the real problem, that see-saw called life will continue to sink toward the ground until you crash. All of the alcohol and drugs in the world cannot solve a chemical dependency problem.

While you are attempting to identify the real problem you must resist your temptation to give up and quit trying. This happens a lot in marriages and in the search for a job. Couples get tired of fighting all of the time and call it quits. The real problem is not the fights but their inability to yield to the other and each trying to be the boss. If you can't seem to find a job, the real problem is not that there is no work available. The real problem is that you have quit looking too soon.

Frequently, you must also swallow your pride, admit that you can't

125

handle it alone because the problem is bigger than you can handle, and ask for outside help. This presents another problem. Who do you ask? The remaining chapters will help you with that problem.

The second step in the problem-solving formula is to brainstorm solutions with all of the people involved in the problem. As you are doing this ask yourself these questions: (1) what resources will it take to balance the scale and (2) which of those resources are available to me at this time?

If the crisis is a large one, you will need to have a larger number of resources available to help you keep your life balanced. For example, if your stressor is alcohol dependency or any other type of compulsive behavior, you will need more than one resource to keep the scale from tipping over. You may need your family, counselors at a substance abuse program, Alcoholics Anonymous, and a loving church group to help you get over your crisis. Your family may need the advice and help of friends, family, community support groups, and a loving church family.

However, only certain people should be consulted as you brainstorm possible solutions. For example, it would be better to find the resources to handle a relationship with your spouse at a family counselor's office than from the men at work or from neighbors. Many men, thinking that they were going to be divorced soon, have spent hours trying to convince their family and friends how terrible their wives were. Later, after they had worked through their difficulties, these same men regretted sharing the "family secrets" with people who didn't need to know them. Many affairs have been started by someone asking a friend of the opposite sex how they should handle the problem they are having with their spouse.

Third, examine the long-term consequences of each possible solution. This includes thinking about how your decision will affect others. For example, going through the discomfort of marriage counseling might be a better solution to the problem of an unhappy marriage than getting a divorce. This is a prime example of using an outside resource to help you determine what the real problem is and to assist you in making the decision about which solution to try first.

Fourth, pick the best-looking solution and try it. Then evaluate the results. If that solution does not work, go back to step one and try again.

Developing a new way of life called settled living

Using problem-solving skills to keep your life in balance means developing a new way of living that will probably be different from what you've ever experienced before. It's called settled living and involves (1) keeping your commitment to ethical living, (2) staying off alcohol and drugs, and (3) working steadily so that you can support your family. Former inmates who practice settled living stay out of prison.

Facing stressful moments, crises, and problems are as much a part of life as breathing. Unfortunately, because your old ways of doing things are so ingrained within you, every time you are faced with one of life's stresses or problems, you are going to be tempted to go back to your old ways of doing things. Habits are hard to change.

You are like that baby eagle who is being taught how to fly. As long as you do it your way, you will continue to fall toward an inevitable crash. The resources that you discover while using the problem-solving model are your mother eagle. Use them. What you will discover, if you look hard enough, is that there are a lot of people, both inside and outside this prison, who are willing to keep you from crashing and after a fall will be willing to help you back up until you have learned to fly on your own. They want you to learn how to be as free as an eagle.

Work can be a valuable resource to help you handle life's stressors and to keep your life in balance. It provides money and enables you to support your family. Work provides self-esteem, especially if you can look back and see that you have done a good job at whatever you do. The workplace can provide good companionship. But watch out; many workplaces have dishonest people who will entice you to do dishonest things.

Your community can offer many valuable resources to help you keep your life in balance. There is the state Employment Service, the Health Department, the Welfare Department, and mental health facilities. Some universities offer free or reduced counseling, both for marriage and family problems and for individual problems.

One of the best resources that you can use to keep your life in balance is church. But it can't be just any church, it must be a special church. It needs to be a church that teaches God's moral values; one that will accept you just the way you are and will make you feel welcome. It needs to be a church

Chapter 5

that provides for the needs of your wife and children so that you can worship together as a family.

Throughout the week, let your mind dwell on the things that you learn from the teachings of the church. Dwell on whatever is true, whatever is honorable, whatever is right, whatever is pure, whatever is lovely, whatever is good, or anything that can be praised. This is important because what you think about and dream about is what you will become in the future.

Remember; everything that you do in life starts with a dream that says, "I wonder what it would be like to (fill in the blank) ." Your dreams are your goals in life. An actor named Ronald Reagan dreamed about playing his greatest role: President of the United States. He used problem-solving skills to develop resources that enabled him to climb the steps necessary to reach that goal.

One of my dreams and goals is to make every place that I live a better place simply because I have been there. This book and the educational programs that go with it are part of the fulfillment of that dream. This material had its beginnings after I failed a course in graduate school, was dropped from one program, and had to change directions. We had invested everything we had so that I could have a chance to go to college and graduate school. But now my dream had turned into a nightmare. This created a major crisis for me, and for my family.

While looking for resources that would help me decide which way to go, a friend told me of a need in the Alabama Department of Corrections for family life education. Unfortunately, there were no funds available from the state or church to pay the costs. He felt that my unique background in law enforcement, ministry, and family life education made me qualified for the job.

Even though I had been involved in family life education for years, producing Alabama's first family life programs for inmates was a bigger task than anything that I had ever handled in my life. After discussing these programs with the people that would be involved, I discovered that I would have several resources available to help me:

1. The huge Auburn University Library had all of the professional journals and books that I would need and a computer hookup that would let me find the articles about inmates and their families much faster.
2. Auburn University's Department of Family and Child Development agreed to provide supervision for the project.

This gave me access to some of the top professors in family studies and marriage and family therapy in the nation.

3. Much of the material that I had developed during the previous years as a family evangelist could be adapted to these new programs.

4. The Alabama Department of Corrections agreed to allow me the opportunity to try it. They placed me under the direct supervision of Dr. Paul H. Van Wyk, the chief psychologist at the prison, as a mental health intern.

5. Since there were no funds available to pay for this project, and since it would require my full time, my wife was willing to work many hours of overtime so that we would have the funds to produce this material.

You are reading this material because I used the problem-solving formula to help me through the greatest crisis that I had ever faced in my life.

Individual failures do not make you a failure. The only person who is a failure is one who quits trying and refuses to make the necessary changes in their lives.

Out of my failure came two dreams (1) the dream of writing this book so that inmates would have access to the material and (2) becoming as good at helping inmates get out of prison as I used to be at locking people up. Because I didn't quit and was willing to make the necessary changes, I was still able to earn my Master's Degree from Auburn University.

Another valuable resource is your family. They are also going to have to find new ways of doing things after you are released. They still remember the old you, and their ways of doing things are just as ingrained as yours are. It is just as hard for them to change as it is for you to change. Remember, if there is no change in the family system, it can drive you back to your old ways; back into hard living and crime. Nurture your family, care for them, and most importantly, love them.

Giving your family the gift of love

Love is giving a part of yourself that is the best you have to offer, asking only that the gift be accepted. True gifts of love never harm; they are never given for selfish reasons; and they have no strings attached to them. True

Chapter 5

gifts of love ask only that they be accepted and allow the receiver to decide how the gifts will be used.

One of the best gifts that you can give your wife is to be affectionate and caring all of the time and not just when you want sex. Being affectionate and caring only to get sex is not being loving, it is being selfish.

Your children want your gift of time; time to be with them and do the things that *they* like to do. That doesn't mean helping you mow the lawn or watching Monday Night Football. It means doing the things that they like to do, like having a tea party with your little girl, or pitching the ball to your son.

If you reject gifts of love you have rejected the giver of the gift and not the gift itself. Here's an illustration: One evening back in 1985, I was studying hard for my final exams. My five-year-old son was being so good that I hardly noticed him just sitting at his desk, writing on a piece of paper.

At bedtime, my son came to me and gave me a piece of paper with some writing on it. I took it, thanked him for it, put in on my desk, and took him upstairs. After we prayed together, I kissed him and tucked him in for the night. Feeling proud of myself for being a "good daddy," I returned to my desk, wadded up the piece of paper, threw it into the trash, and returned to my studying.

Later my wife asked me if I had looked at the piece of paper. After admitting that I hadn't, she told me my son had spent the evening sitting at his desk and painstakingly writing the numbers 1 through 164 on that piece of paper. He was so proud that he was studying and being "just like his daddy." I suddenly realized that by throwing away that "useless" piece of paper I had actually thrown my son away. He had just given me the most precious gift a son can give his father: three hours of his time and his undying loyalty to his dad.

Needless to say I dug down into the trash and recovered that piece of paper. I still have it. I use that piece of paper to remind me of the times when I can be unloving. Looking back, how many times have you been like me and rejected your children, family, or friends by rejecting their gifts of love? Rejecting love kills relationships.

A true gift of love is a part of yourself that is the best you have to offer and asks only that the gift be accepted. It allows the recipient to decide what to do with it, with no strings attached.

Accepting gifts of love will cause the relationship to grow. As you exchange gifts of love that ask only that they be accepted, you will learn to work together. Your selfish nature will start to disappear and you will grow closer. By digging that piece of paper out of the trash, apologizing to my son, and then complimenting him on his effort, I became closer to my son. Do you need to make some apologies and go back and thank some people for their gifts that you have rejected?

Your family needs that kind of love. The nice thing is that you can start the cycle by beginning to display true love. You don't have to wait until they make the first move; you can start by offering true gifts of love. A loving, caring family relationship is one of the best resources available to keep yourself from coming back to prison once you are released.

Here are your keys to freedom

It takes two keys to keep the door to freedom open. The keys to freedom are respect and responsibility. If you take these keys and use them you will never have to worry about living behind a locked prison door for the rest of your life.

True freedom always begins with respect for the rules of society. Every society has rules that must be obeyed if you want to remain in that society. For example, close family relationships are possible only when each member respects the rules of ethical living. A concert pianist must respect the rules of music or nobody would listen. An airline pilot must respect the rules of the Federal Aviation Administration to pilot a 747 with hundreds of people aboard. If you want to drive and get where you are going in one piece, you must respect the rules of the road. Respecting the laws of society allows you to walk the streets freely and without fear.

Then comes responsibility. You alone are responsible for the decisions that you make. No one can make you angry; you choose to get angry. No one can make you strike out either with your words or with your fists; you choose that response. No one can make you take that first drink when you get out of here. If you do, it will be because you have chosen to take that first drink or smoke that first joint. It will also mean that you have chosen to take the hard-living road, and that will cost you your freedom.

Being responsible is realizing that punishment is the logical conclusion for all criminal activity. When you are a responsible person you will understand that if you choose to violate the law, you are asking society to put you in jail.

You choose to make each and every decision that you make. You must choose where you are going to work. You must choose how dependable you are going to be. You must choose who your friends are. You must choose how good of a family man you are going to be. You alone are responsible for those decisions.

Do you really want out?

Every inmate says "yes." In fact, they can usually tell you the date they expect to be released. There's a difference between being released from prison and remaining free. If you are going to get out and then come right back, why get out in the first place?

The real question is, "Do you want to remain free?" When you are ushered out the front door, you are going to have to take one of two roads. There are no other options. Now that you know what to look for you will recognize their markings. The road that looks the nicest and is the most familiar is called hard living. It is frequently traveled by newly released inmates. Unfortunately, those who use this road discover that it's really a loop that will lead them back into prison.

The other road is called settled living. It is not as well-marked and is a lot harder to travel. It's worth the extra effort because the longer you stay on that road the better your chances are of permanently ending your criminal career. It is the road that leads to true freedom.

Staying out of prison once you are released is a choice; your choice. When you leave this place, you will be the one to decide which road you will take. This is a choice that only you can make, and you alone are responsible for that decision.

Chapter 6
What's In A Name?

A good name is to be more desired than great riches, favor is better than silver and gold.

—Proverbs 22:1

If you are (or have ever been) an inmate, and you're tired of living with your past, here's a simple task you can do that will help you to change that.

Find a clean sheet of paper and fold it in half. Write your name on the top half. Then on the bottom half, write down every crime you have ever been convicted of in your life. Unless you show it to someone, nobody but you will ever see that piece of paper. Now refold it and place it in the back of this book. Later in this chapter you will be shown how to separate yourself from your crimes and create a new, good name for yourself.

Chapter 6

The meaning of a person's name

Before you picked up this book, the name Daniel J. Bayse probably didn't mean a thing to you. There is a possibility that you have seen the name on a church bulletin somewhere or even seen me in a prison where I have taught a class. There is even a remote chance that we met while I was a trooper. Every once in a while I meet an inmate who says, "Don't you remember the day you locked me up?"

Throughout this book, I have shared many personal things about myself and my family. I've shared some of my successes and my failures and how my faith has helped me through my trials. I've shared this information with you because even though you may have never seen me and even though you didn't realize it, I knew that you would start forming an image of me the moment you first saw the cover of this book.

Even though I've tried to make myself a likeable person, the image you have of me may be a positive one, and it may be a negative one. And from now on, every time you see or hear my name, you will again see the image of me that you have created in your own mind. However, others reading this same material may disagree with your assessment of me. There are several reasons why others will see me differently than you do.

One day when I was a trooper I was called into the sergeant's office to answer a complaint from an irate citizen. The woman making the complaint said that even though she had deserved the ticket and I had been polite to her, she felt that my face was so ugly that I should not be allowed to continue wearing a State Police uniform. I guess the State Police disagreed because I wasn't fired. What image had she formed of me during our brief encounter on the side of the road?

For some, the image formed is either positive or negative because I'm overweight or underweight by their standards, because I talk too loudly or too softly, or because of some other physical characteristic. How frequently do people judge the character of a person simply because of the color of their skin or their nationality?

The fact that I am a minister may affect the image that you have formed of me. Because of the recent moral failures of some well-known evangelists, there are a lot of people who don't like evangelists these days. In other words, the behavior of other ministers has affected my name.

How about the fact that I was a state trooper? Again, the image that you assign to me is determined partially by your image of police officers as a whole. Almost every inmate can tell of instances where they were mistreated by a police officer. As a result, for many, the words police officer mean, "Don't trust him, he's out to get you."

My name is more than "just a handle" to you. Although my name gives you a way to identify me, what you think about when you hear the name Dan Bayse is more than just a name. You have already assigned your opinion of me to my name, and your opinion is based on whether you like me or not, and you will use this same process with all of the people that you meet, just as others will use this same process every time they meet you.

A person's name is more than just identification. It's an invitation that says, "Examine what I've done in the past, my history; that's what you can expect from me in the future." What you and I have done in the past is the name we've made for ourselves.

People see different qualities in the same people

Salvador Minuchin, a well-known family therapist, claims that what you will see in people will be determined by whether you like them or not. There is truth in the old saying, "You only have one chance to make a good first impression."

Everyone has a good side and a bad side. If you like someone, you will tend to focus on their good side while ignoring the things about them that are not so good. If you see a friend behaving like a jerk—which everyone does occasionally—you will blame his bad behavior on something other than him. You may think, "He's just having a bad day," or "He is not in a good mood today because his boss or his wife just chewed him out." After all, you value your own judgement, and you wouldn't like someone who wasn't nice. By looking only at his good side you can prove yourself right.

All of this changes if you dislike the person. If you dislike him, you will see only his negative side and ignore the good that he does. Again, you must prove yourself right. You respect your own opinions and feel that you wouldn't dislike anyone who had good qualities. The way to prove to yourself that he is of no value is by ignoring any good that he does and focusing on his bad side.

Here's another example. History proves that Adolph Hitler was one of the most evil and cruel men who ever lived. During World War II, he heartlessly ordered millions of people murdered simply because he thought their race was inferior.

However, millions of Germans loved Adolph Hitler because his leadership provided jobs and brought the country out of a recession. He had a mistress who thought he was special enough to live with. She and many Germans were able to look at the good side of Adolph Hitler while ignoring the bad side.

Names are more than just a handle. Every person who hears your name will think about more than what your face looks like. They will also think about your reputation in the community, their opinion of you, and whether they like you or not. They will then tell others the label that they have assigned to you. That label tells them and the world what they think your character is, based on their opinion of you.

Because of your crime, you have created a bad name for yourself in your community. You can rebuild your name, but it will take a lot of time and a lot of hard work on your part.

Rebuilding your name starts when you can admit to yourself who you are. Like you did in Chapter 1, admit that "I am a convicted criminal. I was convicted of _____." Remember, saying these words simply admits the facts about something that happened in your past; it says nothing about what you are right now or what you will be in the future.

You can't change what has happened in the past, but you can change your future. Your future will be determined by the decisions you make about your attitudes, values, and behavior patterns. You alone are responsible for those decisions and are the one that will be held accountable for your actions. As you make those decisions, you are also deciding what you want your name to mean.

It won't be the probation officer's fault if you get caught with "dirty urine" or get arrested for assaulting your wife. It will be because you decided that it didn't matter if your name was "drug user" or "wife abuser." Yes, it is hard to "just say no" to drugs. Especially when "all" of your friends are using them and you want your name to be included as part of their group. Maybe you need to find a new group. Controlling your temper with your wife may be even harder than saying no to drugs.

It has taken all of your life to build your name into one that says, "I can't be trusted to obey society's rules." It will take you the rest of your life to create a new name for yourself. But that's okay because today is the first day of the rest of your life. If, starting today, you begin doing the things necessary to create a new name for yourself, soon people will start remembering the new you instead of the old you.

A word of caution: Every time that you go back to your old ways, people will think, "I knew that the changes weren't real; I knew that they wouldn't last." You can help convince people that your changes are real if, after you have acted improperly, you can identify the specific ways that your actions harmed them and ask them to forgive you.

Rebuilding your name means learning to control your temper

Nobody can make you angry. Not your wife. Not your children. Not your employer or anyone else. Anger is a feeling; a reaction to what is going on at the moment. How you act when you are feeling angry is your choice. If you chose to assault others with words or with your fists, it will be because you have chosen to allow your anger to control you instead of you controlling your anger.

Say you and a fellow inmate are having an argument about which television show to watch. As the argument continues and tempers flare, you become so angry that you are about to strike him. Suddenly someone yells, "The captain's coming!"

As he enters the dorm, the captain walks up to you and says, "The warden wants to see you in his office immediately." On the way up there, he tells you that there has been a review of your case and that there is a possibility you will get an early release.

What is going to happen to your anger between the dorm and the warden's office? Are you going to show your anger to the warden like you were showing it to your fellow inmate just seconds before? Or, even though you still feel angry down inside, are you going to control your temper and be kind and polite to the warden? You *are* in charge of your temper, and you can learn to control it.

Everyone feels angry at times. It's one of those feelings that tells you that something is wrong and that you have a problem. When this happens, mature people use their problem-solving skills to deal with the problem rather than doing what their emotions are telling them to do. As a result, they can choose to treat people with respect even when they are angry.

In fact, the ability to act differently than how one feels is one of the differences between children and adults. Children act according to the way they feel at the moment. If they become angry, they blow up. Children are only nice to those who are nice to them or if they think being nice will get them something that they want. They want what they want when they want it.

Mature adults control their tempers instead of allowing their tempers to control them. They choose ways of dealing with their anger other than hitting, hurting, or lashing out and instead will use that anger to motivate them to find a solution to the problem causing the anger. A mature person can even choose to truly love their enemies instead of giving them what they deserve.

Treating people with respect is not being a coward. It takes an extremely mature adult to give someone love after they have acted ugly. Walking away from an explosive situation is using your problem-solving skills, not being a coward. It is realizing that the long-term consequences of striking back are worse than the short-term consequences of having to listen to some immature hothead tell you how much of a "chicken" you are.

Rebuilding your name means developing goals

Before you can rebuild your name, you must develop specific goals based on your dreams and create a plan of action about how to accomplish those goals. For this you use your problem-solving skills.

First, you must decide what you want your name to mean and then create some specific steps for achieving that dream.

For example, my goal, my dream, is for the name Dan Bayse to mean:

1. A Godly man, of good character, and someone who can be trusted.
2. A good husband to my wife and father to my son.
3. Someone who is dependable and faithful—someone who can be counted on to do a good job.
4. A minister of the gospel.
5. Someone who can teach people how to get along with their families and society (which includes inmates).

Notice the order that I placed my goals and my dreams. First, I want my relationship with God to be right, then my relationship with my wife and family. After these come my work relationship. The priority that you establish to accomplish your goals will tell you what is the most important part of your life.

Now that I have established my goals, a plan can be created that could help to make these dreams come true.

Being a Godly person begins by accepting God's forgiveness and studying His word. Then, whenever faced with a decision about how to act or what to say, deciding to be someone who can be trusted to submit to God's moral laws.

Good husbands are those who are kind and loving to their wives and children. This doesn't come naturally, especially to those who grew up in troubled homes. But there are many courses, seminars, and books available that teach marriage and parenting skills. Marriage and family relationships will not improve until the decision is made to start using the solutions offered by these resources. Some will work, and some will not. Use the ones that work; forget the ones that don't.

How could I accomplish the goal of being dependable and faithful at work? By being the person who the boss can give a job to and consider it done the moment he gives it, and by doing the best that I am capable of doing.

To accomplish my dream of becoming a minister, I needed additional education if I wanted to be effective. This I have done by investing four years to earn a Theology degree. Additionally, I needed to meet the requirements of the church.

Adding the words counselor and Certified Family Life Educator to my name required that I continue my education through graduate school and meet the requirements of the National Council on Family Relations. If I achieve my dream of receiving a Ph.D. in Counselor Education so I can be even more effective, it will take more education, and thus even more years in college.

Before I could start college I had to first break a heavy chain that was placed around my neck in high school; one that said, "You're not smart enough to go to college." College was a real struggle for me, and if I hadn't kept my eyes on my goals I would have dropped out and never finished. You may have to do the same to achieve your goals.

Keeping my eyes on my goal gave me the strength to take jobs that I didn't particularly like just to earn my tuition. Keeping my eyes on my goal allowed me to sit at my computer and keep writing this book, even though I had no promise that it would ever be published.

Most jobs, like the ministry, require special training if you want to put the title before your name. I had to complete the state police academy before I could use the name trooper. Electricians must be trained, as must construction workers, teachers, etc.

There is nothing to stop you from going back to school when you get out or finding that special job that you always wanted. It starts with a dream and using problem-solving skills to make it happen.

You need to have *specific* dreams and goals. As you try to reach those goals there will be times when the struggle seems harder than you can manage. If you keep your eye on your goals, you will be less likely to fail.

Rebuilding your name requires a commitment to change

If you want to rebuild your name, you have to make a commitment to change. This change must start inside your soul and work its way out. This change begins when you realize that you *are not* the most important person in the world.

Most inmates think that they are Number One. Don't be fooled by that mentality. If you are looking out for Number One, you are thinking, "I'm the one in power, and I make all the decisions. I can do anything I want; say anything that I want, anytime and anywhere I want; and there is nothing you or anyone else can do about it, period!"

Then you meet someone else that is looking out for Number One. They are also thinking, "I'm the one in power and make all of the decisions. I can do anything I want; say anything that I want, anytime and anywhere I want; and there is nothing you or anyone else can do about it, period!"

Both of you can't have it your way. One of you has got to give. The power struggle between people who are "looking out for Number One" is the root cause of all interpersonal conflicts.

Unfortunately, if you are looking out only for Number One, you can't give in because your ego won't allow it. You will feel that yielding to that other person would be a sign of weakness and would prove that you are no longer Number One, and you are not about to let that happen. Unfortunately, the other person also feels the same way.

What's In A Name?

The resulting fight is actually to determine who can overpower the other and then claim to be Number One. The conflict starts with heated words, then angry accusations filled with profanity, then violence and will continue to worsen until someone finally surrenders.

If you are always looking out for Number One, you are the one who is going to get hurt. Let's go back to the illustration about the argument in the dorm. Even though you know the captain is coming, you go ahead and hit the guy because he would not change the channel to the one that you wanted to watch. Who would be hurt the most, you or the guy you were fighting with?

When you leave this place and return home you are going to start making love to your wife again. What if, in your lovemaking techniques, you continue your practice of looking out for Number One, do it "slam, bam, thank you ma'am" style, and forget that a woman needs more than that? In the long run, who is going to be hurt more, you or your wife?

What if your boss gives you something to do that you don't want to do, and you say, "I am not going to do it. I am tired of you bossing me around. You can take this job and shove it!" Who is going to be hurt more, you or the boss?

As you rebuild your name, the next thing that you will need to do is change your focus from yourself to others. This is the very heart of ethical living. You are important, but people do not exist to meet your needs. Once you realize that your family and friends do not revolve around you, you can start treating others like you want to be treated.

You know when you are about to do something wrong. At that point you must make a decision: Do I look out for Number One, or do I respect their feelings? When you do anything that would hurt another individual, you are saying to that person in a loud voice, "Your feelings don't count!"

Changing your focus from yourself to others means developing the ability to understand how your actions will make your family, friends, or victims feel. If you ask yourself, "How would I feel if someone did that to me?" you will be less likely to act impulsively to meet your own needs.

If, for example, before forcing someone to submit to your sexual needs, you could picture your victim being as angry with you as you would be if someone did it to you, then you would be less likely to commit the crime. If you can realize how dirty and violated the victim of a burglary will feel when they realize that someone has placed their hands all over their belongings and how this will make them fearful for years to come, you will be less likely to break into their house or business. When you can see the mother of a teenager crying over the body of her son who died from an overdose of the drugs that you sold him, you will no longer be able to deal in drugs. This is because you are now realizing that their feelings do count.

Seven things that will keep you from changing

The next step in rebuilding your name is to recognize the things in your life that can prevent you from changing. Here are some of the more common ones that cause inmates the most trouble:

1. *Being selfish.* That's putting your own needs above the needs of others. This is simply a continuation of always making yourself Number One.
2. *Resentment of authority.* This is also another continuation of looking out for Number One. It is going around with an attitude that says, "I, Me, Numero Uno, can do anything or say anything I want, and you can't tell me what to do." The problem with this attitude is that you get used to pushing your self-proclaimed weight around. Then, when you run into someone who really does have the authority to tell you what to do, such as a correctional officer, a police officer, or an employer, out of habit you will either argue or refuse to comply with their instructions. Who will get hurt the most?

    This is why respect for the rules of society—which includes respect for authority—and taking responsibility for your own actions are the keys to freedom. Think about it: If you can't respect the silly rules in this place, how are you going to be able to respect the silly rules on the outside? True freedom always starts with respect.
3. *Habitual lying.* If you are still lying, you haven't changed. Once you catch a person in a lie, do you trust them anymore? Have you admitted that you earned your right to be here? Many haven't and then wonder why the parole board won't believe them when they say they have learned their lesson. Telling only part of the truth is also lying.
4. *The inability to tolerate frustration.* How many fights have

you seen here in this prison because the television was too loud or too soft? How many fights have you seen because an inmate did not like the way someone looked at him?

5. *Violence and anger.* A changed life is not filled with violence and anger. It's been said that you can tell how big a man is by how much it takes to make him angry.

6. *An inability to show true love.* A lot of inmates feel that love is what other people do for them. They will give love only when they expect that they will get something in return. That's not love, that's selfishness and looking out for Number One. You're not being a loving person if you are still demanding that others give you your own way.

7. *A lack of responsibility.* People will know when you are finally becoming a responsible person when you stop blaming others for the improper or criminal things that you have done and start accepting the responsibility for your own actions. It's learning to say, "I was wrong," and "I blew it."

Have you stopped making excuses about your criminal behavior? If you haven't, your road to change will suddenly come to a dead end. Although alcohol, drugs, the company you kept, a lack of love or too much love when you were growing up, living in the ghetto, your inability to find a job, or whatever may have played a part in your decision to commit your crime, you can't blame anyone but yourself. You did your crime because you wanted to and may have enjoyed it while you were doing it.

Crime does harm society, and society demands that criminals be punished. In their book *Convicted,* Charles Colson and Daniel Van Ness describe the intense pain felt by victims of crime. As you listen to angry victims who are fed up with crime and their inability to participate in the justice system, what you will hear them saying is, "I want that criminal to have to walk a mile in my shoes. I want him to feel what I felt after I became the victim of his crime."

Unfortunately, most inmates have lost the ability to do that. In fact, most criminals never think about the harm their crime does to others. Your ability to live as free as an eagle will largely depend on your ability to put yourself in other people's shoes and to realize how much harm crime does to the victims.

Put yourself in my shoes. When I first moved to Alabama, my wife and I invested all of our money to rent an apartment, pay deposits, and pay my first semester's tuition. We only had one car, and my wife needed it to get to work. My only means of transportation was a woman's ten-speed bicycle.

One night someone stole that bicycle. The thief thought only about the few dollars that he could get for the bicycle. He never thought about the pain that it caused a middle-aged college student who lost his only means of transportation and who had no money or insurance to replace it. Last year, someone broke into our car and stole my wife's and my son's only winter coats. Both had been gifts. How much pain does that cause?

One Christmas morning when I was a trooper, I was called to a home by a woman who was so hysterical that all she could do was give her address. When I arrived, I discovered that someone had broken into the house while they slept and stolen *all* of their Christmas presents. Even though that was years ago and those children are now grown, I wonder if the pain that they experienced that Christmas morning has ever gone away.

It takes a new inmate less than 24 hours to learn that prisons are full of crooks. If this prison is like most, and someone sends you a box of candy, chances are you will not get to enjoy them all because someone will steal them. It hurts when people steal your things, doesn't it?

Years ago, I rushed a two-year-old girl to the hospital for an emergency hysterectomy because of the damage her father did while molesting her. She's a young woman now. Even if she survives and appears to be normal, the pain of not being able to have children because of what her father did to her will be with her for the rest of her life. Do you have memories of mean and cruel things that your parents did to you while you were growing up? Do they still hurt?

I had to go to the home of a bus driver and tell his wife and children that he had been stabbed to death by a passenger. That morning, the driver made a decision. Instead of fighting off the attacker and saving his own life, he put the safety of his passengers first and brought the bus safely to a stop. He died a hero. Regardless of how they die, it still hurts when a family member or close friend dies because of the criminal acts of others, doesn't it?

Frequently you will hear inmates say, "Don't sleep on your stomach," or "If you drop your soap in the shower, don't bend over and pick it up." These make cute jokes, but how does it feel when another inmate attempts to force you to have sex with him or simply scans your body from top to bottom while you are in the shower? You feel violated, like someone has invaded your privacy. If you give in to their demands and have sex with them, with or without a struggle, how do you feel when it is over? Dirty?

What's In A Name?

When you are a victim, the way you feel is the same way that all victims feel. The bad feelings that you feel when these things happen to you are the same bad feelings that your victim felt when you did your crime to them.

As you learned in Chapter 3, there is a "second victim" to your crime—your family. You would probably say that you love your mother. Then why did you hurt her by becoming a criminal? Do you remember how much she cried at your trial? She cried because your crime hurt her severely. You did that to her—not the court and not the "system."

The simple truth is that if you don't change your ways and start thinking about the harm that crime does to others, you will be no good to your family. They won't be able to depend on you to provide emotional or financial support. And if you hurt them again by committing more crimes, which will earn another sentence, the next time their pain will be so great that they will probably abandon you. If this happens, you will spend your new sentence all alone, with only your fellow inmates as friends, and it will be all your fault.

Guilty or Not Guilty?

As you read the last section, how did it make you feel? Bad? In the last chapter you were taught that bad feelings tell you that there is something wrong. They don't tell you what the problem is, only that there is something wrong.

That bad feeling, which at this moment seems to be coming from the deepest part of your soul, is called guilt. Guilt is nature's way of reminding you that what you have done is wrong. In fact, you deserve to feel guilty and disgusting because the crime that you did makes you guilty and disgusting. In his book *Emotions, Can You Trust Them?*, James Dobson says, "Guilt is a message of disapproval from your conscience, which says, in effect, 'You should be ashamed of yourself!'"

Think about what is on that sheet of paper that you were asked to fill out at the beginning of this chapter. Look at it. Right now, even if you lied about the crimes that you have committed and didn't put them on the piece of paper, those crimes are staring you right in the face. At this moment, you are being reminded of your crime(s), and your mind is forcing you to watch yourself committing them. As you watch, you realize that you didn't belong there, and that what you were doing was wrong. It looks ugly, doesn't it?

You do have a conscience, and it still works. Listen to your conscience.

Chapter 6

The crimes listed on that sheet of paper are what your victim, the police, the courts, and society think about you. That is the name that you have made for yourself. Are you proud of that name? If not, are you ready to change that name?

Only when you can see how dirty and disgusting you really are can you begin to do something about it. Only when you see the dirt and guilt in drugs, alcohol, murder, rape and other sex crimes, or any other type of crime will you be motivated to change.

"Wait a minute," you say, "You don't understand. I didn't get a fair trial. The lawyer didn't do a good job." It doesn't matter now. The words of a judge and/or jury aren't what makes people guilty. People become guilty at the scene of the crime. Besides, we're not talking about what happened in the courtroom. We're talking about the things that only you and God know about and that your conscience is reminding you of now. If you were found guilty of all of the things that you are being reminded of at this very moment, how much time would you have to serve?

IF you can now see, and admit, how dirty and disgusting you really became the moment you committed your crime(s), you are ready to change.

IF you are ready to separate yourself from your past and make a new name for yourself and are willing to learn more about keeping your commitment to learn how to practice ethical living, take that sheet of paper and tear it in half so that you have your crimes in one hand and your name in the other. Now tear up the part with the crimes listed on it into little pieces and throw them in the trash.

Now all that is left is a clean piece of paper with your name on it. Your crimes are the things that have happened in the past. They are the old name you made for yourself, but now they are gone.

This means that starting right now, you need to start creating a "new name" for yourself, one that means dependable and faithful. This commitment goes far beyond the commitment that you made in Chapter 4 to practice ethical living. It means that you will stop making excuses about your past and admit that you did your crime because you wanted to and that you enjoyed it while you were doing it. It means admitting that you didn't care about how it harmed society, your victim, or your family.

It also means that starting today, you will do these two things for the rest of your life (1) you will never again do anything that you know to be morally wrong and (2) you will do *only* the things you know to be morally right. You know the difference between right and wrong.

This means that you must take action and use a bold new approach.

What's In A Name?

These commitments lead to activities that are incompatible with crime. They may include regular church attendance. It means getting involved in community activities. This commitment means always being considerate of others. These things can start right here in this prison, today.

This commitment means deciding to engage in activities designed to help others rather than hurt them. Besides giving you a new name, there is another reward for helping others. Doing good to others will make you feel better about yourself. Learning to listen will make you aware of other people's needs and will make you less likely to focus on your own needs.

Do you want a new name? You still have the half sheet of paper with your name at the top. If you are willing to do the work to make a new name for yourself, write the words "dependable" and "faithful" under your name. Then add today's date. Keep that piece of paper and think of it as your new "birth certificate." If you keep your commitment and allow this to become your new name, you will never have to worry about ever committing another crime for the rest of your life.

A resource that will make your life incompatible with crime

Making commitments is easy; keeping them is hard. Here is another resource that will help you keep your life balanced and incompatible with crime.

Find someone who is straight, someone you can trust, someone who knows all about you and still accepts you just the way you are, and make yourself accountable to that person. Make sure that this person is willing to accept the responsibility and the trust that you are asking for and is strong enough to help you past your transition points.

As you look for this special person, look for someone who is willing to share personal things about themselves that will help you through your trials. This person may be a minister, a counselor, a fellow inmate, or an old friend. No matter who it is, they must be someone that you can open up your soul to without fear of rejection.

Brag to that person about the times that you were tempted and resisted. Confess your failures, what your learned from your mistakes, and the resources that you are going to use to keep them from happening again.

Make a deal with that person that whenever you are tempted to do something that is morally wrong that you can call them and talk it out. Don't let pride stand in your way. Pick up the phone and call that minister, counselor, friend from the Alcoholics Anonymous group, or whoever is willing to fulfill that role.

Make yourself accountable to your wife. Let her know where you are and who you will be with at all times. Wouldn't you be less likely to be unfaithful to her if you knew that you had to tell her everyone that you saw and spent time with each day? Let her know that you want to be her husband and want her to help you keep from going back to hard living.

After you get out, use your probation officer for what he or she is there for: to help you stay straight. Don't allow your ego and pride to stand in your way. If you broke your leg you would gladly wear a cast to hold the bone in place until it healed: you would gladly learn how to walk with crutches. Being accountable to others will be a totally new way of life for you, so why be ashamed to admit that you need help in staying straight?

When my son was trying to learn how to walk, he would totter all over the house and the yard as long as he had a hand to hold onto. One day as we were walking down the sidewalk, his tiny hand slipped from my grasp and he plopped onto the ground. Immediately he looked up at me, and his little hand shot up like a bullet. I reached down, he grabbed hold of my hand, and off we went again. As long as my finger was there for him to hold onto, my son felt secure.

Soon, my son felt brave enough to let loose and try a couple of steps on his own. But every time he would start to wobble, out would go that little hand looking for someone to keep him from falling. One day, my son discovered that he didn't need a hand any more. He had matured enough to walk on his own.

By making yourself accountable to someone else, you are giving yourself a hand to grab until you are strong enough to walk on your own. It is a resource that can help you to keep your life balanced.

Have you forgiven yourself for what you've done?

Whenever you do anything criminal or morally wrong, a debt is created with God, with society, and with the victim(s). As you learned in Chapter 4, forgiveness is not forgetting. You don't have the ability to do that.

What's In A Name?

Forgiveness is a decision to quit blaming people for the harm they have done and to begin treating them like the offense never happened—while still holding them accountable for their actions. There is a difference between accountability and blame. Webster's Dictionary defines blame as speaking evil about someone, or accusing and condemning them. Accountability is requiring the person to repay their debts according to the rules of God and society.

Unforgiving people continually blame others. They speak evil, ugly words of condemnation that accuse people of all kinds of harm. It's easy to tell when you are around an unforgiving person. They are always talking about the harm that other people have done to them. Unforgiving inmates will blame their families, their victims, the police, the attorneys, the courts, the "system," and society for the things that are wrong with their lives. Some inmates try to blame God for their crime by saying God failed to take away their evil desires.

If you are an unforgiving person, it will hurt you more than anyone else. For example, if there are people in your life who you haven't forgiven, those people will be with you all of the time. They will be the first people that you think about in the morning and the last people you think about before you go to sleep. Those people will even haunt you in your dreams. As your hatred of them grows, it will turn to bitterness and will burn within you until you are literally consumed.

Your hatred of them for what they did, no matter how bad it was, doesn't hurt them at all. They don't know how you feel; and even if they did, it would not affect them like it does you.

You are also one of the victims of your own improper actions. Your improper and immoral actions made you guilty the moment that you committed them. You can't forget them because you don't have the ability. You can try to hide those guilty feelings under anger, depression, denial, or just plain lying, but they won't go away. Your conscience simply won't let you forget the moral failures in your life. Forgiveness is the only way to get rid of the guilt.

Chapter 4 gave you the steps to forgiveness. Clear your conscience by confessing the wrongs you have done to the people involved. Then do what is necessary to repay your "debts" to your family, to your victims, and to society by doing your time and making any needed restitution. Once that is done, accept the fact that you now have a clean slate and that your debt is paid. Then stop punishing yourself and start living the rest of your life as if your moral failures never happened. That's hard to do.

Forgiveness also means that you will quit blaming yourself for your failures. Stop blaming your alcoholism, your family, or whatever for your own improper actions. This also means that you will stop putting yourself down.

Make yourself accountable by acknowledging your guilt. Accept the fact that what you did was dirty and disgusting and that you may need to make restitution to your victims. Admit that you are paying your debt to society. Learn from your mistakes, make the commitment not to make the same mistakes again, and keep on going. Keep your eye on your dream.

One last thing. You can't be forgiven for the harm that you have done unless you are willing to forgive others. Nobody will forgive someone that has an unforgiving spirit.

Building a new image for yourself

Are you ready to rebuild your image of yourself? Good self-esteem and a feeling of completeness require four things: to feel loved, to feel accepted, to feel competent, and ethical living.

You will feel loved when you know that the group you are in will treat you with respect. It may take some time, but you can change how a group treats you by treating the others in the group like you want to be treated. You get people to love you by loving them first. You get people to treat you with respect by treating them with respect first. If you wait until others start treating you with respect before you start being nice to them, you're going to have a long wait.

Have you ever heard the saying, "What goes around comes around"? This has many applications in interpersonal relations. For example, if you blow up at someone, and they blow up right back, what will that do to your relationship? What if you blow up at someone and they continue to treat you with respect? The chances are that you will treat them with respect the next time.

You will feel accepted by the group when you can convince others to do things your way without using force and without any threats. This will never happen until the others around you know that you have considered their feelings and that the action you have proposed is in the best interests of all concerned. Remember, you may need to switch groups before this can happen. A wolf will never feel accepted in a flock of sheep.

Ethical living is a combination of the other three. This is living in such a way that your name means "dependable" and "faithful." This is living in such a way that you never have to worry about a guilty conscience. It's living in such a way that your life can be an open book; one filled with true love, forgiveness, and trustworthy actions.

In your attempt to live up to your commitment to ethical living, remember the resource that you learned about earlier: make yourself accountable to others for your actions, and make sure that the people that you make yourself accountable to are straight and can be trusted to help you.

Once you realize that you are a person of worth, you will suddenly realize that you have something to offer society. Think about the trades that you already know or the jobs that you have done here in the prison system.

"But," you say, "I don't know how to do anything." Baloney. Can you sweep a floor? Can you clean a toilet? People pay good money for others to clean up after them. Can you push a lawn mower? I earned the money for one semester in college by calling real estate firms and asking them if they had houses for sale that needed their lawns mowed. You can do the same. Can you use a pick or a shovel? Construction companies are frequently looking for people who are willing to do hard work. Helping others by sharing what you know is a good way to prove that you are someone of value. This can start right here in this penitentiary. Participate in the GED program, either by working toward your GED certificate or by tutoring another inmate so that he can get his GED. You will discover that when you help someone else, you will learn more than the person you are tutoring.

Once you realize that you are a person of worth, you may realize that you are good enough to continue your education. Explore the possibilities of going to a trade school or to college. You might be surprised how little they cost and how much financial aid is available to help you attend. You might even find ways to start that educational process while you are in prison.

Once you realize that you are a person of worth, you will be able to dream again. Everything you will ever accomplish will start with a dream, a dream that says, "I wonder what it would be like to [fill in the blank]?" Once you have the dream, you can use your problem-solving skills to discover ways to fulfill those dreams. Then the possibilities are limited only by the size of your imagination. Following your dreams will help you to learn how to live as free as an eagle.

Chapter 6

Making your new name stick

Now that you have decided that your new name will mean dependable and faithful, you must develop a way to convince others that you will keep that commitment. Once you have cleared your conscience, forgiven yourself, and have formed a new image of yourself, you can start doing the things that will make your new name stick. Bill Gothard of the Institute of Basic Youth Conflicts says, "Success in life is not measured by what we are or what we have done, but rather by what we are and have done compared to what we could have been and could have done."

You may be thinking, "I would like to do a whole lot more than I am doing now, but no one will give me a chance to do anything." Here is a secret way to get your boss to give you more important jobs with greater responsibility. It is so simple that few people try it.

If you are faithful in doing the little jobs that people give you, soon you will be trusted to do bigger and more important jobs. For example, suppose your first job is with a janitorial service. You are assigned the task of making sure that all of the wastebaskets are emptied in the building that your crew cleans each night. If you did that every night, everyone would be happy. But what if, instead, you decided to start doing even more than what was required of you? After you finish your work, you look around and see if one of your fellow employees is running behind in his work and jump in and help him. When it comes time for a promotion, who do you think the boss will promote, someone who does the minimum amount of work required, or someone who has proved himself to be faithful in the little jobs?

M. R. Weideranders found that this is not the way that most inmates act after they complete their sentences. Instead, even though most are able to find work almost immediately, they usually stay on the job for only a few weeks before quitting or being fired. The usual reason is because the former inmates return to their hard-living lifestyle and refuse to follow the company's rules.

In order to rebuild your name, you are going to have to prove that your new name is dependable and faithful. You do this by staying on the job. You get to work on time. You give the boss a full day's work while you are there, and then you go home at quitting time instead of going to the bar.

Being known as dependable and faithful does have its rewards. Promotions within companies are given to those employees who work hard and play by the company rules and to people who have time with the company.

But what if "everything" goes wrong?

"Murphy's Law" says, "If anything can go wrong, it will; and at the worst possible moment." When things go wrong, if you go back to your old way of doing things, you are going to crash. Remaining dependable and faithful and using your problem-solving skills to find the resources that will keep your life balanced will keep you from failing. Keeping your commitment to practice ethical living and to never again do anything that you know to be morally wrong will keep your conscience clear and keep you out of prison for the rest of your life.

Remember, when a person hears your name they will automatically think about more than what your face looks like or the words your parents placed on your birth certificate to identify you. Besides these things, they will also think about your reputation in the community, your character, and whether they like you or not.

What do you want your name to mean? It's your decision, and you alone are responsible for the choices that you make.

Chapter 7
"Hey Man, I Need To Feed My Family"

(And other ways to find a job that don't work)

There is nothing better for a man than to enjoy his work, because that is his lot.

—Solomon, 935 B.C.

Like it or not, your time in prison is coming to an end. When that happens, just like that baby eagle, you are going to be kicked out of your nest. Suddenly, you are either going to learn how to fly, or you are going to crash. If you want to live as free as an eagle, one of the things that you must learn is how to find, and keep, a job.

Robert Homant followed inmates for ten years after their release from prison. During this study, *none* of the men who stayed on their first job for

154

one year were ever arrested for anything during the entire ten years. In contrast, that same study found that 86 percent of the offenders who lasted less than one month on their first job were arrested again. Many other researchers report similar findings.

Believe it or not, most inmates do not have any trouble finding work after they are released. The problem is keeping the job once they have found it. In 1981, Mark Wiederanders studied the employment patterns of recently released California inmates. Although 95 percent of the ex-offenders were able to locate jobs shortly after their release, the majority of them did not stay on the job. While 31 percent were fired, most (69 percent) quit. When asked why, 68 percent said that they left because they didn't like a boss or coworker, and 53 percent said that they could not conform to the work schedule.

How can a former inmate find a job he can stay at for a year? What kind of jobs are available to you? What are some of the common problems that newly released inmates face while trying to find the right job? How can these problems be avoided? What rights to employment do inmates lose because of their conviction? What rights do they still have? What can be done if their rights are violated?

You have not lost your rights to employment

Having a criminal record is often a severe handicap in trying to find a job once you are released. However, the handicap is usually the ex-offender's attitude and not his criminal record. Many inmates, usually the ones on the hard-living road, come out of prison with a chip on their shoulder that says, "I've done my time, and now you owe me a job." Employers don't want people with that kind of attitude.

You have not lost your right to employment simply because you are a convicted criminal. Minorities are protected by Title VII of the 1964 Civil Rights Act, which bans discrimination because of race, color, religion, sex, and national origin. In the 1957 case of *Schware v. Board of Examiners*, the Supreme Court ruled that the equal protection clause of the Fourteenth Amendment to the Constitution required employers to prove that a person's past crimes would have some bearing on the job before they could be excluded from that job.

Chapter 7

Federal law, backed by court decisions, says that there are five things that must be considered before a prospective employer can refuse to hire ex-offenders because of their criminal record:

1. The time elapsed since the crime was committed.
2. The offender's age when the crime was committed.
3. The seriousness of the offense.
4. Any evidence of rehabilitation. [HINT: Participate in every helpful program that the prison offers and save all of the completion certificates.]
5. If the nature of the crime has a direct bearing on the ex-offender's fitness for the job.

Allen Gosh, enforcement supervisor for the Equal Employment Opportunities Commission, says that employers do have the right to ask a prospective employee if they have ever been convicted of a crime and that the employer can take the answer into consideration when deciding if they are going to offer them employment.

However, if challenged, the employer must then prove that they did not discriminate against the ex-offender solely because of his criminal record. If the company can't show a relationship between the crime and the job, the company would be held responsible. If found guilty of illegal discrimination because of one's criminal record, the company may be required to hire the ex-offender, train them, provide them with back pay and seniority rights, or other compensation and benefits.

An employer has the right to refuse to hire you (or fire you later) if you lie on your application or during your interview. If this happens and you sue, the courts will back the employer and you will have lost your right to ever have a job with that company. This will also further damage your work record. How many companies do you think will hire a man after he has just been fired from another company for lying?

Your criminal record will prohibit you from having certain types of jobs. For example, federal courts have upheld the right of police departments not to hire convicted felons. They have ruled that police departments have this right to assure the appearance of good character and integrity among police officers and to avoid any appearance that police officers can't be trusted.

Don't expect to be hired by a day care center if you are a convicted child molester or sex offender.

"Hey Man, I Need to Feed My Family"

Don't expect to be hired as a bank teller if you have been convicted of armed robbery, extortion, or embezzlement.

Don't expect to be hired as a bill collector if you have been convicted of murder.

Don't expect to be hired as an apartment manager if you have been convicted of theft.

Don't expect to be hired as a clerk in a pharmacy if you have been convicted of a drug offense.

On the other hand, the courts have actively enforced the civil rights of ex-offenders. One company was found to have acted illegally when they failed to hire a black applicant for a bus driver position because he had been convicted for attempting to accept a bribe while working as a police officer. Another company was found to have violated Title VII of the Civil Rights Act when it failed to hire an ex-offender as a laborer because of a prior conviction for robbery.

Eric Matusewitch says that, over the years, courts have also ruled that ex-offenders could be employed as civil servants, licensed private detectives, and with security agencies.

Your state employment service is willing to help you

Every state has an employment office. You will find them listed in the white pages of the telephone directory under the state government listings. These offices are there solely to help people find jobs. In fact, some of the larger offices may even provide an employment counseling program to match your skills and interests to the jobs that are available. It is paid for by the state.

Bob Armstrong, chief of special services for the Alabama Employment Office, says that it is not much harder to place a convicted criminal into a job than it is any other person *if* two things are done. First, they must show a proper attitude that says to a prospective employer, "I want to work." And, they must be honest about their past. His words could probably be repeated by employment officials across the country.

Many jobs and occupations require that the individual be bonded. Some truck drivers, certain sales personnel, some delivery people, and many jobs that require the handling of money require security bonds. Unfortunately,

157

Chapter 7

many times private insurance companies are hesitant to write bonds for former inmates. However, many states have a bonding program specifically designed to help inmates find a job regardless of the crimes that they have committed in the past.

If you would qualify for a job and a company is willing to hire you, but can't because their insurance company will not bond you, your state may issue the bond so that you can get the job. Usually, there are no set limits. Each bond is tailored to the needs of the individual and the company. States know that employment is extremely important for former inmates, and they will do everything within their power to help you find work.

However, your state's employment service *cannot* get you a job. They can tell you were the openings are. They can furnish you with an appointment for a job interview. But they cannot make the employer hire you. You will have to do that by convincing the employer of your worth.

Using problem-solving skills to find the right job

Finding the right job is a problem. Whenever you have problems, use the problem-solving formula to find a solution that will eliminate the problem.

First: identify the real problem. In this case the problem is that you need to find a job that you can stay on for one year and that will allow you to provide for your family's needs.

Second: brainstorm solutions with the people involved in the problem. Consider your personal characteristics as you brainstorm the possible jobs that interest you. Since people do not have the ability to see themselves as others see them, try talking with your family members, friends, or counselors and discover where your talents really are.

For example, do you work best around a lot of people, or do you work best when you are given a job to do and left alone to do it? Do you need a lot of supervision, or can you be depended on to work without supervision? Do you need additional training to develop your potential to its fullest? None of these characteristics are better than the other, they are just different. You need to consider your individual needs and desires while you are doing your brainstorming.

How many different jobs can you do? What are the skills that you presently have? It might help if you wrote down every place that you have ever worked and describe your job. This would serve two purposes: to help you identify your skills and to give you the information that you will need to talk with a prospective employer. Find a book that teaches you how to write a resume. Then use it.

Who do you already know that would have the information about the type of work that you are looking for? Many people, including inmates, have been able to find work because a friend told them about a job that might be available if they applied for it. What is available through the state employment service?

Before you start looking, you need to decide if you are looking for a temporary job or something that is a possible career. Looking for a career job doesn't mean that if you accept it, you will make a commitment to stay there until you retire. It simply means that the job looks attractive enough to you that you *might* consider staying there until you retire.

When you are talking to prospective employers, make sure that you ask if the position that you are applying for is a temporary position or a permanent one. This will save you from being shocked later when the job ends. For you, permanent jobs are better. But if jobs are hard to find in your area, take the temporary job. It's more important that you work.

Third: examine the long-term consequences of each possible job. Consider the types of job that would fit into your personal value system. For example, a recovering alcoholic shouldn't work in a restaurant that serves alcoholic beverages. If you think gambling is wrong, you shouldn't look for a job at the dog track. In examining the long-term consequences of a particular job opportunity, ask yourself what you expect to be doing five years from now and examine these life goals while making the decision about the job. For example, you might not mind digging ditches for one summer if it will give you the money to go back to college in the fall, even though your life goal is not to be a construction worker.

Fourth: pick the best-looking job and try to get it. Apply for that job. If you are turned down, go to the next place on your list. If you get to the end of your list, go back to step one and start over.

A short description of the job search

You're all ready to go. You have your list of prospective employers and you hit the streets.

Interview Number 1: "I would like to work for your company." The reply: "NO!"

Interview Number 2: "I would like to work for your company." The reply: "NO!"

Interview Number 3: "I would like to work for your company." The reply: "NO!"

Interview Number 4: "I would like to work for your company." The reply: "NO!"

Interview Number 5: "I would like to work for your company." The reply: "NO!"

Interview Number 6: "I would like to work for your company." The reply: "NO!"

Interview Number 7: "I would like to work for your company." The reply: "NO!"

Interview Number 8: "I would like to work for your company." The reply: "NO!"

Interview Number 9: "I would like to work for your company." The reply: "NO!"

Interview Number 10: "I would like to work for your company." The reply: "NO!"

Interview Number 11: "I would like to work for your company." The reply: "NO!"

Interview Number 12: "I would like to work for your company." The reply: "NO!"

Interview Number 13: "I would like to work for your company." The reply: "NO!"

Interview Number 14: "I would like to work for your company." The reply: "NO!"

Interview Number 15: "I would like to work for your company." The reply: "YES!"

The problem comes when you stop with interview 4, 8, or even 14, get frustrated, and give up instead of using your problem-solving skills. You must not stop until you get to a "Yes." Each "No" means that you start the problem-solving process over again. Refusing to give up and continuing to look for a suitable job may be the hardest things that you have ever done.

Ask not what your employer can do for you

Prospective employers can be divided into two groups: those who don't care about your criminal record, and those who do. Your job is to find the ones in the first group and forget about the ones in the second group.

"But," you say, "I have my rights. The Equal Employment Opportunity Commission or the courts will require them to hire me." Possibly so. But considering how important it is for you to stay on your first job for one year, wouldn't you be better off if you could find someone who knows about your past, accepts you just the way you are, and is willing to give you the same chance that he or she would give anyone else? Even if there are only a handful of employers in your community that wouldn't care about your criminal record, your job is to find those few and forget the others.

Be confident when you go into the front door of the business. After talking with the state employment office, friends, or a job counselor, you know that you have the skills needed to do the work at that place of business. Now all you have to do is convince that employer that you have what he needs.

Although it is important, you aren't going to the interview to find out what the company can do for you. The purpose of a job interview is to give you a chance to explain what you can do for the company. A company's sole purpose for hiring people is to make money from their employees' work.

The company is not a charity. They probably won't give you a job simply because you need to feed your family. They are looking for people who are willing to work and want to help make the company profitable.

How should I dress for the interview?

You will only have one chance to make a good first impression. So wear the nicest clothes that you have. Make sure that they are appropriate for the type of job that you are applying for. Let your clothes give the boss the idea that you are there dressed and ready for work. This means that blue jeans and a sweatshirt would not be appropriate if you were going for an interview as a salesman in a men's clothing store. On the other hand, a suit and tie wouldn't be appropriate if you were applying for a job as a roofer. If you are applying for a job at a large construction site, it might help if you showed up for the interview wearing matching work pants and shirt, steel-toed boots, and a hard hat.

Regardless of what you wear, make sure that your clothes are neat, clean, and pressed. Make sure that your shoes are shined. Make sure that you are clean. Take a shower just before you go. Use deodorant. Brush your teeth and use mouthwash. Make sure that your hair is clean and brushed. One of the quickest ways to turn an employer against you is to show up dirty, with body odor and bad breath.

Wear your "Sunday manners." Be on time. Be polite and considerate of the office staff and employees. Answer the questions politely.

What will a prospective employer ask during an interview?

To comply with federal law, they will first ask to see your social security card and a picture identification card such as a driver's license.

Then, before an intelligent decision can be made about offering you a job with their company, employers have legitimate questions that must be answered. Except for things such as your name and address, everything that they will ask during an interview can be reduced to these four questions.

1. *"Why are you here?"*

    They want to know why you chose to apply at their company instead of another company. What are you expecting to find at their firm that you couldn't find somewhere else? What are you expecting them to do for you if they hire you?

2. *"What can you do for us?"*

    Translated, this means, "What can we expect from you if we hire you?" and "What special skills do you have that will make us more profitable?" You are going to be in competition with all of the other applicants. To win the competition and get the job, you are going to have to convince them that their company will be the winner if they hire you for the job instead of someone else. They also want to know that you will be loyal to the company and believe in their product or service.

3. *"What kind of person are you?"*

    This means, "Will you fit in with the other employees?" Companies want trustworthy people who have a desire to create a name for themselves that means dependable and faithful.

"Hey Man, I Need to Feed My Family"

4. *"Can we agree on a salary?"*

Most employers start people at the bottom of the ladder. Higher pay comes after people prove that they can be trusted to do the seemingly unimportant jobs and have demonstrated loyalty by building time with the company.

People who already know the answers to these questions before they walk into the interview room will have a better chance of being hired.

What should you do if an interviewer asks you questions during a job interview that you feel are illegal or indicate that the company is discriminating against you because of your past criminal record? If this happens, you have three options.

The first is to answer the question honestly and ignore the fact that it may be illegal. There is a chance that the employer simply does not know all of the latest laws about nondiscrimination. You could choose to give them the benefit of the doubt. It could also be that the employer doesn't care about your past and is just testing you to see how honest you will be.

The second would be to answer the question this way: "I don't think that what you are asking is part of the job requirement, is it?" This would let the interviewer know that you are aware of your rights and should make him or her stop asking such questions. Employers, especially at larger corporations, know that they must prove nondiscrimination if challenged.

If you feel that the company illegally refused to hire you because of your criminal record or discriminated against you in some other way, the third option is to report them to the Equal Employment Opportunity Commission (EEOC). They have a nationwide toll-free number that you can use (1-800-USA-EEOC).

It is important that you report any suspected discrimination in hiring immediately. EEOC has strict guidelines about the deadline for reporting alleged discrimination and for making decisions. If you fail to meet the deadline, you lose your chance to have them review your case.

In making the decision about how to answer an employer's questions or calling the Equal Employment Opportunity Commission, you must decide if the prospective employer cared about your criminal record or was simply prejudiced against you. If you decide that you were discriminated against, you must then decide if that particular job is worth the hassle involved in filing a claim. Do you really want to work in a place that does not want to have you there?

Chapter 7

How to handle rejection

There may be many Nos before you find that one magical Yes. Each time you get turned down, go back to your problem-solving skills.

1. Identify the problem: I need a job.
2. Brainstorm solutions: How can I find out what other jobs are available?
3. Examine the long-term consequences.
4. Pick the best-looking job and turn in your application. If it doesn't work and you don't get the job, go back to step one.

If you are rejected, resist the temptation to go back to your old ways of doing things. Don't display your anger toward the interviewer by storming out of his office and slamming the door behind you. He or she won't care, and all you will do is end your chances of ever working for that company.

Instead, respect the rules of society. If you feel that you were discriminated against, and you really want that job, then contact the Equal Opportunity Employment Commission. Let them be the judge. They will be honest with you.

Don't go out and get drunk, get in a fight with your wife and/or children, kick the dog, or do some other inappropriate activity. Be man enough to admit that the rejection hurts. If you feel like crying, do it. Find the person that you are accountable to and ask for help. Use them as your crutch. Take each rejection as being taught how to fly. Keep your eye on your goal, and soon you will be able to live as free as an eagle.

People are willing to give you work and to allow you to grow within the company if you are honest with them, if you are faithful and dependable, and if you show the proper attitude.

Here's an example. The owner of a large masonry company routinely gives ex-offenders a job, if they are willing to work. He starts them as laborers at $5 an hour. Carrying blocks and mixing mortar is hard work. He claims that starting new people this way lets him know who is really interested in working and who simply likes to do the least they can get by with.

If they are interested, he teaches them how to lay concrete block. When they can follow the string line and keep the blocks straight, their salary is increased to $8 an hour. Then he will teach them how to lay bricks. When they can build corners and can work totally without supervision, their salary is increased to $12.50 an hour. The owner of this company says that it takes a motivated person approximately one year to reach top pay with his company.

The most important person who can help you is you. Resist the temptation to give up and stop trying. Use those problem-solving skills to find the resources that will help you keep your life balanced.

Employers have legitimate concerns about you

One of the greatest fears that every employer has is that one of their employees will do something that will damage the company name. Company owners know that the company name is more than just a handle. The know that every time people hear that name, they will also think about their reputation, their opinion about the quality of the product, and whether they like the company or not. Company owners are also painfully aware that dissatisfied customers love to tell everyone they meet about the problems they have had with that company or their product. Because of this, companies have worked long and hard over the years to build a name for themselves. They know that sloppy workmanship and discourteous employees can quickly destroy their good name.

Here's an example. A plumber spent twenty-five years building his business. Builders knew that even though he might cost a bit more, he could be counted on to do a good job, and it would be done right the first time.

He began getting more business than he could handle by himself. So he hired two plumbers and furnished each with an apprentice and a new, fully equipped truck. Besides being paid generous wages, each new plumber was promised a nice bonus if he was able to complete his jobs ahead of schedule.

One of the new plumbers seemed to outshine the other. On the surface it looked like he was the ideal worker because he worked many long hours and completed the jobs in record time. Because of his diligence, he received many bonuses. Unfortunately, this new plumber became more interested in earning the bonus money than he did in doing the quality work. As a result, his work grew increasingly sloppy.

During his first three months of employment, this new plumber installed the plumbing in fifteen apartments and ten houses. All of it reached the stage of final inspection at about the same time. As the water was turned on for the first time, the building inspectors discovered that every one of the jobs done by this new plumber had leaks.

Chapter 7

A closer inspection revealed that many wrong sizes of pipes had been installed because this new plumber frequently substituted whatever he had on the truck for what the plans called for to save time. Drains had been improperly installed. Water lines burst at the couplings. Faucets leaked. Hot and cold lines were reversed. But worst of all, much of the work had to be redone.

The owner of the plumbing business was hurt by the loss of an employee, the cost of his materials, the salary and bonuses that he had paid the new plumber, and three month's worth of time. But what hurt him even more was the loss of his good name in the community. As builders learned about the problems, his name no longer stood for quality service. That plumber watched twenty-five years of work to build a good name go right down the drain. When you apply for a job, that new employer will want to know that you won't do the same thing to him.

Another concern that employers have is that you won't be able to do the job because you don't have the skills or experience. After all, many people exaggerate their abilities. They also fear investing the time, effort, and expense into training you, only to have you leave after a few months.

Employers also fear that if they hire you, you won't put in a full day's work. They fear that you will be one of the people who are constantly calling in sick or will skip days when you don't feel like working.

Because of the reputation created by previous ex-offenders, there is a big concern that you will not get along with other employees. You've heard the saying, "One bad apple spoils the barrel." Often, all it takes is one person with a sour attitude to ruin the morale of the entire workplace. Employers are concerned that you may be that person. They are looking for people who are willing to put the needs of fellow employees above their own and will treat people the way they want to be treated. This is important because workplaces just cannot function without cooperation among employees.

Because so many former inmates decide to take the hard-living road when they leave prison, employers fear that you will either be unwilling or unable to follow instructions. They want employees who know that the keys to having the freedom to work at their establishment are (1) respect for the rules of the company and (2) taking responsibility for your own work.

If the personnel officer recommends that the company accept your application, he or she is also putting his or her name on the line. The company trusts his or her judgement to hire the right people. Even though he or she may never admit it, he or she fears that if they hire you, a convicted criminal, you will let him or her down. He or she's afraid that after you start work you will start demonstrating the character flaws associated with hard living and disrupt the work place. He or she fears that your supervisors will begin complaining that you are dishonest, lazy, someone who shows up drunk or "spaced out," a liar, or someone who spreads rumors and stirs up the other employees. If this happens, his or her supervisors will call him or her an idiot for hiring you. Nobody likes to hear the words, "I told you so." Nobody likes to look bad to their supervisors.

What employers are looking for are people who enjoy working, are fun to have around, and will be an asset to the company.

Taking the hard-living road to work

Research shows that many inmates choose to take the hard-living road on their release and usually return to prison within three years. Men on the hard-living road are always looking for signs to remind them that they are Number One. They like to be reminded to "get all the gusto that you can"; "have it your way"; or "you deserve a break today."

These men tend to strut around like they're the only rooster in a henhouse, angrily scratching in the dirt, crowing a lot, but not accomplishing anything. Hard-living people think that talking tough, yelling, fighting, threatening, and using a lot of profanity will make people think they are tough. Power, for this type of person, is measured by their ability to force others to do things their way.

We know that this is actually an abuse of power. Real power comes when you can convince others to do things your way without resorting to force.

Ex-offenders who travel this road seem to have a preoccupation with the problems and the drama of everyday life. Hard-living people feel that asking for help is a sign of weakness. As a result, their pride won't allow them to accept help, even when it's offered. "After all," they'll say, "our problems are different, and you just wouldn't understand." Their refusal to use problem-solving skills prevents them from finding the resources that would keep their lives in balance. Problems build until there is so much pressure that everyone in the family is ready to explode. Whenever people reach their capacity to handle stress, all it takes is one little insignificant thing to topple the entire load.

The attitude that accepting help is a sign of weakness especially affects hard-living men when they go to work. People who feel that they are

Number One think they have the answers to every problem in the world and will not try anything except their own way to solve their problems. You can push on a 20-ton rock all day long, then push harder and harder the next day, and it still will not move. You are going to have to have some help and perhaps another approach.

Hard-living men can't accept supervision. In fact, they will frequently react to constructive criticism with feelings of rage, shame, or humiliation. The feeling that they're Number One and their own boss will not allow them to respect the company rules. As can be expected, these men stay in continual conflict with their supervisors and fellow employees.

Hard-living people consistently take advantage of other people to get what they want. They think that their "special" circumstances entitle them to special consideration—these guys even think that they shouldn't have to wait in line like everyone else. They'll brag to everyone about how great they are, but their work record doesn't back up their claims.

Their inability to recognize how their improper actions hurt others makes them unpleasant to be around. These guys will even get angry when a fellow worker takes a day off to care for his sick child. If a fellow employee gets injured on the job, instead of expressing sympathy or offering to pitch in and help carry the load until she recovers, they will complain about how much it is increasing their own workload. But if their kids get sick or if they get injured, you had better not treat them the way they treat others.

Needless to say, people on the hard-living road don't make very good employees or very nice people to work beside.

The settled-living road to freedom

The narrow road called settled living is harder to travel. Those who follow it are able to successfully end their criminal careers and will continue to distance themselves from their former prison life. Settled living is a lifestyle based on using the keys to freedom. Because these people are willing to respect the rules of society, they are free to enjoy long and stable marriages and enjoyable work careers. Years later, friends will find it increasingly difficult to believe that they are former inmates.

If you follow the road called settled living you will develop a general sense of "rootedness" in your community; you'll feel like you belong there. You'll discover that even though all churches have hypocrites, you have a much greater chance of making the right kind of friends at a church than

"Hey Man, I Need to Feed My Family"

you will at the local bar. Settled living means getting involved in community affairs, such as participating in a neighborhood clean-up, in a neighborhood watch program, or attending the parent-teacher meetings at your children's school.

The settled living road includes a desire to practice ethical living. You'll want to live in such a way that you never have to look over your shoulder or worry about the parole officer's suddenly ordering you to "fill the cup." You will no longer worry about drugs or alcohol being found in your system because you don't use them anymore. You'll remember your days of chemical dependency and understand that all it would take would be one drink, one hit of heroin, one snort of cocaine, one toke on a joint to again start the cycle leading back into alcohol or drug dependency—and for you, back into prison. You'll be able to resist the temptation to go back to your old ways because it would put you on the entrance ramp to the superhighway called hard living.

Because you want your new name to mean dependable and faithful, you will enjoy doing things that prove you trustworthy. This will enable you to endure the stress associated with staying on your first job for a year. You will want your boss to know that he can depend on you to do a good job and to know that you will not quit the first time that the job gets frustrating. Bosses like that kind of person. Your wife will like knowing that you can be faithfully depended on to "bring home the bacon."

Settled living includes being a respectable member of your community. People will not have forgotten about your crime. Even though it happened over 20 years ago, how many people still associate Senator Edward Kennedy's name with his crime at Chappaquiddick. You are going to find that people have long memories, especially if they think you did not get what you deserved.

Settled living means knowing that your life will not come to an end because of your crime. Even though your dream will have to change, you can be successful if you spend the rest of your life rebuilding your name by doing only what you know to be morally right and by practicing ethical living.

Charles Colson did just that. In 1974, in the aftermath of the Watergate scandal, his life suddenly changed from being one of President Nixon's most powerful advisors to being an inmate in a federal prison in Montgomery, Alabama. He made himself accountable for his actions, served his time, and used his experiences to develop a new dream. Prison Fellowship, an international prison ministry devoted to helping inmates recover from prison life, is the result of that dream. He used his problem-solving skills to make that dream come true.

Settled living includes a concern for others. Wives, children, employers, fellow employees, and everyone else like to be around people who demonstrate their concern for the needs of others. People respond to true acts of love.

Settled living includes using your keys to freedom—at home, at work, and in everything that you say and do.

Using the keys to freedom at work

Being free to continue working after you are released means learning to respect the company rules and taking responsibility for your own actions. The reason that most recently released inmates quit or are fired is because they refuse to observe the company's rules or because they do not get along with fellow employees.

Instead of respecting the company schedule, they create their own schedule by coming in late, if they come in at all. They will create their own work rules by ignoring their supervisor's instructions and doing only what they want to do—when and if they want to do it. They'll even try to become the boss by bossing the boss around. Then, frustrated because the job is not going like they want it to go, they will quit; provided the boss doesn't get tired of their attitude and fire them first.

Here's one inmate's story that is, unfortunately, typical. Because of his background in construction work, the state's work release program was able to place him as a laborer with a company that installed underground pipe. This inmate knew that if his work performance was satisfactory for six months, he would be released on parole. He also knew that this company routinely hired inmates after their release and paid them well.

Each morning the company picked him up at the work release center, then returned him after work. He would spend his day in a ditch shoveling out the dirt that the backhoe missed and bragging about his former skills as a heavy equipment operator. One day, when the backhoe operator called in sick, the boss asked the inmate if he would like the chance to run the backhoe for the day. "Sure," he said, "if you're willing to pay me to do it. I'm not going to run a piece of equipment for ditch-digging wages!"

Here is a classic example of the power struggle between two people to determine who is going to be the boss. The boss was saying, "Because I'm

"Hey Man, I Need to Feed My Family"

in a bind, I'm willing to give you a chance to prove yourself." Many people have begun successful careers after jumping at the opportunity to fill in for someone who had become sick or injured.

But this inmate needed to be Number One. His attitude told the boss, "*My* rules say that if you want that backhoe run today, you are going to have to bow to my demands." It is standard practice in business to never agree to pay someone higher wages until *after* they have demonstrated an ability to do the task. The boss had only known this inmate for two months. For all he knew, this inmate may have been lying about his experience and wouldn't even know how to start the backhoe, much less be able to dig a straight ditch.

The inmate won the argument; the boss did not require him to operate the backhoe. Since there was no one to operate it, work was canceled for the day, and the inmate was returned to the work release center. The next day, the inmate discovered that he no longer had the freedom to work at the construction site because the company had canceled his contract. Then, because of the way he exploded after the boss refused to yield to his demands, he was reclassified and sent back to a medium security prison. What do you think happened to his parole chances?

Still angry, the inmate announced, "I'm not going to work for any man for nothing, would you? I've got my pride. That man was just trying to take advantage of me because I'm an inmate. He knew I could operate that piece of equipment, but refused to pay me what I was worth because he was greedy and wanted to pocket the extra money."

His pride cost him his freedom. If this inmate had jumped at the opportunity to prove that he was as good as he said he was, then later talked to the boss about a promotion and raise, do you think the boss might have agreed? We'll never know.

This inmate lost an opportunity to begin his parole with a current work evaluation that could have said, "Because this man proved himself faithful in the little jobs that we gave him, we quickly promoted him from laborer to equipment operator. We found him to be a good worker who is willing to take additional responsibility when the need arises."

But instead, by refusing the boss's request, he lost his freedom. The inmate still won't accept responsibility for his own actions: he still blames that boss for his return to prison.

There are other ways of refusing to respect the rules. When you are tempted to lay off the job, take that drink, take those drugs, cheat on your wife, steal, or whatever, find the person that you have made yourself accountable to and hold on to their strength. Make sure that person is straight. Let that person be your helping hand, your crutch that will keep you from falling.

Then, every time you are tempted to return to your old ways, think about the harm it will do to others. How much did that inmate harm his family and the other employees who lost a day's pay by refusing to operate the backhoe on the boss's terms? How would things have been different if he had used the problem-solving formula and considered the long-term consequences of his action?

Although sometimes it's not possible, it's important for you to stay on your first job for one year after you are released, even if it's a job that you don't particularly like. Most inmates, like the previous one, have trouble respecting the rules. Proving to yourself and others that you can live by the rules of that company for one year can make the difference between continued freedom and returning to prison.

Avoiding the pitfalls

In 1983, Frederick Englander found that when newly released ex-offenders (and notice the "ex") are suddenly forced to pay for their own food, clothing, and shelter, they are more likely to steal. Remember, if you decide to steal or commit any other type of crime, even if it is to eat, the judge might take that into consideration and might only give you half of the sentence that he normally would. Then you wouldn't have to pay for your food any more. The state will buy it for you, cook it for you, and give you a spoon to eat it with.

If, after you get out you find yourself without a place to stay, food to eat, or clothes to wear, instead of stealing, find a community service organization that will be willing to help you. Call the Salvation Army, local churches, the welfare department, or a local crisis center. Find out what types of emergency aid they offer. They're a crutch; swallow your pride and accept their offer. It's better than nothing, and much better than doing something that would land you back in jail.

If you have to accept a low-paying job or have trouble finding work immediately, you may be eligible for food stamps. Eligibility for food stamps is based solely on the family's gross income less certain deductible items such as rent or house payments, utilities, and childcare if both parents work. At the time of this writing, owning a home did not affect a family's

"Hey Man, I Need to Feed My Family"

eligibility for food stamps as long as they are still living in it. The food stamp program does not discriminate against former inmates.

The amount of food stamps given to any particular family is based on their need. In making a determination of need, family size, savings, and any other resources will be considered. In 1990, if you made less than $150 per month, you could be placed in a special category and obtain your food stamps in five days. Otherwise it takes approximately thirty days to receive your first food stamps.

The eligibility requirements and amount of aid furnished change frequently. If you think you might be eligible, you will have to ask. The people in charge of the food stamp program will not come to you.

Your ability to find the right job and to be able to stay there will largely depend on two things. First is the image that you have of yourself. What you think about yourself is what you will become. Do you see yourself as a criminal, or as a an ex-criminal with something to offer society? With proper planning and using problem-solving skills, you can make your dreams become a reality.

Secondly, your ability to respect the rules of society and take responsibility for your own actions will determine your ability to find and keep a job. You can do it!

Chapter 8

"... And They Lived Happily Ever After"

(And other fairy tales that are not true)

Once upon a time there were two knights. One was named Sir Macho and the other Sir Wimpy. Each was the king of his own castle and lived by his own laws. Their wives always obeyed them and did everything that they were asked to do—without complaining. Their children always minded and were perfectly behaved. (Remember, this is a fairy tale.)

One day Sir Macho and Sir Wimpy were caught plundering the land and the people. As a result, the king rewarded both of them by allowing them to live with some other knights at the Big House for a while.

While living in the Big House, Sir Macho listened intently to the other knights. He wanted to learn how to be more efficient at plundering the land and how to use the loopholes in the king's rules whenever he had to appear

174

before the king's courts. Every once in a while Sir Macho wrote letters to his princess, who was waiting for him back at his castle. In those letters, Sir Macho told her that he would be glad when he returned so that things would go back just like they were before he was sent to the Big House.

Sir Wimpy was different. He attended all of the king's classes that were available at the Big House. He especially liked the one called, "How To Be A Gentleman." Sir Wimpy stayed up late each evening writing long, mushy letters to his princess, who was also waiting back at his castle. In those letters, Sir Wimpy told his princess about the events of the day, what he was learning in his classes, and how things would be different when he returned. Many pages were filled with the dreams that he had about the future and the specific plans he had developed so that his dreams could come true once his time in the Big House was over. Sir Macho and many of the other knights made fun of Sir Wimpy and picked on him constantly.

The time at the Big House came to an end for Sir Macho and Sir Wimpy. Early one morning they put on fresh new armor and bid the other knights at the Big House good-bye. As they walked out of the front gate, each of their princesses came running to them with open arms. Instantly, with one magical kiss, their family relationships were revived. They both got into their chariots and rode off into the morning sun, and they lived happily ever after.

The real ending to the fairy tale

All fairy tales end with the words, ". . . and they lived happily ever after." But as Paul Harvey would say, "Now for the rest of the story."

Sir Macho rode his chariot to his castle and hung up his armor. Each day he required his princess to polish it and to wait on him hand and foot. "After all," he would say, "I am a knight and the king of my castle." Sir Macho liked to strut around at the local gathering house so that everyone could see his freshly shined armor. He also wanted to keep up on the activities of the other knights.

Sir Wimpy, on the other hand, rode his chariot to his castle, hung up his armor, and never wore it again. He didn't try to hide the armor, but he didn't show it off. Instead, it stood quietly on a stand in the hall reminding him of his promise to retire from knighthood. He knew that putting the armor back on, even for a minute, would be breaking that promise, and he might have to live in the Big House with the other knights again. Frequently he would

Chapter 8

talk to his children, his princess, and his friends about the mistakes that he made while he was a knight and the lessons he learned at the Big House.

Sir Wimpy and his princess would lay awake at night to discuss the plans that he had made and how they might accomplish them. Sir Wimpy listened to his wife's ideas and her dreams about how she would like for things to be. He told his princess everything that he had done that day and everyone that he had seen or been with. He enjoyed doing things that would meet her needs, even if it meant putting aside what he needed.

One day, as Sir Wimpy was driving his chariot to work, he saw Sir Macho all decked out in his shiny armor. But instead of being in his own chariot, he was being driven in one of the king's Tijuana Taxis. The royal paper said that the king was so impressed with Sir Macho's work at plundering the land that he rewarded him with more time in the Big House with his fellow knights.

Both knights swore that they would live happily ever after. Sir Wimpy made specific plans and found ways to make those dreams come true. Sir Macho just did what he had always done. Which knight lived happily ever after?

The moral of the story

By now you have realized that this is not a story about knights, kings, and days of chivalry. This is a story about two men who lived by their own law and not the laws of society (the king's rules) and who liked to murder, rape, rob, or do whatever else they wanted (plundering the land). They were caught and prosecuted by the state (the king) and sentenced to prison (the Big House). The knight's princess was his wife, and "Tijuana Taxi" is CB slang for a state trooper's car.

Being rewarded for plundering the land is another way of saying that time in prison is the logical reward for murder, rape, robbery, and the like. After all, having to pay one's debt to society is the natural and proper ending to all criminal activity. In the end, the king gave Sir Macho what he asked for—more time in the Big House.

The knights of the Big House were other people who had earned time in prison because of their criminal activities. In this story, Sir Macho used his time in the penitentiary to learn how to be a better criminal and how to use the loopholes in the law to get away with his crimes. It obviously didn't work. Instead, he reaped what he sowed.

". . . And They Lived Happily Ever After"

The armor is something that you put on so that you can do what you want to do without having to worry about getting hurt. Sir Wimpy's not trying to hide his armor symbolized not trying to hide his past criminal record. Even though he didn't brag about it, he freely discussed his past mistakes with his family and friends. In doing this, he was careful to explain to them that what he had done was wrong and the things that he had learned from his mistakes. Sir Wimpy knew that this would help keep him from making the same mistakes again. Anyone who doesn't understand the mistakes that they have made in the past is doomed to repeat them.

In this "fairy tale," one of the knights refused to change and stayed on the road we have called hard living. He returned to prison. Sir Wimpy used the techniques taught in this book and was able to successfully end his criminal career. Who do you think really lived happily ever after?

Are the names backwards? Isn't Sir Macho the real wimp?

Living "happily ever after" is a decision

The decisions that you make will determine if you will be able to "live happily ever after" once you are released from prison. Just as nobody can make you get angry, nobody can make you happy. In his book *Happiness Is Not An Accident*, Richard DeHaan explains that happiness is something that you must plan for, work for, and then let happen.

As you learned in Chapter 5, people have four sides: a spiritual side, an emotional side, a mental side, and a physical side. Each of these play an important role in deciding if you are going to be a happy person. If all four sides are working together in harmony, you will be happy. Unfortunately, if one of the sides is missing, your happiness will escape.

Your spiritual side contains your moral values that tell you right from wrong. It is where you house your belief in a higher power that wants things to work out for the best and will help you if you call. Your conscience is housed here. It is the side of you that says, "Don't do it" whenever you are tempted to do anything that is morally wrong.

There are many things in life that feel good while you are doing them but result in unhappiness, misery, and even death. Things such as drugs, alcohol, affairs, lying, cheating, criminal activity, overeating, overpowering or taking advantage of people, and looking out only for Number One fall in this category.

Based on what you do with these and other temptations, your spiritual side will give you one of two messages: (1) "Good for you! You resisted the temptation and you should be proud of yourself!" or (2) "You're guilty, and you should be ashamed of yourself for what you have done!" Both messages have a profound effect on your personal happiness.

Your spiritual side is your guide to ethical living. It is the side of you that tells you to do what is right simply because it is the right and moral thing to do. Your spiritual side also helps you to be satisfied with whatever you have while dreaming of better things to come.

Listen to your spiritual side and you will never have to worry about a guilty conscience. Keep it clear by using the steps to forgiveness given in Chapters 4 and 6. You can't be happy as long as you have a guilty conscience. On the other hand, if you have a negative outlook on life and on people and do things you know are morally wrong, you will be unhappy.

Your emotional side is where your feelings are, and they play a very important role in your happiness. Your feelings are neither right nor wrong, they are simply your *reaction* to the things that are going on in your life at a particular moment.

Good feelings generally mean that everything is going okay. For example, if you've just had a pleasant visit from your family, your reaction to the experience will be good feelings. It's normal for good feelings to follow after you have done something nice for someone else or have resisted the temptation to do something that you know to be morally wrong.

Bad feelings usually tell you that you have a problem. They don't tell you what the problem is or how to solve it. For example, your mind's reaction to being chewed out by a supervisor will be bad feelings. It's normal for bad feelings to follow whenever your conscience reminds you that you have done something morally wrong or have hurt someone. In each of these cases, these bad feelings should motivate you to use your problem-solving formula to find out what the problem is and to find a solution to the problem. It's hard to be happy when you are having bad feelings.

If you want to constantly feel bad, make the decision to always allow your emotions to control your life. Then, how you feel at any particular moment will be controlled by your temper, your depression, your urges, and what others think and say about you. The pain caused by unkind or harsh words will, at times, seem almost more than you can bear. You'll feel good only when people are treating you nicely and when everything is going fine.

If you allow your emotions to control your life your mind will change constructive criticism into thoughts such as, "I'm no good; I can't do anything right," or "I must really be an awful person." Feelings of guilt will overpower you, and if you try to drown them in drugs and alcohol it will only add to your misery. This will happen because you have decided to let your emotions rule your life.

If you let your emotions rule your life, you won't even be able to accept gifts of love because you will feel that (1) "They don't really love me," (2) "They're just doing it because they feel sorry for me," (3) "They're just repaying what they owed me," or (4) "I deserved that gift." As a result, you won't appreciate the gift, and the person offering you the gift will feel rejected. If this continues, the love may die, and you will become even more unhappy—even to the point of despair.

Since feelings follow actions, you can learn to be happy by changing what you think about. Simply dwelling on things that are true, honest, just, pure, lovely, and worthy of praise can change your entire outlook on life. Happiness will follow if you continually go through the steps to rebuilding your self-image that were taught in Chapter 7. This will allow you to feel loved, accepted, competent, and to practice ethical living.

Your mental side is the process that you use to make decisions and is totally under your control. It is where you decide about which words to use, the way that you act, the attitudes that you will display, and the values that will guide your life. Your mental side is where you decide what you want your name to mean, the image that you want to present, and what your character will be. Then, after you have decided who or what you want to be, your mental side will devise ways to help you to accomplish your goals. Your mental side can evaluate your mistakes and let you learn from them.

By now, you have realized the pain that you have caused others because of your crime. Because of this, your emotions tell you how awful you are. However, if you have a clear conscience, you can respond with (1) "I was responsible for what I did," (2) "I'm getting the punishment that I earned by doing the criminal act," and (3) "When I leave here, I will have paid my debt to society for what I've done." Whenever necessary, your mental side can tell your emotions, "Shut up!" That's because you have decided to start a new chapter in your life that can judged by moral laws and to be held accountable to society for your actions.

Your mental side can choose to act and think differently from the ways that you have done in the past. Instead of doing what your emotions are telling you to do, you can choose to use your problem-solving model. You can also choose to do only those things that you know to be morally right so that you will never have any reason to have a guilty conscience. Or you can fill your conscience with guilt by choosing to do things that you know to be morally wrong. You cannot be happy as long as you have a guilty conscience.

Your physical side is your body. Keeping yourself in good shape will make you feel better deep inside of your very being. For example, if you are depressed, a good workout in the gym or a brisk walk will help your body to release endorphins. You will feel good, and that helps you to feel happy.

On the other hand, abusing your body makes you feel lousy. How do people feel after they have abused their body with an all-night drunk? It's simply impossible to be happy when you've got a hangover, isn't it?

Giving yourself the gift of happiness is hard work, but you can do it! Each of the four things required for happiness is something that you can control. Living happily ever after means taking care of your spiritual life, your emotions, your mental health, and your body.

As you search for happiness, remember this old saying: Your mind is the only thing that can make a hell out of heaven and a heaven out of hell.

Things you need to consider before going home

Before you go home and try to resume living with your wife, you need to answer the following question: Would you have put up with your wife if she had done the same criminal act that you did or the same amount of time in prison that you have? You're asking your wife to forgive you, but would you be able to demonstrate your forgiveness of her by treating her like it never happened if she were in your shoes?

If the answer to either of these questions is "No," and your wife is still standing beside you, you have just discovered that she is more loving than you are. How long has it been since you told her that you love her? How long has it been since you have acknowledged the sacrifices that she has made for you while you have been in prison and thanked her for putting up with you? Wives, and children, need to be told on a regular basis these words: "I love you, and I appreciate what you have done for me and our family." *Be specific.*

Your wife needs to know that it was not her fault that you are here. It wasn't her nagging or not nagging that made you a criminal. It wasn't her fighting or not fighting. She needs to hear you say that you became a criminal because of what you chose to do.

Remember; she didn't have to stand by you. She could have divorced you and had every right to do so. She has been standing by you because she loves you and still believes in you. You need to thank her for that love.

Don't ask to be forgiven if you are not a forgiving person. It just won't happen.

Facing their unresolved anger

As the time of your release comes closer, your family must again deal with the things about your arrest and imprisonment that caused them a great deal of pain. Even if they have forgiven you, your family has not forgotten how your criminal activities hurt them. They don't have the ability to do that. Although they may not admit it, each member of your family has a complete record of those hurtful things tucked away in the family bank account. The hurtful things that still make them angry every time they think about them are the debts that you need to settle if you want peace and harmony in your home when you get out.

Your wife and your children may display some lingering resentment because of what your crime and imprisonment has done to the family's finances. She may still be trying to pay the attorney, and you may still have fines and restitution to pay. How much did she have to sacrifice to pay for your collect long-distance phone calls? How much did it cost her to come to this desolate place in the middle of nowhere just to spend a few hours talking to you? Could she afford to send you those special gifts that you asked for, or did she use the money that she would have normally spent on your children to do things for you?

Your wife may have some built-up anger about the difference between your living conditions and her living conditions. Compared to how some inmates' families live, this prison could be considered a country club. You've been provided with free laundry, free haircuts, free medical care, free clothing, and three hot meals cooked for you each day. Your family may have had to skip doctor's appointments, wear used clothing, and live in substandard housing because of a lack of money. Minimum-wage jobs and welfare don't allow for any extras. Then you wonder why she seems to get angry whenever you try to tell her how rotten your prison is! What about hers?

If you were a physically, emotionally, or sexually abusive parent, your children may actually be afraid of you. While you were in prison they were safe from you. They will be afraid of what might happen the first time you are alone in the house with them. You are going to have to convince them that they have nothing to worry about. If you want them to love you, you are going to have to start loving them first.

If you want your family to forgive you, you're going to have to do more than ask for forgiveness. You're going to have to show them that you understand exactly how you have hurt them. It's going to be up to you to convince each member of the family that they can share painful memories with you without fear. You're the one that caused the pain, and you are responsible for helping them get over the pain. You can make the transition into your home much smoother by settling these debts *before* you get out.

Listen as they describe their feelings, and avoid the temptation to say thinks like, "That's silly," or "But what about what you did to me?" You can help your family overcome their anger by saying the magic words, "I was wrong; Will you forgive me?" whenever necessary and by keeping your commitment to practice ethical living. As they learn to trust you, your family will be able to start treating you like your crime and imprisonment never happened.

Stresses of reuniting with your family

One of the main stresses that you are going to have to face when you leave this penitentiary is renegotiating your place of leadership within your family. During your imprisonment, your wife learned that she can live without you. She has been the head of your family while you were gone. You forced her to learn how to be independent. She wants your help; not your dictatorship. If you see her as your equal partner, then you will be able to function together as a team. If you use problem-solving skills instead of trying to overpower each other, you will be able to find solutions that are best for the entire family.

But if you go in like Sir Macho did and sit on your throne assuming that simply because you are the man you are automatically the boss, you're going to start having problems. Most Sir Machos make their royal throne a recliner placed directly in front of the television. Whenever they feel like being at home, there Sir Macho sits watching what he wants to watch while ordering

". . . And They Lived Happily Ever After"

his wife and children to fetch him a "cold brew" or whatever else his heart desires.

If you behave like this when you go home, your wife is going to buck your self-assumed authority. She is going to stop being nice to you and become a nag. She is going to become distant and start withholding her emotional support, her financial support, and even sex. If you try to make things like they were before you were sent to prison and go back to only looking out for Number One, she is going to go back to her old ways of doing things and shut you out of her life.

If you want to keep this from happening, remember this: Treat your wife like a thoroughbred and she won't become an old nag.

Reuniting with your children is going to cause you stress. You are not used to being around children all the time. In case you have forgotten, children can get on your nerves very quickly. What is it like here on visiting day when the children get cranky because there is nothing here for them to play with? While you are in prison, you only have to put up with it for a few hours. When you get home it is every day.

Like the rest of your family, your children have grown used to not having you around. They are used to the way their mother disciplines them. They have their own friends. They have settled into a new lifestyle since you left. You are going to have to earn their friendship and your place of leadership when you get home. You have let them down once before, and it will take time to rebuild their trust.

You can do this by demonstrating true love to your children. You are going to have to show them that you care about their needs, are interested in what they are doing, and that you are willing to spend time with them. Accept the little gifts of love that they bring to you. Don't be like the father who fussed at his little girl for giving him a sloppily wrapped empty box, only to find out later that she had blown kisses into it. By rejecting her gift, he rejected his daughter.

If you're like a lot of inmates, when you get home, you'll try to treat your children exactly the way you remember treating them before you left. Your children aren't the same as when you left. They've grown up. You can't treat a teenager like you would a child, and you can't treat a child like you would an infant. It won't work and will cause a lot of problems.

Chapter 8

Giving your children a chance to be successful

In her book *Your Child's Self-Esteem*, Dorothy Briggs claims that the key to successful parenthood is helping your children to build high self-esteem. The ability to have good self-esteem is one of the few things in life that doesn't discriminate against people because of their race, sex, age, occupation, or social status. In fact, anyone can have its quiet sense of self-respect and its feeling of self-worth. Parents have the responsibility to give their children the gift of a good self-image by teaching them they are loved, accepted, and competent, as well as how to practice ethical living.

As shown in the diagram on page 185, starting at the moment they are born, and maybe even before, children begin climbing the steps that will eventually lead to adult living. Each one of these steps is an important stage of development in the child's life. Parents have a powerful influence on their children's ability to successfully climb these steps. Notice that each one supplies one of the ingredients of a good self-image.

The first step begins on the day the child is born. Babies are cute, but they're also a lot of trouble. They wake you up in the middle of the night, cry a lot, spit up all over you, smell when their diaper is dirty, throw their food on the floor, and do lots of other equally nasty things. Then they laugh at you while you clean it up. No one enjoys changing a diaper overflowing with diarrhea or listening to babies cry for seemingly hours on end while they're cutting teeth.

The primary thing that infants need to learn during this first stage of development is that others can be trusted to love them even when they are doing things that make them unpleasant to be around. It doesn't take you long to find out who loves you and who doesn't when you are totally dependent on others for your care. The ability to trust others to treat you with respect at all times is the basis of all loving relationships.

A baby's cry is a request for help or attention. This is the only way that they have to tell you that they're tired, hungry, hurt, wet, messy, scared, or simply lonely. The way to stop them from crying is to find out what they need and meet that need. Young babies who can trust their parents to check on them every time that they cry will feel secure and loved. As a result, they will cry less. More importantly, they will have a strong, solid foundation of love and trust to build the rest of their lives on.

Unfortunately, many babies aren't loved during this time. Child neglect and abuse are rampant. Parents have been known to shake their children

". . . And They Lived Happily Ever After"

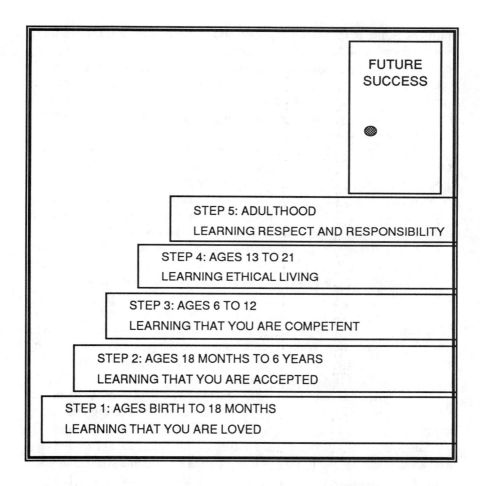

FUTURE
SUCCESS

STEP 5: ADULTHOOD

LEARNING RESPECT AND RESPONSIBILITY

STEP 4: AGES 13 TO 21

LEARNING ETHICAL LIVING

STEP 3: AGES 6 TO 12

LEARNING THAT YOU ARE COMPETENT

STEP 2: AGES 18 MONTHS TO 6 YEARS

LEARNING THAT YOU ARE ACCEPTED

STEP 1: AGES BIRTH TO 18 MONTHS

LEARNING THAT YOU ARE LOVED

violently, injure, or even kill them simply because they cried during the middle of the night. Even though babies can't talk about their feelings, down deep inside they know that their parents can't be trusted to love them, and the only way babies can express their disappointment and fear is by crying, and crying, and crying. Children who grow up without being loved have a shaky foundation and will enter adulthood with an inability to trust others.

The second step begins at about 18 months and continues until the child is approximately six years old. During this stage the child changes from a baby into a young child. It is a parent's duty to teach their children that they are accepted during this stage.

Children need constant supervision during these years. They make a lot of mistakes, break things, are clumsy, and talk out of turn. It takes a lot of love to accept a child and guide him or her through this stage without losing one's cool. Guiding children through this stage requires two things: (1) praising them when they do things right and (2) correcting them when they do things wrong. Parents who consistently do these two things say to their children, "I accept you just the way that you are, but I love you too much to allow you to stay that way."

Your children will live up to the name that you give them. If you continually tell your children that they are no good, clumsy, untalented, ugly, or whatever, you will scar them for the rest of their lives. When you are tempted to use that type of language in describing your children, think of the number of scars that you are still carrying around because of the cruel statements that your parents made to you when you were a child.

The third step begins when the child is about six years old and continues until about age 12. It is the parent's duty during this stage to teach their children that they are competent people, both in physical skills and in social skills.

As children start school they suddenly have to learn how to act in large groups and how to please an entire new set of adults—teachers and school officials. An important task for parents during this stage is to teach their children that they are competent people even when they fail to achieve their goals. It's teaching each child to learn from their failures and that individual failures do not make you a failure. It's teaching a child that true competence is measured by achieving as much as you are capable of doing and not by being the most popular, the strongest, or coming in first all the time.

The fourth step begins as the child enters his or her teen years and lasts until around age 18 to 21. Your job as a parent during this stage is to teach them ethical living. You can't teach your children ethical living, but they will learn it from you. They will learn about ethical living by seeing if you practice what you preach.

Children tend to adopt the same attitudes, values, and behavior patterns as their parents. This means that if you want your children to practice ethical living, you must give them a good example to follow. This means being painfully honest with them about the mistakes that you have made in your life. Admit your mistakes and tell them about how the mistakes hurt you and what they cost you. Admitting one's mistakes is one of the hardest things a man can ever do. Sit down with or write your children, and tell them the specific mistakes that you have made in your life and what those mistakes cost you and the family. This is part of your responsibility to teach your children that accepting the consequences of your actions is part of life. Here's an example of how it could be done:

> *Son, as I watch you grow up, I see a lot of you in me. When I was your age, I was a pretty good mechanic. I could make a car go faster than anyone else around. I got tired of having to learn the stuff in the English and history books. So I quit school and got a job. It wasn't long until my old classmates graduated and started coming to work where I did. I realized that suddenly they were getting the promotions and I was getting passed over. I became stuck in low-paying jobs. That last year of high school seems awfully short now. Did you know that most inmates did not finish high school? I didn't until I got here.*
>
> *Son, please stay in school. Find someone who can help you. Don't make the same mistake I did. I love you and I don't want you to wind up like me.*

Would your son be more likely to listen to something like that or "You get your tail back in school, and I don't want to hear another word about you dropping out!"?

Being honest with your children and sharing your life story will build trust in your family bank account and will strengthen your relationship with them.

Stage Five is the final step. The people who have the greatest chance of going through the door of success are those who have a good self-image and who know that the keys to freedom are respecting the rules of society and taking responsibility for your own actions.

Even though you've blown it, it's never too late to start giving your children the gift of a good self-image. Even if you have made every conceivable mistake possible in rearing your children, starting today, begin teaching your children that they are loved, competent, and accepted by you. Admit your mistakes and start practicing ethical living. Then provide a proper example for them to follow. This can help to undo some of the damage done by previous parenting mistakes.

The purpose of discipline

One of the most important things for children to learn before they are grown is that improper actions have penalties and that choosing to do improper things is asking for those penalties.

Chapter 8

The proper discipline of children can be simple, if you follow these simple rules. First, you and your partner decide what the family rules are going to be. This includes setting the penalty for violating those rules. This also includes talking to your children and explaining the rules and the penalties to them. Then, when the children decide to violate the family rules they will already know in advance what the penalty is for that violation.

Then, allow the children the freedom to stay within the rules. They need to learn that any violation of the family rules creates a debt in their family bank account that can be cleared *only* by receiving the penalty that they earned and that it is your responsibility as a parent to give them what they earned. Giving the children the discipline that they earned proves to that child that you love them and builds trust within the family.

If parents are consistent with their discipline, children learn that a decision to misbehave is also a request for the consequences that go with that behavior. This also means that the discipline they receive is something that they asked for and that you can be trusted to enforce the "family law."

Think about it: How would your life be different today if, during your childhood years, someone had taught you that if you violate the rules that you were asking to be punished? How would your life be different if you had been taught that every action has consequences and that deciding how to act is also asking for the consequences that naturally follow?

The purpose of discipline is to teach children that respecting the rules of society and taking responsibility for your own actions are the keys to freedom. You can help your children break the chains that bind them *to your past* by being honest with them when you call or write them. Tell them that sometimes daddies misbehave just like they do. Tell them that sometimes even good daddies do bad things. Tell your children that you are in prison because the state is giving you the punishment that you asked for when you committed your crime.

Teaching your wife what you are learning about the proper discipline of children is one way to start rebuilding your relationship with her. Tell her about this material. She can get additional helpful hints in books such as *Discipline With Love* by James Dobson (Tyndale House, 1988). Then, when your wife starts using proper discipline methods, back her up. Tell your children that she is doing that because she "loves you too much to allow you to act that way."

Effective methods to discipline children

There is no one form of discipline that is the correct method to use. Every child is different, and because of these differences, you will have to develop different methods of discipline for each child. Here are some forms of discipline that have been found effective in the past.

Scolding can be a very effective method of discipline. However, scolding is not screaming at the child. To effectively scold your child, kneel down to the child's level so that you can look them straight in the eye. Once you have their attention, firmly explain to them exactly what they did that was wrong, why it was wrong, and how they should handle the situation differently if it comes up again.

Here would be a good time to start teaching your children problem-solving skills. Even at a young age, children need to be told more than "Don't do that." They need to be told why. For example: "I said don't do that because that jar may fall over and break if you touch it." There are times that a child needs to be told "Don't do that because I am your parent, and I told you not to." Children need to be taught to respect authority.

Time Out is when you make your child sit in a boring place for a specific amount of time. Experts recommend one minute for each year of age. For example, a three-year-old would have to sit in the chair for three minutes. Have a special time-out chair and teach the child that when you say the words "time out" that they must go to that chair and sit there for the specified amount of time. Make sure the chair is not in a place that will scare the child.

If they get out of the chair during a time out, give them additional minutes. Some people purchase a timer so that the child knows exactly when they can get up, and the child will have nothing to look at except the time ticking slowly away. Do not send your child to their room where they can play, and do not allow them to read during this time. Time out only lasts for a few minutes, and the purpose of having a time out is to teach your child that having your freedom taken away is one of the things that naturally happens when you break the rules. Would you be in prison today if your parents had taught you this principle when you were young?

Removal of privileges is another way to say, "I love you too much to allow you to continue acting that way." For example, a child might have his Saturday morning cartoons taken away from him. A teenager might be required to stay home for the weekend and do chores for her infraction of the family rules. The possibilities are limited only by your imagination. Just make sure that the punishment fits the crime. For example, requiring a teenager to stay home all weekend and paint the house would be too much for forgetting to take out the trash.

Spankings can be an effective method of discipline *when all other methods have failed*. First comes a scolding, then a time out. If the behavior continues after the time out, then the child receives a spanking.

Or, consider reserving spankings for times when your child's behavior endangers their own or someone else's safety. For example, if a child runs out in the street without looking, a spanking would teach the child to associate this with pain, and they would be less likely to do it again. In this case, the pain of a spanking would hurt less than the pain of being hit by a car. There are those that disagree because they believe that it teaches a child to use violence. If you use spankings, remember that if it leaves marks it is considered a beating and is considered child abuse. Spankings should not be your only form of discipline and should be used only as a last resort.

Many parents have a rule in their home that if their children get a spanking at school they will get another one when they get home. This is a bad rule because it places the child in a position where it would be more beneficial to lie than to tell the truth. If the child lies about it, he or she won't get another spanking unless the lie is discovered. This teaches children that you can avoid punishment if you lie. Is this what you want to teach your child? Couldn't the additional spanking be considered double jeopardy?

Regardless of the form of discipline that you use, its purpose is to teach your children that you love them too much to allow them to act in certain ways.

The key to effective discipline is consistency. If your child knows that when the family rules are broken they will always receive the discipline that they earned, your child will be less likely to break the rules in the future.

In order for your discipline to be the most effective, your child needs to see you as being a warm, loving parent who is concerned for their needs. Ross D. Park found that punishment alone, without telling the child the exact reason why the discipline was necessary, was ineffective. Children need to have the reason for the discipline explained to them both before and after receiving the appropriate punishment. They need to know that your love for them will require you to repeat the discipline, which may be harsher the next time, if they violate the family rules again. After the time of discipline is over, give them a hug and remind them that you love them.

Even though you knew the penalty for breaking the law, you chose to do your crime. By committing your crime, you asked the state to discipline you, and they complied. Isn't your incarceration a way for the state to say, "We love you too much to allow you to continue acting that way"? When your time of discipline is complete, don't you want to hear your family say, "We love you, and you are still a part of the family"? That's what your children need to hear when their time of discipline is over.

Parents who are as eager to praise their children when they have done things correctly as they are to punish them when they have done wrong usually find that a lot of discipline isn't necessary in the first place.

The proper use of anger

Anger is a normal, healthy, and useful emotion. Everyone gets angry, including God. The Bible says that God became so angry that He flooded the entire earth. On the other hand, because Moses lost his temper *one time*, he lost his chance to live in the Promised Land. Moses and countless others have ruined their lives by doing what their temper was telling them to do instead of doing what they knew was right.

There are many things in life that you should get angry about. If your wife is raped, you should get angry and demand that the rapist be held accountable according to the laws of society. If your child is rebellious and slaps his mother, you should be angry and hold the child accountable for his actions by providing the appropriate discipline that says, "I love you too much to allow you to continue acting this way." It's not your anger that gets you into trouble, it is what you do with your anger that creates problems.

Frequently people get in trouble because they focus their anger on the wrong thing, and as a result a lot of people get needlessly hurt. For example, many men become angry with their wife instead of her attacker after she has been raped. Women do not ask to be raped. When I was a state trooper people used to get angry and blame me for their speeding ticket—sometimes they even said nasty things about my mother. Many men have gone home and abused their wives, children, and/or pets after having a fight with their boss.

In each of these cases there is a legitimate reason to feel angry. But instead of focusing on the real problem, the anger was vented in an inappropriate way. Anger is one of those bad feelings that tells you that something is wrong and that you have a problem that needs to be solved.

Anger's purpose is to motivate you to use your problem-solving skills

Chapter 8

to find a solution to the problem that is causing the anger. Then you can bring your life back into balance. For example, if your wife is raped or is the victim of any other crime, your anger should motivate you to support her as she cooperates with the police, testifies in court, and struggles to survive emotionally as she attempts to put her life back together again. Your anger at your children's improper behavior should motivate you to find the most effective forms of discipline for each of your children. Your anger at a failing family relationship should motivate you to find a family counselor who might be able to help you resolve your differences.

In his book *The Marriage Builder*, psychologist Larry Crabb says that everything we do has a goal. It may be something as big as climbing the ladder of success and becoming a millionaire or something as small as being able to go to the bathroom whenever you want. Whenever goals are blocked, anger follows.

Frequently this starts a pattern. As a person's goals are blocked, frustration increases, and they respond by becoming more aggressive. How many fights have you seen because one inmate stayed on the phone too long? Plenty! The reason for the anger is because the other inmate's goal of using the phone was blocked.

Anger in homes works the same way. Here's an illustration. You have decided that you want to watch the ball game on television. Your wife wants you to do the dishes. Each of you have different goals for how you want to spend your time. Her desires are blocking your goal to watch the game and your desires to watch the game are blocking her goal of getting the dishes done. Because of these blocked goals, the two of you have become angry.

Now you must make a decision about what to do with your angry feelings. You could choose to blow up, cuss her out, scream at the top of your lungs, jump up and down, and/or threaten her. After you have done all of that, she'll probably stop asking you to do the dishes.

But just because she gave in and you won the fight, her anger will not go away. You overpowered her and blocked her goal. As a result, while you are watching the game, you will probably have to listen to pots and pans banging in the kitchen. Then, if she fixes it at all, your dinner will be a silent one—and cold. And you probably won't get any that night.

What if you had said instead, "Let me finish watching the game, and then I'll do the dishes"? This statement is a way of explaining to her that you desire not only to have your own goals met, but also that you are willing to meet her goals. If she agrees, you had better not forget to do the dishes.

Can you see why respect is so important? If your goal is to provide for the needs of your family, then you won't mind missing a ball game if your family's needs are more important. Respect for the needs of your family will give you the freedom to have a happy marriage.

How to decide if something is worth fighting over

Sometimes it's best to yield to the other's desires, and sometimes it's better to be unyielding, even if it means a fight. There is a way to decide if something is worth fighting over. As you make that decision ask yourself this question: Which is more important, being right or the relationship?

For example, if your three-year-old spills a glass of milk, ask yourself if it is more important to be understanding and build the relationship up or to be right. If your relationship with the child is more important, you will say, "That's okay, we can clean it up. Everyone spills things every once in a while. Let's try to be a little more careful next time, okay?" On the other hand, if all you care about is your own feelings you might scream something like, "You are clumsy! I can't even trust you with a glass of milk!" Even though that statement is absolutely true, it will damage your relationship with the child. Suppose that you notice that your teenage daughter's date has been drinking heavily when he arrives to pick her up. In this case, even though your daughter may be angry, it's more important to be right and cancel the date than to allow her to be driven around by a drunk driver and risk death or injury. In fact, you shouldn't even allow him to drive. Instead, take him home.

Suppose that your wife tells you that she doesn't want you attending the Alcoholics Anonymous meetings or going to church any more. If they are helping you to stay on the road called settled living, you *must* go to those meetings. The entire family would be hurt if you went back to your old ways. If you are chemically dependent, or if you are relying on the moral values that you are learning at church to keep you straight, then it is more important to be right. In this case you couldn't afford to give in to your wife's demands.

But consider something. It may be that your wife feels that you are using every spare moment to be with these groups instead of spending time with her. She knows that your time away from her is damaging your relationship.

Asking you to quit going to the meetings may be the only way that she knows to say, "Quit hurting me; I need more of your time."

What you may need to do at this point, instead of stubbornly walking off and going to the meetings, is to renegotiate how much time you spend in these outside activities—even if it means finding a counselor that could help the two of you resolve the relationship problems. It takes a strong person to admit that they don't have all of the answers all of the time.

Violence in homes

Violence is uncontrolled anger. Violence occurs when one person who is looking out for Number One meets another person who is looking out for Number One and neither will yield. Then one or both resorts to force to get their way. Unfortunately, this is frequently the way that many families enforce their rules.

Underneath the use of violence is a loud statement that says, "How dare you question *my* authority!" In violent homes, the next scene would look something like the old Batman television series and have the words *Slap, Slug, Hit,* or *Wham* printed over it.

There are other ways of enforcing the family rules than by hitting. What if the COs were told to enforce all of the rules in this penitentiary with physical force? If you questioned their authority, they would be allowed to slap you across the face or scream insults at you. Suppose after a correctional officer told you to turn the television off you said, "The program goes off in three minutes, I'll do it then." The correctional officer could grab you by the ear, throw you down on the floor, take his belt off and beat you. If this happened, wouldn't you quickly ask a court judge to remind the prison officials about the amendment that forbids cruel and unusual punishment?

Isn't this the same way a lot of families enforce their rules? Many children have been abused with ugly and hurtful words simply because they spilled something on the floor. Untold thousands of children, and even wives, have been slapped around because they dared to question a ruling by the self-appointed king of the house. Countless beatings are started each day because children didn't obey an order quickly enough to suit their parent's wishes.

Men who abuse their families do not see them as people of value. In fact, any man who uses violence in order to force his family to obey his orders has reduced them to being of less value than an animal. Becoming violent is not showing your family love. If you ever become violent in your home you have forfeited any rights to their companionship and given your wife grounds to divorce you.

Many affairs start when the wife of a violent, abusive man finds someone who is loving, caring, and kind to her. Some men feel that beating their wives will make them leave their lovers and come back to them. They can't they see that it was their abuse that drove their wives away, and by leaving, these wives are only making permanent what their husbands had already done.

Affairs are wrong. Discovering that one's spouse has been unfaithful is one of the most painful experiences anyone can ever have and leads to some of the most savage fights. If you discover that your wife is having an affair, don't become violent. Instead, use your anger to motivate you to find a solution to the problem. One alternative would be to find out from her what it would take for her to come back to you and hope that she will reconsider. Let her know how much it hurts to see her with someone else. Offer to see a family counselor and make the changes that need to be made. Then, even though you will never forget the affair and will feel angry about it for a long, long time, demonstrate your forgiveness by treating her like it never happened. Another option is to end the relationship. Violence is not the best solution to adultery or any other problem.

Differences between how happily and unhappily married couples communicate

In her book *Intimate Relationships*, Sharon Brehm claims that most couples, whether happily married or not, usually do not intend to make their spouses unhappy, upset, or angry by what they say to each other. The difference is that happily married couples expect their mates to communicate in positive ways, while unhappily married couples expect their mates to communicate in negative ways.

For example, after you have dressed for work one morning your wife looks at you and says, "Do you really think that shirt looks right with those pants?" If you are happily married, you would think something like, "I love the way she cares about me; she's really concerned about the way I look." Your reply would be something like, "What do you think would look better?" If you are unhappily married, you would think something like,

Chapter 8

"That dumb broad thinks that I'm color blind." So the words out of your mouth might be something like, "There you go again, treating me like a child. Don't you think I know how to dress myself?"

Even though it's the same message, can you see how the interpretation of the message changes it? Whenever we hear people talk, we have a tendency to assign what *we think* they are trying to say instead of finding out from them what they are really trying to say. In doing this, we hear only what we want to hear. In this illustration, the unhappily married man assigned his wife ideas about what she said and accused her of bad motives because of what he thought she was thinking. On the other hand, the happily married man went off to work wearing a different shirt and felt the assurance of his wife's love.

You can make your relationship happier or unhappier simply by changing what you expect to hear from your spouse—helpful messages or critical messages. Since she's probably not trying to make you feel bad, simply looking for the positive side in everything that she says will make your relationship a lot happier.

The way they handle complaints is another important difference in the way happy and unhappy couples communicate. Happy couples deal with one complaint at a time; unhappy couples cross-complain.

For example, you and your wife are lying in bed at night and you feel romantic. When you ask her if she wants to make love, she replies, "I don't want to make love to you because you have bad breath." If you have a tendency to cross-complain, you will respond with, "Well, I do not like the amount of money that you spent for the dress you just bought." That is not the way to convince your wife to make love to you.

If you were a happy couple, you would gladly get up and brush your teeth and thank your wife for telling you about your breath. This is because you realize that she is telling you something that would enhance the relationship. After all, who could enjoy sex while having to smell bad breath? Wouldn't you really rather make love to someone who is enjoying it than someone who isn't?

If the amount that was spent for clothes is an issue, it can be brought up at a later at a more appropriate time. If you want to be happy, deal with and resolve one issue at a time.

The way they argue is different. In unhappy couples, each member feels that they must always win the argument. As a result, arguments continue until one of them finally surrenders and lets the other have their way.

". . . And They Lived Happily Ever After"

Unfortunately, in a marital relationship whenever one person wins an argument, both lose. This is not the way to build a relationship.

For example, you want to go fishing this Sunday afternoon. So you tell your wife, "I am going to go fishing Sunday." She wants to have lunch at her mother's house, so she says, "We are going to mother's house for lunch." If neither is willing to yield or use their problem-solving skills, the argument must continues until someone surrenders. It will become a no-win situation.

Satisfied couples negotiate. They understand that anytime two or more people live together there will be times when they do not agree. Conflict is an essential aspect of intimacy. It provides a way to resolve issues in such a way that each can show that they are listening to the other person and are responsive to their needs. When this happens relationships grow stronger.

You could say, "What if I go fishing and we go to your mother's for supper?" She might reply, "What if we still have lunch at mother's, then you and dad could go fishing while I visit with mom?" Notice that neither of these statements is a command. Each is a question that allows room for further negotiation and takes the goals of the other person into consideration while allowing for their own goals to be met. In this exchange, it is obvious that both the husband and the wife care about what the other wants to do. This type of exchange helps to build satisfying relationships.

Happy couples have the ability to have "good fights." A good fight is one where the goal is for everyone to win. Each spouse may not get everything that they want, but they are both willing to put the needs of the relationship above their personal needs. In a good fight, everyone involved can state their own feelings without having to fear being attacked by the other people involved.

People involved in good fights avoid words like *always* and *never*. For example, instead of saying, "You *always* treat me like a child," you could say, "I *felt* angry when you corrected me in front of my boss because I *felt* you were treating me like a child." Both of these statements cover the same incident. The first statement places blame, passes judgement, and will usually lead to a defensive, argumentive answer. The other simply expresses a feeling and allows the other to make a response that would improve the relationship.

Good fights don't become "historical." Unless it has a direct bearing on the question being considered, don't bring up things that happened in the past. Once an issue is resolved, never bring it up again. It will only serve to weaken the relationship.

Happy couples have memorized the two most important sentences known to mankind (1) "I was wrong; will you forgive me?" and (2) "What can I do to make things right?" And they use them frequently. No wonder they're happy.

The kind of husband your wife needs

When you get home, you will not have any chance of having a happy marriage unless you can become the type of man that your wife needs. Your wife needs a man who is willing to be a true leader. This is a man who will treat his wife like what she is, his queen. He will walk beside her and not try to rule over her. Together they will make the decisions that affect their little kingdom called home.

Your wife needs a man who is going to be loyal to her no matter what the cost. You will always believe in her, always expect the best of her, and will always stand your ground defending her.

Your wife needs a man who will never give her any reason to be jealous. Sharon Brehm defines jealousy as the fear of being replaced. You need to live in such a way that your wife will never fear that she is going to be replaced.

Your wife needs a man who is strong enough to admit that sometimes he needs help from a higher power, from his family, and from the others around him. She needs a man who is smart enough to realize that he does not have all of the answers; a man who is willing to go to marriage counseling and make changes if things are not going right.

Your wife needs a man who will work to support his family and to do his share around the house. Not to *help her* with the housework. It's your house too, and it is your responsibility to keep it clean.

Your wife needs a man who will discipline the children in a way that says, "I love you too much to allow you to act this way."

Your wife needs a man who is willing to take care of her sexual needs. This is a man who will ask her what she wants and then do it instead of taking what he needs. She needs a man who understands that for her sex begins in the morning when she first gets up. For most women, sex is part of the total relationship and not just something for her to do for a couple of minutes just before you turn over and go to sleep at night. You might want to buy a book about female sexuality and read it when you get out. Your relationship will be enhanced when you learn more about your wife's sexual needs.

". . . And They Lived Happily Ever After"

Your wife needs a man who will give her a part of himself that is the best he has to offer, expecting nothing in return except that your gifts of love to her be accepted. She needs a man who will accept the gifts of love that she provides for him. In short, your wife needs to be loved and to know that she fills a special place in your heart that nobody else in the world can fill.

And he lived happily ever after?

Sir Macho and Sir Wimpy both swore that they would live happily ever after once they were released. Sir Macho did not change and took the hard-living road once he was released. Soon he was escorted back to the Big House in one of the king's Tijuana Taxis. Sir Wimpy chose to change and traveled along the road called settled living. He is still out and living "happily ever after."

You have the same choices as Sir Macho and Sir Wimpy. You can choose to live happily after once you leave this place. Or you can choose to put the invisible chain back around your neck and go back to your old way of doing things. If you do, you won't live happily ever after because you will probably be back in prison within one year.

You *can* live the rest of your life as free as an eagle. Even though it will probably be the hardest thing that you have ever done, all it will take is for you to use the tools furnished in this book and use them to learn how to fly. The choice is yours, and you alone are responsible for the choices that you make.

Go for it! As you try to reenter family life and society on the completion of your prison sentence, may God bless you and give you the strength that you need to follow your dreams.

A Message To The Families Of Inmates

As *Free As An Eagle: The Inmate's Family Survival Guide* would not be complete unless it contained information that would help the family members and friends left behind. If you have a family member in prison, this chapter is written just for you. Its purpose is to help the families of inmates survive their own personal prison sentence and to help inmates see how their families feel about their criminal behavior.

Even though the first eight chapters have information that applies to the inmate, they were written as if the rest of the family read along. This chapter speaks to the families while the inmate listens in.

It is hoped this chapter will stimulate many hours of loving, open, honest, and healing communication between inmates and their families. Painful as it is sometimes, this is the only way that family relationships can be healed.

You are not powerless against the system. Prison walls cannot prevent you from having a close family relationship. In fact, your family can actually become stronger while one of its members is in prison.

Use this book to help improve your relationship with the inmate. Buy your own copy and have a copy sent to the inmate. Then discuss its contents with your inmate. Although some prisons will not allow you to carry this book into the prison, most will allow publishers, book stores, churches, or prison ministries to mail the book directly to an inmate as long as they use a printed company letterhead envelope or label. In some cases, prison chaplains are allowed to deliver books to inmates. Call the prison and ask them if one of these methods would be acceptable. Ordering information is in the back of the book.

Chapter 9

"What Are We Going To Do With Him?"

If you love someone, set them free. If they come back, they're yours. If they don't, they never were.

—*Anonymous*

Every time an inmate is sentenced to prison, family members ask this question: "What in the world am I going to do with him?" This question is really several questions rolled into one. Is he worth saving? Do I dump him, or stand by him hoping that he'll change? How can I tell if he's really changing? How can I get over the pain that he has caused me? What can I do that will help him change into a person who has the ability to stay out once released?

Underneath these questions are two even bigger questions: "Doesn't anyone care about me?" and "How can I survive while he's in prison?" If you have a family member in prison, this chapter should help you to find the answers to these and other questions.

A modern parable

Once upon a time there was a man who owned a large grocery store. He had two sons. The oldest, Square John, was straight-laced and hard-working. He always did everything that he could to make his father's business better. He spoke to the customers when they arrived, carried out the groceries, and always had a smile. Square John didn't mind unloading trucks, stocking shelves, sweeping floors, or even cleaning the rest rooms.

Wild Bill, the other son, was different. True to his name, he liked to party and to act big and important. "You're only young once," he would say, "and I intend to enjoy every minute of it! Besides, I've got better things to do than stock shelves, mop floors, and bow down to a bunch of fussy old women and bratty children!" Needless to say this caused some friction in the family.

Wild Bill was always trying to think of a better way to make money than working for it. He constantly made fun of his dad and brother for working so hard. Over and over he would tell his dad, "If you would just let me handle the finances, I'd make us a million by next week—then we could retire." Dad would try to tell Bill that the good name that he had created in the community was worth much more than money, but Bill didn't listen.

One day Bill said to his dad, "I'm tired of the grocery business. In fact, I don't want to be part of this family anymore! I'm tired of fighting with you about how *you* want me to run *my* life. I'm leaving. I want to go out in the world and make my own name for myself, and I don't want to wait until you die to get my inheritance; I want what's coming to me NOW!"

Sadly, Dad agreed to Bill's demands. After having the company and all of his possessions appraised, Dad withdrew all his savings and borrowed money until he had an amount equal to half of everything that he owned. Then, he and his two sons met at his attorney's office. There, with tears in his eyes, Dad signed a new will that left the remainder of his possessions to Square John on his death and presented Wild Bill with a large check. This arrangement left Dad with no money in the bank for retirement and huge loans to pay back.

With the check in his hand, Wild Bill gleefully jumped into his shiny

"What Are We Going To Do With Him?"

new silver Mercedes convertible and roared out of town—leaving Dad and John with shelves to stock and floors to mop.

Once he arrived at the big city, instead of going to work, Wild Bill lived off his inheritance. He liked wild parties, wild women, and wild times, and he had plenty of all three—until the money ran out. Then he discovered that banks repossess cars and fancy houses when you don't make the payments, drug dealers don't like credit, and wild women can't be counted on when the chips are down. Then the worst part! Without an education and no skills, all he could find were dirty, back-breaking, minimum wage jobs with either long or irregular hours.

One day, while serving soup at a rescue mission, Wild Bill started thinking about his family. "Dad treats his baggers better than this. If I go back, maybe he would give me a job." So he decided to hitchhike back home and say to his dad, "I'm sorry I was so mean to you; would you consider hiring me as a janitor and letting me have my room back until I can get back on my feet?"

After days of hitchhiking Wild Bill finally reached the edge of town. As he walked toward the store, his dad rushed out of the store, ran across the parking lot, and hugged him so hard he thought his ribs would break. Through the tears Bill begged his dad to forgive him for all of the hurt and damage he had done to his family. But all Dad could say was, "Bill, I'm so glad you're home. You're still my son, and I still love you."

That night Dad threw a party to welcome Bill home. He roasted the largest prime rib he had in the store with all of the trimmings. All of his family, neighbors, and friends were invited to attend. Everyone came, except Square John.

Dad left the party for a few minutes and went to see Square John. "John," he said, "nothing's changed between you and me. The store and everything that I have will be yours when I'm gone. Bill has to live with what he's done, and he has to live with the name he made for himself. Bill says that he's learned his lesson and is asking for my forgiveness and my help as he tries to build a new name for himself. I'm going to do it. I'm going to give him another chance and even let him work here if he wants. He's going to have enough trouble rebuilding his name in the community without us making it harder for him. He's still my son, and I'm glad he's home! Come on, John, we've got a party to go to! We need to welcome Bill home and hope for the best."

This is more than just a story about a man with two sons and a grocery store. It is also a story that symbolizes the family of every inmate who is presently living, or has ever lived, inside of a jail or penitentiary. It's a story about power struggles, rebellion, and greed. It's a story about repentance and recovery. But more importantly, it's a story about love, forgiveness, and starting over. This story answers the question: "What are we going to do with him?"

The criminal mentality

In this story, Wild Bill had many of the characteristics of the criminal mentality. The first is that he was a man who declared that the rules of society and of his family did not apply to him. That's called "Looking out for Number One."

You can always tell a person who is looking out for Number One, you just can't tell them much. That's because they're always strutting around crowing, "I'm Number One! I can do anything that I want; say anything that I want, anytime that I want, anywhere that I want, to anyone that I want; and there's nothing you or anyone else can do about it—period!"

There's nothing wrong with wanting a different occupation from your father. In fact, if research is right, many inmates and their families would be better off if they did do things differently than their parents. But there is something wrong with an attitude that says, "My needs are more important than anyone else's." There is something wrong with an attitude that tells those in authority, "Your rules don't apply to me." These two attitudes formed the basis of Wild Bill's attitude and the average criminal's personality.

Committing a crime involves four things:

- seeing something that you want but have no right to have
- declaring that nobody has the right to tell you to control your urges
- declaring that the rules of society don't apply to you, so you can violate them without paying the penalty
- abusing your power and taking it

Another way that Wild Bill is like the average criminal is that he didn't care that his actions and attitudes could ruin his father's business and the family's name. The rules of society say that if you want to succeed in any business you must take care of your customers. Wild Bill's attitude said that

"What Are We Going To Do With Him?"

"I'm doing them a favor by being here, Besides, I'm not going to belittle myself by bowing down to them."

How many businesses do you now avoid because of *one* bad experience that you had with *one* employee of that business? That's especially true if the bad experience was your first visit to the store. First impressions last, and you only have one chance to make a good first impression.

Wild Bill's same inconsiderate attitude is displayed every time someone does a criminal act. Just as Wild Bill had no idea how much it hurt his dad to see him drive away in the shiny new car, as a group criminals don't have the ability to understand how their actions hurt their families. It's more important to them to get what they want when they want it, regardless of the harm it does to others. Once a criminal's trial is over and he's gone, the families are left behind to live with the damage that he did to the family name. And it hurts—especially if his crime was in the papers and on the newscasts. The truth is that our actions *always* affect the others around us.

Quit making excuses for what he did! This only reinforces his belief that his actions did not hurt you. Instead, tell the truth. All criminals, including your inmate, do their crimes because they want to do them and probably enjoy them while they are doing them. Like a child who gets caught with his hand in the cookie jar, the only part they don't like is getting caught and punished.

Another way that Wild Bill is like the average criminal is that he didn't care that meeting his needs would ruin the family's finances. Not many inmates really stop to realize how much their crime, trial, and imprisonment really cost the family. Bail bondsmen are expensive; 10 percent of $10,000 is $1,000. Some now charge 15 percent or more. That's a lot of money—and you don't get it back. Lawyers are expensive, and criminals always want the best one in town.

Employers have a tendency to fire men after they have been charged with a crime. Then the paycheck stops, and if he was the only one working, suddenly the family doesn't have any money.

Children are expensive. My 1989 study showed that approximately 70 percent of the inmates in an Alabama prison left an average of three children behind. How much does it cost the families of these inmates to support these children? Off he went to prison, leaving the family deeply in debt while making it impossible for him to help support his own family.

Inmates want visitors. Unfortunately, most prisons are located in remote places that are not served by public transportation. Does he care how much trouble it takes to drive to the prison or how much it costs to drive there?

Chapter 9

How much do his collect long-distance calls cost? Does he call when he wants to, or does he wait until after 5:00 p.m. or on weekends when the rates are lower?

Like Wild Bill, criminals ask to be removed from their families. People become guilty of their crimes the moment that they commit them. People also ask for the consequences of their crime the moment that they commit them, which includes possible imprisonment and removal from their homes.

For example, every time an illegal drug is sold, a thief or robber commits his crime, or a sex offender rapes someone or molests a child, he is asking the state to allow him to live in prison instead of living at home. At the moment that a person commits a murder he is asking the state to never allow him to live at home again.

For the wives of inmates, what this means is that if you decide to divorce him, you *will not* be abandoning him. You will only be making permanent what he has already done. Legally and morally, you are not required to remain married to him, because he abandoned you the moment that he did his crime and earned his place in prison. This also means that there are only two reasons for you to remain married to him—because you love him, and because you want to stay married to him. Come to think of it, those are two of the best reasons to stay married to anyone.

Both Wild Bill's and the average criminal's actions prove that they don't really love their families. True love *is not* taking advantage of someone else's feelings to meet your own selfish needs. Think about the nerve, the gall, the audacity, of a son to walk up to his father and say, "I don't want to wait until you die to get what's coming to me; I want it NOW!"

Isn't this basically the same as what criminals say to their families whenever they decide to get involved in criminal activity? Isn't forcing the family to pay the bondsman, hire the lawyers, make up for the loss of income, and to support him while he is prison saying, "Even though I'm going to do everything in my power to hurt this family and even though it will leave the family deeply in debt, I want you to give me at least half of everything that we have before I go"?

To people like this, love is measured by how much others do for them. Love becomes something that you give to people only when you want something from them. It's saying, "You be nice to me and I'll be nice to you." That's not love—that's selfishness. As is explained in Chapters 4 and 5, true love *is not* something that you feel. True love is something that you do. Love is giving a part of yourself that is the best you have to offer, expecting nothing in return except that the gift be accepted. It never harms and is never given for selfish reasons. If you reject a gift of love you have rejected the giver of the gift and not the gift itself. Accepting and exchanging gifts of love will cause the relationship to grow.

It's easy to tell if someone really loves you. Are they constantly asking you to give them the best that you have to offer while giving nothing in return? Are they nice to you only when you've given them something? Do they intentionally do things that would hurt you physically, emotionally, or sexually? Do they usually put their own needs above the needs of others? Do they try to force you to stay in the relationship? If the answer to any of these questions is "yes," then they don't love you.

So what! Since love is something that you do, anyone can start the loving process. In fact, if you're waiting for him to start the loving process you've just proven that you don't truly love him. If you want to start the loving process in your family relationship, think, "What can I give to him that is a part of myself that would meet his needs while expecting nothing in return except that the gift be accepted?" Then do it! In a loving family relationship each member of the family can be trusted to consistently give of themselves to meet the needs of the others.

True love never insists on having its own way and knows that you can't force someone to remain in a relationship.

True love never fails.

The kind of family an inmate really wants

It was obvious that Wild Bill knew that his family was unwilling to compromise their values. And when he hit rock bottom, what did he want? He wanted a family with rock-solid moral values. Wild Bill was willing to make the changes in his own life so he could be part of that loving family system again. That's the kind of family that you can have, if you are willing to display true love.

You can tell when an inmate starts to change when he has learned the same lessons that Wild Bill learned before trying to go home. True change comes from within. Even though it took losing everything that he had to wake him up, Wild Bill learned to quit making excuses about his past improper actions and admit that he did them because he wanted to and enjoyed them while he did them; to realize how much his improper actions had hurt others; to allow his guilty conscience to motivate him to make the

Chapter 9

necessary changes in his life; and how to make and carry out plans for putting his life back together.

Wild Bill also learned the two most important sentences known to man: "I was wrong; will you forgive me?" and "What can I do to make things right?"

Before going home, Wild Bill realized that you can't turn back the clock and erase the history that you have created for yourself. You have to live with the consequences of your own decisions. Wild Bill blew it, and he knew it. He didn't even try to go back to having things the way they were before he left because he had thrown that life away. He also knew that his family wouldn't allow it.

When he returned, all that he had left was a bad reputation, a job, and a family who was willing to give him another chance. Come to think of it, that's enough.

Family members are some of the most important people in an inmate's life. In fact, families can have more of an impact on an inmate's rehabilitation than *all* of the programs presently being offered within any prison walls. Prison programs are important: They can help an inmate change into the man he needs to be if he is going to make it on the outside. But they're not enough by themselves. As Chuck Colson, chairman of Prison Fellowship, said in an interview: "People cannot make it coming out of prison unless two things happen. One is a change in their hearts. Two is somebody on the outside that will help them."

Men with strong family ties have the fewest parole failures. In 1979, Eva Homer found that over 50 years of research had shown that there is a strong positive relationship between the strength of the family and social bonds with the ex-offender's parole success. Today's research continues to support this.

Having family members who are willing to visit him in prison can make the difference between an inmate being able to remain out of prison once released or his coming back. Homer's article also presented evidence that only 2 percent of those with three or more regular visitors had to be sent back to prison while on parole. On the other hand, those with no visitors were six times more likely to reenter prison during the first year of parole than those with three or more visitors.

Families can help to keep inmates from becoming prisonized. This happens when he tries so hard to become part of the "prison family" that he starts accepting the norms, values, and behavior patterns of other inmates. (See Chapter 2.) When this happens, he will start thinking like a career criminal. Since what you think of yourself is what you will become, if he starts thinking like a career criminal, he will, in fact, become one.

By staying in contact with him, you can provide your inmate with a focus on returning to the outside and living in the free world once again. You can help him change his criminal thinking patterns into those of a good family man. This is extremely important because if he wants to stay out once he's released, he *must* change into a man who (1) can maintain a close family relationship, (2) stay off alcohol and drugs, and (3) be able to maintain steady employment.

But try as you will, you can't make an inmate do those things once he's released. Besides, it's not your responsibility to change the inmate in your family. Just like the rest of us, he is responsible for his own actions, for the decisions he makes, and for the consequences that naturally follow.

Even though you can't force him to change, you can change your relationship with him by changing the only person that you have the power to change: YOU! Then, as you change, others around you will also change.

As you make your decisions about what to say or how to act, realize that they will have one of two effects on the relationship. They will either build the relationship up or they will tear it down. There is no middle ground. (See Chapters 3 and 8.)

Families are the building blocks of society. Strong families are built on trust, openness, and mutual sharing. Weak and poorly functioning families are built on secrecy.

Families are victims of his crime

Just as Wild Bill's family was a victim of his improper actions, if you have a family member in prison, you are also a victim of his crime. And like all victims, your life will be forever changed because of his improper actions.

Not only did you have to suffer the pain of losing a family member, but you also had to endure the demoralization and stigma as people started treating you differently because of his crime. Not only do you feel lonely as you deal with the readjustment of your relationship, but you also have to deal with the shame that you feel.

It hurts when old friends suddenly drop you or people whisper behind your back and point at you when you walk by. It was probably especially painful to find that some people are less likely to trust you because they

Chapter 9

associate you with his crime. Many wives also have to go through the additional humiliation of having to take a low-paying job or going on welfare for the first time in their lives.

His crime and the imprisonment that he earned also has an impact on the wife's relationship with her parents and in-laws. Often the wife's parents will display great resentment toward the incarcerated son-in-law because they feel that he's the one that is causing their daughter all of the grief. She may hear statements like, "Why don't you dump the bum and find someone decent?" Since she doesn't want to hear things like that, she stops going to see them.

On the other hand, the inmate's parents frequently blame her. She may have to tolerate statements such as, "This is all your fault. If you had been a better wife he wouldn't have done those terrible things." If this happens, it's common for the wife to retaliate by blaming them and saying things like, "If you hadn't kept meddling in our business we would have had a better marriage," or "You're the one who raised him; if you had been better parents he would have known better." By now, neither is talking to the other and the relationship is severed. The inmate's children have not only lost their fathers, but also their grandparents.

If this happens, this leaves the wife in a difficult dilemma. She still loves her husband and misses him, but at the same time is very angry at him for what he has done. She's lonely, hurting, and needs some support. She needs someone who can help her construct a new relationship with her husband given her new situation. But instead, she now has three troubled relationships: the one with her husband and with both sets of parents.

To get away from the pain, wives frequently withdraw into suicidal thoughts, alcohol or drugs, or into their own private hell.

A parent's absence because of imprisonment has special problems for children. They want sympathy but sometimes find that other children aren't sympathetic with their loss. Instead, their friends feel that the they should be happy because the "awful" man is gone. "After all," the other children will say, "your daddy is supposed to be in prison, so why do you miss him?" Research shows that children of inmates usually start having greater discipline problems, and their achievement in school usually suffers.

Because of her own feelings of shame and confusion, wives are sometimes reluctant to tell their children the whole truth about their father's arrest and conviction. Instead, she may tell the children that their father is in the army, in the hospital, working out of town, or whatever else she can think of that will make his disappearance seem acceptable.

Usually the children know that this is a lie. They may have overheard the parents talking, seen the arrest, or been told by someone at school or in the neighborhood. This causes even more problems for the mother. The foundation of good family relationships is the ability of each family member to trust one another. Now the children know that neither parent can be trusted. Their father can't be trusted to care for them, and mother can't be trusted to tell them the truth. It's tough living in a place where no one can be trusted.

Children have their own set of guilt-ridden feelings that they must work through. They are going to be upset, confused, and sad because they have lost their father. They don't understand everything that is going on. Children have a tendency to feel that the bad things that happen in a family are their fault. They fear that the reason that daddy went away was because he stopped loving them. They may feel angry at their mother for not being able to keep daddy at home or because they think she sent him away.

Whenever children become upset, confused, or afraid, their behavior is going to change—for the worse. A common reaction to fear and uncertainty is anger and hostility. Parents will probably see their children start to display more aggressive behavior or withdrawal. It's their only way to cry out for help in understanding. Unfortunately, all of this happens at a time when their mother is at the end of her rope. As a result, neglect and/or physical abuse are common.

Helping each other to get over the pain

First, families should understand that the children's increased difficulties are a reaction to their father's crime and imprisonment. (See Chapter 2.) Both the children and the family have sustained a great loss: the "man of the house," their financial security, and their name. Both the family and the children need to grieve together.

Wives and grandparents, save the false front for your neighbors; let your children see you grieve. Help your children through the grieving process. Don't hide your feelings from each other. Admit to each other that you hurt, that you're upset, and that you are angry. If each person doesn't work through their own feelings of loss and the loneliness caused by his imprisonment, as well as their anger over the changes in their daily routines and rituals, they will become a prisoner of their own feelings. When this happens, the stress will continue to build until they finally explode.

Chapter 9

To keep this from happening, have open and honest family discussions about how you feel about everything that has happened. You might say, "What good will that do? Talking about it won't change his sentence or let him come home." No, you can't change his sentence, but sometimes it helps just to have someone listen, and to care.

The solution when there is no other solution is "dump time." Dump time is when you simply need someone's shoulder to cry on. When you ask for some dump time you're not trying to solve a problem, and you don't want any advice. You and/or the children simply want someone to listen and to care.

When you are talking to the children, don't lie about where their father is or why he is there. That's a tightrope—on one hand you want to be honest, but on the other hand you don't want to destroy the confidence and faith that they have in their father. It is important that children feel that their fathers love them and still care for them.

Here's one way you can tell the children: "Son/daughter, even good daddies can do bad things. Your daddy saw something that he had no right to have, and he broke the law and took it. When he did, he earned his right to live in prison. He broke the trust that we had in him and it hurts very much."

When you talk to the children about his crime, don't glorify it. Describe the crime in their language. Here are some examples: "Your father is in prison because he killed someone." "Your father is in prison because he hurt someone very badly." "Your father is in prison because he took something that wasn't his." "Your father is in prison because he was selling illegal drugs."

If they ask you, "Why did daddy do it?" tell them the truth. "Your daddy did his crime because he decided to do it and because he wanted to do it. Now your daddy is being punished because he was being very naughty."

Be honest when they ask, "When is daddy coming home?" Put it in terms that they can understand. For example: "We hope that daddy will be home by your tenth birthday," or "I don't know, but it will be a long, long, time;" or for life without parole: "Honey, the judge said that daddy will never get to come home again."

Make sure that the children understand that what their daddy did is not their fault. This is especially important if their father is in prison because the child was a victim of his or her father's criminal activity.

Dealing with increased discipline problems

Even though the increased discipline problems with the children may be their reaction to their father's imprisonment, whenever a child misbehaves parents or guardians have only two choices: (1) to provide the appropriate loving discipline that says, "I love you too much to allow you to continue acting that way" or (2) to abuse their power. The purpose of discipline is to teach children that whenever they choose to break the rules they are also asking for the consequences that go with it.

Here is a simple discipline method that works. The parents set the rules and the appropriate punishment for breaking the rules. (See Chapter 8.) Make sure that the form of punishment selected is appropriate for that particular child. For example, asking a two-year-old to sit still for 30 minutes is something that is impossible. Putting a six-year-old on restriction for a month isn't effective. By the time the month is over they have forgotten why they were on restriction.

Once the rule, and the penalty for its violation, is explained to the children, permit them the freedom to stay within those rules. Never enforce a rule if the child doesn't know what the rule is. This means that you will have to say, "The next time you do that, here is what will happen" many times. Then, whenever the children choose to disobey the rules give them the discipline that they earned.

Every time that you discipline your children, follow this procedure: (1) remind them of the rule that they broke; (2) remind them that they knew what would happen if they broke the rule; (3) give them the punishment that they earned; and (4) when it's over and they've settled down again, hug them, remind them of the rule again, and tell them that you loved them too much to let them continue acting that way.

Dealing with the family's physical needs

You will find that it is easier to deal with your own increased problems when you can admit to yourself that you are a victim of his crime. Unless you helped him do it, you *are not* guilty of his crime. Even if you helped him plan his crime, it's not your fault that he is in prison. He's in prison because he made a conscious decision to break the law and earned his right to live in prison. His selfish act forced you into your present predicament and caused you to have the additional problems that you now face because he is in prison.

You have a choice. You can act like a helpless victim, wringing your hands while saying "poor, poor, me," and quit trying. Or you can take charge of the new situation and start looking for ways to do something about your new set of problems.

For the wives, the first order of business is to take care of the family's physical needs of food, clothing, and shelter. If you are not already working, Chapter 7 gives several helpful hints about how find a job, how to use the state employment service, and how to get food stamps. You can find information about low-cost housing and other assistance that is available to you at the welfare department.

Finding child care while you work can be a problem. Use the Yellow Pages, check the want ads, and ask your neighbors who they use. Many churches now have day care centers. Visit the centers, ask for references, and check with other parents to see if they are pleased with the care their children are receiving at that center or with that individual. When selecting child care, remember that it is important to the development of each child that, if possible, the same person take care of the child every day.

Many churches have clothes closets that provide free used clothing simply for the asking. Goodwill Industries has stores that sell used clothing and furniture. Yard sales are an excellent source of children's clothing, toys, and all sorts of household items that can be purchased at bargain prices. Check the want ads for times and locations.

Your local health department may be able to furnish your family with their necessary vaccinations and other medical services free of charge. All it takes is a phone call to find out what is available.

Charities such as the Salvation Army, the United Way, and some churches provide assistance to families in emergency situations. Usually, the amount of aid that they can give an individual family is small, but if you have run completely out of food, are about to have your power cut off, can't afford medical treatment, or are unable to purchase needed medicine, they may be able to help. You can find their telephone numbers in the Yellow Pages listed as Charitable Organizations or Social Service Organizations. Call these organizations: If they can't help, they may know of someone who can.

The over 39,000 Lion's Clubs furnish free eyeglasses to needy adults and children, including the families of inmates. In some cases the Lion's Clubs can even furnish free eye surgery. Contact your local welfare department, public school, or any member of a local Lion's Club to find out how to apply for this assistance.

Dealing with your emotional needs

Once you have taken care of the family's physical needs, you can then begin taking care of your own emotional needs by dealing with the shame and humiliation that you feel. You will feel a sense of release when you can admit to yourself that "My (husband, son, father, etc.) is a convicted criminal." As you read in Chapter 1, this says something about his past and nothing about what he will be in the future. *He* must decide if he is going to be a criminal in the future, and he alone is responsible for that decision.

A common complaint of wives is a feeling that they're going crazy. That's normal! Your world has been turned upside down. Suddenly you were shoved into a single parent role. Your children are causing you additional child-rearing problems. You've had to adapt to an entirely new lifestyle that was forced on you. Actually, you would be crazy if you didn't feel like you were going crazy.

Now that he is in prison, how do you handle his changing attitudes? Does he seem to understand how you feel, or does he act as if his crime didn't happen? Is he considerate of you, or is he becoming more demanding? If he doesn't know how you feel about these things, you need to tell him. You handle these and other problems with him by being open and honest with your feelings. You have no right to be angry with him if he doesn't know exactly why you are angry with him.

How do you feel about his crime? Angry? Certainly! You wouldn't be normal if you didn't. There is nothing wrong with getting angry. Everyone does. However, as seen in Chapter 8, the purpose of anger is to motivate you to find a solution to the problem that is causing the anger—*not* to give you permission to blow up.

You may find that you will need professional help as you deal with your feelings about his crime. If you can't afford a private therapist, call the local mental health department. Many universities have psychology, counseling, or marriage and family therapy centers that offer free or reduced-cost help. Many, but not all, ministers are good counselors. Some larger churches even have professional counselors on their staff. All it takes to find out what is available from these sources is to pick up the phone and call them.

Take care of yourself and don't neglect your own personal growth while he is gone. One way to handle the loneliness is to find a church or social club that will accept you just the way you are and welcome you into their fellowship. Unfortunately, not all churches or social groups will welcome the wife or family of an inmate. People's prejudices get in their way. But keep looking; you'll find a group where you feel accepted.

Finding true friends

You can be a part of 100 groups and still feel lonely. Groups fulfill your need to be accepted, but don't always take away the loneliness. To take away the loneliness you need to develop friends until you have at least one, but preferably two, true friends. True friends are people whom you can share every intimate detail of your life with without worrying about being rejected *and* without having to worry about being featured in the next issue of the *National Enquirer.*

There's an old joke: What are the three fastest forms of communication? Answer: (1) telephone, (2) telegraph, and (3) tell-somebody-else. That's a cute joke, but if you want true, intimate friends that's exactly what you are going to have to do. You are going to have to start sharing appropriate information about yourself with others. As you do, friendships will grow one step at a time until you have true friends.

Step One: Making acquaintances. You're just starting to see each other so you talk about things that are public record: your name, address, children, job, the weather, your parents, and even your age. Some "friends" are only willing to talk on this level. But that's okay. You need many friends on this level.

Step Two: Casual friends. As you get to know each other a little better, you can begin sharing common interests, problems, desires, ideas, and even opinions. During this stage you can even risk talking about "hot" topics such as religion and politics. That's because casual friends accept each other in spite of the fact that they don't agree on everything. Instead, they just agree that they disagree on certain topics. You won't find many people who will go beyond this step if you require them to agree with your ideas in order to be your friend.

Step Three: Close friends. By now you enjoy being together and doing things together, and you have begun looking for reasons to share time with each other. You have meals together, visit each other's homes, go to the movies, church, or whatever. Close friends are people whom you can talk

"What Are We Going To Do With Him?"

to about your dreams and disappointments, achievements and failures, joy and pain. It is at this stage that you can reveal that "My (husband, father, son, friend) is in prison because he was convicted of (name of the crime)."

Some people will show more interest here, even if only to satisfy their own curiosity. However, some people won't be able to handle being that close to someone associated with that particular crime and will back away. For example, someone who has been raped or who is a friend of a rape victim may not be able to be friends with a rapist's wife. Someone whose house has been broken into may not be able to be friends with a thief's mother. If they back away or drop you, you may take it as personal rejection, but it's not. As they talk to you they relive the pain of their own experience, and they haven't grown enough to handle it yet.

Step Four: Intimate friends. True, intimate friends can share their innermost feelings with each other without fear of rejection. It's a relationship based on honesty, mutual respect for each other's feelings, and being available when the other needs you—even if it's inconvenient.

Intimate friends never deliberately do anything that would damage the trust that binds the friendship together because each realizes that if the bond of trust is broken the relationship is likely to die. Intimate friends are even free to criticize or correct each other because both praise and criticism are designed to build each other and the relationship up.

After you learn the stages of friendships, the question is, "How can I get people to go through all four steps and become true, intimate friends without getting burned?" You can't! Some people, including most criminals, will use friendships to get their own selfish needs met, and that hurts. However, there is a way that you can tell if someone wants to be your friend or if they're just trying to collect gossip or use you.

You develop acquaintances into intimate friendships through gradual appropriate self-disclosure. This means that as you climb the steps of friendship, you will become willing to share more information about each other. Be careful; if you reveal too much too soon, you'll scare them off. But if you're too secretive you'll come across as being not interested in their friendship.

Sharing private thoughts is a gift of love. As with all gifts of love, you can start the process. But love, which is the basis of all friendships, can only grow when the receiver is also willing to share gifts of love. This means that they will also be willing to share intimate things about themselves that will help you through your trials and problems.

Mutual self-disclosure of private thoughts is a safety valve. It's developing an understanding that says, "We are becoming comfortable enough with our relationship that we can trust each other not to share potentially damaging information about each other." But more importantly, by sharing similar struggles you can let each other know that you are trying to be part of their world.

When you reach a point where your new "friend" isn't willing to reveal any more about themselves, that's as deep as the friendship will go. Don't drop them; over time the relationship may improve. At a later date they may be willing to climb onto the next step of friendship, and they may become the best friend that you have ever had.

Don't put all of your eggs in one basket; don't put all of your hopes for friendship into one or two people. Keep cultivating new friends. Friendships change over the years. Needs and interests change, or you may simply grow apart. If this happens and you lose them, cherish the memory and be thankful that they were there when you needed them. Make sure the friendship didn't end because they gave so much to you but then you weren't there when they needed you. Intimate friendships are a shared experience.

You may want to limit your intimate friends to your same sex. As you get closer to someone of the opposite sex there is often a tendency for the relationship to become sexual. Both men and women will take advantage of a vulnerable person and listen just to get sex. Affairs hurt, and they all start with an innocent flirt. In the end, they cause more problems than they cure.

Working with the prison system

You are not helpless or powerless against the prison system. In fact, learning to work with the prison system is one of the many things that you can do to make your "prison sentence" more tolerable. It's an impersonal system and he's just a number, or so it seems sometimes. However, if you were to work inside a prison you might be surprised to see how personally the staff knows each of the inmates and how much they want to see the inmates succeed when they get out. If you are willing to be persistent and to follow some simple guidelines, you might find them actually pleasant to work with.

If you have a special request, don't be afraid to ask. Even if they can't or won't grant the request, prison officials will talk to you if you call. Here are some simple guidelines that you can use when calling the prison.

"What Are We Going To Do With Him?"

1. Be courteous when you call. You can catch a lot more bees with honey than you can with vinegar.
2. Don't make demands. Simply state your request and the reason that you think it might be justified.
3. Make sure that you're talking to the right person, one who has the authority to grant your request. For example, a correctional officer isn't going to have the authority to authorize a special visit and may simply say "no." Instead, ask the switchboard operator for the name of the person who could grant your request. Then ask for that person by name.

    If the person on the phone is rude and hangs up, call back and ask the person answering the phone who the supervisor is for that department, then request to be connected to that person.
4. Write down the name of each person you talk with. If turned down, ask who their supervisor is, and talk with him or her.
5. Start with the lowest level of supervision that might be able to grant your request, but don't be afraid to go up the chain of command. Ask to speak with the Lieutenant, Captain, Assistant Warden, or Warden. If you think that the chaplain or mental health staff can help, call them. Supervisors stay extremely busy, and it may take you a few tries to talk with a particular individual.
6. Be considerate. If possible, call during the week during regular office hours and give them as much advance notice as possible.

Here is a suggested way to request a special visit at a time other than regular visiting hours. In this illustration you have called the prison and asked to speak with the Lieutenant.

Lieutenant, my name is John Smith, Inmate Joe Smith's father. His brother, Sam, will be flying in from California on Monday and will only be in town for two days. He's not on the visiting list because he lives so far away, and he'll be gone on the regular visiting day. Is there any way that his brother could come see him? What identification would we need to bring?

Then be prepared to answer any questions that the supervisor might have about your request.

Don't expect an immediate answer. The person you talk with may need to check and see if facilities would be available or to clear it with their supervisor. Prison officials may also want to talk with the inmate and see if he actually has a brother named Sam and if he wants to see him.

If you are turned down, don't expect to be told why. For example, the staff may know of a possible riot threat and they don't want to spread the rumor. Or the prison may be short-staffed that day and extra people can't be allowed into the facility. If they say "no" you're no worse off than before. If you consider it really important, don't be afraid to ask to speak with the next level of command.

Don't become a pest. Make sure the request is "special." Don't abuse the system by flooding it with special requests.

Understand that prisons, like all state agencies, work with limited funds. There are lots of things that they would like to do, but simply don't have the money to do them. Frequently civil servants are so overworked that, even if they wanted to, they simply don't have the time to do extra things.

Forming support groups

Another way that you can make your "prison sentence" more tolerable is to form support groups with other inmates' families in your community. Talk with ministers in your community and see if they would let you use their church facilities to create support groups. The church staff might even be willing to supervise such a meeting. If not, they might have someone in their congregation with the background and training who would be willing to lead such a group.

Use free newspaper and radio public service announcements to publicize them. If you provide them with written, short announcements, they'll announce your meeting free of charge.

Once you have found a place to meet, plan and hold regular sessions. During these meetings you will discover that most families of inmates have similar problems that they must face. Using the knowledge gained from others in the group, individual family members will find their own problems easier to handle.

Since everyone in the group has at least one thing in common—a family member in prison—support groups are a good place to develop friendships. Since the others in the group will understand your special problems, these groups are also a good place to find someone who is willing to give you some "dump time."

Support groups are also a good place to learn how to use the problem-solving skills taught in Chapters 4 and 5. The simple four-step formula taught in those chapters will allow you to find a workable solution to every problem that you will ever have in your life.

Finding transportation to visit the prison

Unfortunately, most prisons are built in desolate places that are not served by public transportation. Thus, many families can't afford to visit. Here's some ways that you can solve that problem.

Help your support group charter a bus that can take you to the prison and back on visiting day. For example, in November 1989, Ingram Bus lines would charge $357.10 to take up to 43 people from Opelika, Alabama, to the state prison in Union Springs and back. If you had a full busload, it would cost approximately $8.30 for each person. If support groups from various cities worked together, that company would be willing to make stops in other cities to fill the bus with only slight changes in the charges. Dixie Excursions said that it would cost $125 for a 15-passenger van and $175 for a 22-passenger minibus to make the same trip. This works out to approximately $8 per person for the same trip. All it takes is a few telephone calls to find out what is available in your area.

Some churches or civic groups might be willing to loan their bus or van to furnish transportation for the support group. Ask! If they say no you are no worse off than you are now.

Be willing to form carpools with other members of the support group. By splitting the cost of the gasoline and packing lunches, it can become an inexpensive trip.

Practicing ethical living

Wild Bill knew that if he wanted to be part of his family again he would have to practice ethical living. He knew what his father stood for. He knew that his father considered his good name the most valuable possession that he had in the world. Like Dad did, if you practice ethical living while your

Chapter 9

family member is in prison, you can turn your family into one that is incompatible with crime.

Ethical living is treating others like you want to be treated: fairly, honestly, and with respect simply because it is the right thing to do. In families where ethical living is practiced, each family member can be free to lead their own private lives but will choose to share them with each other.

Healthy family relationships are built on honesty and trust. Picture your family as being like a bank. Any time your actions prove you trustworthy you're building up the "family bank account," and the relationship will become stronger. Any time that trust is broken the relationship is weakened and a debt created in the family bank account. Whenever that account reaches empty or is overdrawn, the relationship is likely to fail.

Ethical living also means learning how to control your temper. Remember, the purpose of anger is to motivate you to find a solution to the problem, *not* to give you permission to blow up. You have no right to be angry with someone unless they know exactly what you are angry about.

Ethical living means learning to share one of the best gifts of love that there is: your feelings. Feelings are neither right nor wrong, they are simply your reaction to the things that are going on around you. What you do with those feeling *is* either right or wrong.

Unless you are willing to share your feelings, you can't tell if the other person cares about you or not. Many times people do or say things and don't realize that they have hurt you. If this happens, you could feel angry and stop speaking to them. But if you do, they will feel that you're rejecting them for no reason, so they pull away from you. A feud is started that may last for years over something as simple as "You didn't speak to me at the mall yesterday."

You can share your true feelings with someone without casting blame. The purpose of sharing your feelings is to let the other person know how they have hurt you or helped you. Since it is a gift of love, whenever you share your feelings, you should ask only that the statement be accepted, but not necessarily agreed with. For example: "I've been hurt so badly that I'm ending our relationship," or "Honey, I don't think I can live without you" are both personal statements that don't have to be agreed with.

As you are sharing your feelings use "I" statements instead of "You" statements. "I" statements share feelings; "you" statements cast blame. For example, you could say, "I feel so angry right now that I'm like an H-bomb ready to explode!" instead of "You've made me so angry that I'm about to explode!" Actually the second statement is a lie. Nobody can make you so angry that you will explode. Choosing to explode is your choice, and you're responsible for your actions when you do explode.

Here's another example: "Right now, I feel so much hatred toward you that I don't know if I am ever going to be able to forgive you." Actually, that's a very personal and loving statement. It shares true feelings without casting blame. You definitely know where you stand with that person. But notice that the words "I don't know if" allows for the possibility of the speaker changing their mind. This would allow the listener to respond with, "What can I do to change that?"

How about this one: "Honey, I'm so proud of you for controlling your temper last week that I'm about to pop." Did you know that it's more important to share positive feelings than to constantly share complaints? The statement, "I liked that long letter that I got from you. Thanks for answering my questions" will get a response quicker than "Why don't you write me anymore? Did your arm break?"

Teach your inmate to see how he has hurt you

All family members have a lot of feelings that need to be worked out before he comes home. Unfortunately, most people are uncomfortable talking about their pain, especially to the person who caused it. It's simply too painful.

Most inmates don't understand how much their crimes have hurt others. Maybe one of the reasons is because the victims don't get a chance to tell them and wouldn't even if they could. Yet one of the keys to inmate rehabilitation is teaching inmates to see things from the victim's eyes. Once this happens, they are less likely to do criminal acts in the future.

You're a victim. You can help to rehabilitate your inmate by teaching him to see your side of his crime. Don't hide your feelings from him. Using everything that you have learned from this book, and without casting blame, let him know how much his improper actions have hurt you.

He needs to know how you feel about when he was arrested. He needs to know how you felt after the police left. How did it feel to have a pistol shoved into your face and to have to sit there under guard until he was carried away? Does he know? Why not?

Does he know how you felt about hearing his name and charges on every newscast or seeing it in the headlines of the paper? Does he know how you feel about his trial and imprisonment? If you want reduce your

Chapter 9

chances of being hurt again, teach him to see the pain that his crime caused you. Then teach him what he can do to make your "prison sentence" easier. Everyone is different and has different needs. You've got to tell him what your needs are. If he responds and starts trying to meet those needs, he cares about your feelings. Praise him for every little success that you see. Don't expect an overnight change.

One way to communicate deep and hurtful feelings is in love letters. A love letter is any letter that shares your true feelings—both good and bad. You can take your time and compose them and say exactly what you want to say. They can be read over and over, so words are less likely to be taken wrong. Even if the recipient screams at the letter, there's less chance of violence (except maybe to a wall or a punching bag). This also gives them time to think about how they want to respond. There are examples of how love letters can be written in the first chapters of this book. Here is an example of a love letter from an inmate's wife.

Hi Honey,

My days are always brighter when I open the mailbox and I see a letter from you. I enjoy hearing about your classes, how much you are learning, and about the little things that happen each day. Thank you for noticing the little drawings I put on the outside of the envelopes. I almost didn't draw them because I was afraid that the other inmates would tease you. I do miss having you around, and I'm looking forward to your coming home.

You're not the only one that feels like you're drowning. Sometimes I feel so overwhelmed that I want to just run away and hide. I got another call from the principal today because Junior was caught fighting again. What can I do to stop him?

My job at the store is nice, but minimum wage just doesn't pay the bills. I'm glad the church has a clothes closet and I'm thankful for the food stamps. I do enjoy talking to you, but could you limit the calls to once a week, preferably on weekend rates?

I'm working a second job now and hopefully I'll make enough money to come see you in a couple of weeks. Seeing you makes the extra work and long trip worthwhile, but I hate coming into the prison. I know that searching visitors is part of their job, but I feel violated when the correctional officers have to touch me.

Honey, you tell me that you've changed and will never again touch any alcoholic beverage, illegal drug, or do anything else you know is morally wrong. I want to believe you, but I've been disappointed before when you didn't keep your promises. Yes, I'll be at the front gate to take you home when you get out. Even though I've decided to treat you like your crime never happened, I'm also going to hold you accountable for your actions.

The day those police officers stormed into our house is a permanent part of my mind. I felt so dirty after they searched our closets and drawers that I washed all of the clothes twice. Junior cried for a week after he found out the "special" camera you got him was stolen and had to be returned. I made up my mind that day that I would never go through anything like that again.

Honey, I'll love you, help you find a job, help you find Alcoholics Anonymous meetings, and sit beside you at public functions with my head held high. But I will never again lie for you—even if it means your return to prison.

You asked me what I needed. I need for you to never again give me any reason not to trust you. Make me a part of your life, and be a part of mine.

Your loving wife,

Keep in touch with each other. You need to write each other at least once a week. Never let it be less than every two weeks. In these letters, share your true feelings—good and bad. Ask specific questions, and expect answers to those questions.

Getting ready for his return

He's the one who forced the family to change—and it has. If he goes back to his old ways when he gets out, he will probably be one of the ones who is back in prison within one year. This means that now is the time to start renegotiating the family contract. Let him know what you are expecting of him when he gets out and the new family roles that you want him to fill. Talk about how much housework that you are expecting him to do, etc.

Let him know that you know that he needs steady employment—and to stay on the first job for at least one year. As you saw in Chapter 7, he needs to prove to himself and others that he can live by one company's rules for a year.

Chapter 9

Help him to dream. Everything that you ever accomplish starts with a dream—one that says, "I wonder what it would be like to (fill in the blank)."

Help him to start dreaming of the specific things that will be part of his life once he's free again (job, problems, family life, etc.) Believe in him. Help him figure out how he can realize his dreams.

Last but not least, be willing to forgive him and welcome him home. Forgiveness is not forgetting; you don't have the ability to do that. Forgiveness is a decision to treat him like it never happened while still holding him accountable for what he has done.

The greatest gift of love you can give someone is forgiveness. It's hard to treat people like it never happened. It's hard to talk about pain and still act loving to each other. Forgiveness is letting God and/or society make him pay for the harm that he has done. Accountability is letting him know that you *will not* tolerate any more criminal activity and that you will turn him in if he commits any.

Wild Bill's dad welcomed him home with open arms and put on a big party. He never once said, "I knew that you wouldn't amount to anything." Instead, he helped him find a job. He helped him patch things up with his brother. But he didn't restore Wild Bill's inheritance. That was gone. You can't get back what has been thrown away. Your old relationship with your inmate is gone. He threw it away and deserted you. You're under no legal or moral obligation to try to create a new relationship with him, except for an obligation of love.

Selfish people frequently take advantage of forgiving people. They want to keep on doing their own evil things and for people to keep on treating them like it never happened. They think that if their victims (including you) forgive them that they won't testify against them.

If your inmate is asking you to take him back without his making any changes in his life, he's asking you to do something that even God won't do. God demands that you show a willingness to change, from the inside out, before he will treat you like it never happened. It doesn't mean that you get your old life back. Instead, you must leave your old life behind and start learning a new way of doing things.

If he's willing to change, he's worth saving. If not, he's better off in prison. Help him, encourage him, love him. Be honest with him and teach him how to love. Forgive him, but teach him accountability. Let him know that you're looking for him to come home.

And when he gets out, welcome him home and expect the best.

Nationwide Resources

There are several nationwide prison ministries, associations, and networks that can provide information and help for both inmates and their families.

Prison Fellowship, P.O. Box 17500, Washington, D.C. 20041-0500, is a worldwide prison ministry that provides a variety of programs through a network of thousands of volunteers to help inmates, former inmates, and the families of inmates. It provides instruction to inmates within prison systems, volunteers who are willing to help inmates make the transition back into the "free world," and in some cases, support and transportation to prisons for families. Their telephone number is (703) 478-0100, www.pfm.org.

Open, Inc. (Offender Preparation and Education Network), 1308 Kynn Drive, Garland, Texas 75041, will provide, for a nominal fee, informational handbooks and tapes to help offenders, their loved ones, and the community at large to understand how the criminal justice system works. The materials are also designed to help offenders learn how to change their values and behaviors so they can get out and not repeat criminal activity. They can be reached at (972) 271-1971.

Friends Outside National Organization, 3031 Tischway, Suite 507, San Jose, California 95128, currently provides a variety of programs, assistance, transportation, and counseling to inmates and their families in California and Nevada, with expansion planned in the future. They also provide information to people throughout the United States about juvenile offenders, working with government agencies, and help families form support groups. They are also available for crisis intervention or counseling during regular office hours. Their telephone number is (408) 985-8807. Like most organizations, they do not accept collect calls.

The Family and Corrections Network, P.O. Box 244, Palmyra, Virginia 22963, is a national professional organization that works to reduce crime by strengthening family ties. Although this organization is not designed to help individual families of inmates, it is a national clearinghouse of research and programs designed to help inmate-family relations. It can share skills and resources with people who provide programs and services for families of inmates. Their phone number is (804) 589-3036.

Al-Anon Family Groups will send any individual an information package about alcoholism and the family if you call 1-800-356-9996 or (212) 582-2000. For the nearest Al-Anon or Alcoholics Anonymous groups meeting in your area, check the white pages of your telephone directory. If your town is too small to have a group, ask the directory assistance operator to check nearby cities.

The National Institute of Corrections Information Center, 1790 30th St., Suite 130, Boulder, Colorado 80301, (303) 939-8877, has a limited supply of the *1989 Directory of Programs Serving Families of Adult Offenders.* Although this directory would not have information that would help an individual family, it might have information that would be useful to a support groups.

The American Correctional Association, 4380 Forbes Boulevard, Lanham, Maryland 20706, is the national membership organization for corrections professionals and others interested in corrections. They sell books such as this one and other materials that are designed especially for inmates, their families, and people employed in the correctional field. Their phone number is (301) 918-1800, www.corrections.com\aca.

To find out exactly what these groups can offer, write or call them. There are people who are willing to help, *if* you ask.

Suggested Readings

Bird, J., and L. Bird. 1976. *Sexual loving*. Garden City, N.J.: Doubleday.

Bolles, R. N. 1990. *What color is your parachute? A practical manual for job hunters & career changers*. Berkeley, Calif.: Ten Speed Press.

Brehm, Sharon S. 1985. *Intimate relationships*. New York: Random House.

Briggs, D. C. 1975. *Your child's self-esteem: The key to life*. Garden City, N.J.: Dolphin Books.

Colson, C., and D. Van Ness. *Convicted*. Westchester, N.Y.: Crossway Books.

Crabb, L. C. 1982. *The marriage builder: A blueprint for couples and counselors*. Grand Rapids, Mich.: Zondervan.

DeHaan, R. W. 1971. *Happiness is not an accident*. Grand Rapids, Mich.: Zondervan.

Dobson, J. C. 1970. *Dare to discipline*. Wheaton, Ill.: Tyndale House.

Dobson, J. C. 1980. *Emotions: Can you trust them?* New York: Bantam.

Dobson, J. C. 1987. *Parenting isn't for cowards: Dealing confidently with the frustrations of childrearing*. Waco, Tex.: Word Books.

Dobson, J. C. 1988. *Discipline with love*. Wheaton, Ill.: Tyndale House.

Half, Robert. 1981. *The Robert Half way to get hired in today's job market*. New York: Rawson, Wade.

Hohman, L. B. 1939. *As the twig is bent*. New York: Macmillan.

Lahaye, T., and B. Phillips. 1982. *Anger is a choice*. Grand Rapids, Mich.: Zondervan.

Pittman, F. 1989. *Private lies: Infidelity and the betrayal of intimacy*. New York: W. W. Norton.

Sack, S. M. 1987. *The complete legal guide to marriage, divorce, custody, & living together*. New York: McGraw-Hill.

Satir, V. 1972. *Peoplemaking*. Palo Alto, Calif.: Science and Behavior Books.

Wheat, E. 1980. *Love life for every married couple*. Grand Rapids, Mich.: Zondervan.

Williams, H. P. 1973. *Do yourself a favor: Love your wife*. Plainfield, N.J.: Logos International.

Bibliography

Ahrons, C. 1983. Divorce: Before, during, and after. In *Stress and the Family, Vol. I: Coping with Normative Transitions.* H. I. McCubbin & C. R. Figley, eds. New York: Brunner/Mazel.

American Psychiatric Association. 1980. *Diagnostic and statistical manual of mental disorders, 3d ed.* Washington, D.C.: American Psychiatric Association.

Aponte, H. J., and J. M. Van Deusen. 1981. Structural family therapy. In *Handbook of Family Therapy.* A. S. Gurman & D. P. Kniskern, eds. New York: Brunner/Mazel.

Bayse, D. J. 1989. *The effect of family life education on prisoner's narcissism, locus of control, and view of ideal family functioning.* Master's thesis, Auburn University.

Blackwell, J. G. 1959. *The effects of involuntary separation on selected families of men committed to prison from Spokane County, Washington.* Doctoral dissertation, Washington State University.

Boszormenyi-Nagy, I. 1986. Transgenerational solidarity: The expanding context of therapy and prevention. *The American Journal of Family Therapy* 14 (3): 195-212.

Boszormenyi-Nagy, I., and G. M. Spark. 1973. *Invisible loyalties: Reciprocity in intergenerational family therapy.* Hagerstown, Md.: Harper & Row.

Boszormenyi-Nagy, I., and D. N. Ulrich. 1981. Contextual family therapy. In *Handbook of Family Therapy.* A. S. Gurman & D. P. Kniskern, eds. New York: Brunner/Mazel.

Boudouris, James. 1984. Recidivism as a process. *Journal of Offender Counseling, Services and Rehabilitation* 8 (3): 41-51.

Boudouris, James. 1985. *Prisons and kids: Programs for inmate parents.* College Park, Md.: American Correctional Association.

Bradley, L. J. 1985. Making the transition from prison to community: Importance of career exploration. *Journal of Employment Counseling* 22 (3): 110-116.

Brodsky, Stanley L. 1975. *Families and friends of men in prison: The uncertain relationship.* Lexington, Mass.: Lexington Books.

Bibliography

Camp, G. M., and C. G. Camp. 1988. *The corrections yearbook*. South Salem, N.Y.: Criminal Justice Institute.

Clark, Duncan. 1989. Chuck Colson: Born again prison reformer. *Corrections Today* 51 (4): 80-84.

Crosby, J. F., and N. L. Jose. 1983. Death: Family adjustment to loss. In *Stress and the Family, Vol. II: Coping With Catastrophe*. C. R. Figley & H. I. McCubbin, eds. New York: Brunner/Mazel.

Czudner, Gad. 1985. Changing the criminal: A theoretical proposal for change. *Federal Probation* 49 (3): 64-66.

Davis, C. A., and B. G. Dawson. 1985. Women, work, and life transitions. *Journal of Employment Counseling* 22 (3): 117-122.

Deturck, M. A. 1987. When communication fails: Physical aggression as a compliance-gaining strategy. *Communication Monographs* 54:106-112.

Englander, Frederick. 1983. Helping ex-offenders enter the labor market. *Monthly Labor Review* 106 (7): 25-30.

Epstein, N. B., D. S. Biship, and L. M. Baldwin. 1982. McMaster model of family functioning: A view of the normal family. In *Normal Family Process*. F. Walsh, ed. New York: The Guilford Press.

Everstine, D. S., and L. Everstine. 1983. *People in crisis: Strategic therapeutic interventions*. New York: Brunner/Mazel.

Finn, R. H., and P. A. Fontaine. 1983. Perceived employability of applicants labeled as offenders. *Journal of Employment Counseling* 20 (3): 139-144.

Fishman, Susan H. 1981. The impact of incarceration on children of offenders. *Journal of Children in Contemporary Society* 15 (1): 89-99.

Fishman, L. T. 1986. Repeating the cycle of hard living and crime: Wives' accommodations to husband's parole performance. *Federal Probation* 50 (1): 44-54.

Friedman, S., and T. C. Ellelstyn. 1965. The adjustment of children of jail inmates. *Federal Probation* 29 (4): 55-59.

Friedman, B. J., and D. G. Rice. 1977. Marital therapy in prison: One partner couple therapy. *Psychiatry* 40:175-183.

Fritsch, T. A., and J. D. Burkhead. 1981. Behavioral reactions of children to parental absence due to imprisonment. *Family Relations* 30:83-88.

Gothard, Bill. 1979. *Research in principles of life*. Oak Brook, Ill.: Institute in Basic Youth Conflicts.

Gupta, P. K., and R. Mueller. 1984. The correction of criminal thinking and behavior through the cognitive-moral approach. *Correctional Options, Vol. 4.* Ottawa: Ontario Ministry of Correctional Services.

Haddock, B. L., and M. J. Sporakowski. 1982. Self-concept and family communication: A comparison of status and criminal offenders and non-offenders. *Journal of Offender Counseling Services and Rehabilitation* 7 (2): 61-74.

Hairston, C. F., and P. Lockett. 1985. Parents in prison: A child abuse and neglect prevention strategy. *Child Abuse and Neglect* 9 (4): 471-477.

Hannon, G., D. Marton, and M. Martin. 1984. Incarceration in the family: Adjustment to change. *Family Therapy* 11 (3): 253-260.

Harrison, R. K. 1969. Jeremiah and Lamentations: An introduction and commentary. In *The Tyndale Old Testament Commentaries.* D. J. Wiseman, ed. Downers Grove, Ill.: Inter-Varsity Press.

Hill, R. 1965. Generic features of families under stress. In *Crisis Intervention.* H. Parod, ed. Washington, D.C.: Family Service Association of America.

Holt, N., and D. Miller. 1972. *Explorations in inmate-family relationships.* Research report #46. Sacramento: Research Division, California Department of Corrections.

Homant, R. J. 1984. Employment of ex-offenders: The role of prisonization and self-esteem. *Journal of Offender Counseling, Services & Rehabilitation* 8 (3): 5-21.

Homer, E. L. 1979. Intimate-family ties: Desirable but difficult. *Federal Probation* 43 (1): 47-52.

Howser, J., J. Grossman, and D. Macdonald. 1983. Impact of family reunion program on institutional discipline. *Journal of Offender Counseling, Services & Rehabilitation* 8 (1/2): 27-36.

Hughes, J. E. 1983. My daddy's number is C-92760. *Journal of Children in Contemporary Society* 15 (1): 79-88.

Hurlock, E. B. 1980. *Developmental psychology: A life-span approach,* 5th ed. New York: McGraw-Hill.

Justice, B., and A. Calvert. 1985. Factors mediating child abuse as a response to stress. *Child Abuse and Neglect* 9 (3): 359-363.

Kaslow, F. W. 1978. Marital or family therapy for prisoners and their significant others. *The Prison Journal* 58 (1): 53-58.

Kaslow, F. W. 1986. Individual therapy focused on marital problems. *American Journal of Family Therapy* 14 (3): 264.

Bibliography

Kaslow, F. W. 1987. Couple or family therapy for prisoners and their significant others. *The American Journal of Family Therapy* 15 (4): 352-360.

Kock, M. A., and C. R. Lowery. 1984. Visitation and the noncustodial father. *Journal of Divorce* 8 (2): 47-65.

Matusewitch, Eric. 1983. Employment rights of ex-offenders. *Personnel Journal* 62 (12): 951-954.

McCubbin, H. I., and J. M. Patterson. 1983. Family transitions: Adaptation to stress. In *Stress and the Family, Vol. I: Coping With Normative Transitions.* H. I. McCubbin & C. R. Figley, eds. New York: Brunner/Mazel.

McGolderick, M., and R. Gerson. 1986. *Genograms in family assessment.* New York: W. W. Norton.

Minuchin, S., and H. C. Fishman. 1981. *Family therapy techniques.* Cambridge, Mass.: Harvard University Press.

Morris, L. 1958. The first epistle of Paul to the Corinthians, an introduction and commentary. In *The Tyndale New Testament Commentaries.* R. V. G. Tasker, ed. Grand Rapids, Mich.: Eerdmans.

Olson, D. H., D. H. Sprenkle, and C. Russel. 1979. Circumplex model of marital and family systems I: Cohesion and adaptability dimensions, family type, and clinical applications. *Family Process* 18:3-28.

Park, Ross D. 1975. Some effects of punishment on child's behavior. In *Influences on Human Development.* U. Bronfenbrenner & M. A. Mahoney, eds. Hinesdale, Ill.: Dryden.

Rauma, D., and R. A. Berk. 1982. Crime and poverty in California: Some quasi-experimental evidence. *Social Science Research* 11 (4): 318-351.

Romero, J. J., and L. M. William. 1985. Recidivism among convicted sex offenders: A 10-year followup study. *Federal Probation* 49 (1): 64.

Schachter, J., and K. D. O'Leary. 1985. Affective intent and impact in marital communication. *The American Journal of Family Therapy* 13 (4): 17-23.

Schneller, Donald P. 1976. *The prisoner's family: A study of the effects of imprisonment on the families of prisoners.* San Francisco: R and E Research Associates.

Schwartz, M. C., and J. F. Weintraub. 1974. The prisoner's wife: A study in crisis. *Federal Probation* 38 (4): 20-26.

Sebold, J. 1987. Indicators of child sexual abuse in males. *Journal of Contemporary Social Work* 68 (2): 75-83.

As Free As An Eagle

Steinmetz, S. K. 1977. *The cycle of violence: Assertive, aggressive, and abusive family interaction.* New York: Praeger.

Swan, L. A. 1981. *Families of black prisoners: Survival and progress.* Boston: G. K. Hall.

Taylor, J. B. 1969. Ezekiel: An introduction and commentary. In *The Tyndale Old Testament Commentaries.* D. J. Wiseman, ed. Downers Grove, Ill.: Inter-Varsity Press.

Thomas, R. G. 1981. The family practitioner and the criminal justice system: Challenges for the 80's. *Family Relations* 30: 614-624.

Vicary, J. R., and R. Good. 1982. The effects of self-esteem counseling group on male prisoners' self-concept. *Journal of Offender Counseling, Services and Rehabilitation* 7 (3/4): 107-117.

Wallerstedt, J. 1984. *Returning to prison.* Washington, D.C.: Bureau of Justice Statistics.

Walsh, F. 1982. Conceptualizations of normal family functioning. In *Normal Family Process.* F. Walsh, ed. New York: The Guilford Press.

Waring, E. M. 1988. *Enhancing marital intimacy through facilitating cognitive self-disclosure.* New York: Brunner/Mazel.

Weideranders, M. R. 1981. Some myths about the employment problems of young offenders. *Federal Probation* 45 (4): 9-13.

Weiner, B., I. Frieze, A. Kukla, L. Reed, S. Rest, and R. M. Rosenbaum. 1971. Perceiving the causes of success and failure. In *Attribution: Perceiving the Causes of Behavior.* E. E. Jones, D. E. Kanouse, H. H. Kelly, R. E. Nisbett, S. Valins, & B. Weiner, eds. Morristown, N.J.: General Learning Press.

Weintraub, Judith F. 1983. The offender as parent. *Journal of Children in Contemporary Society* 15 (1): 73-78.

Wheeler, B. R., and E. Walton. 1987. Personality disturbances of adult incest victims. *The Journal of Contemporary Social Work* 68 (10): 597-602.

Yelsma, P. 1984. Marital communication, adjustment and perceptual differences between "Happy" and "Counseling" couples. *The American Journal of Family Therapy* 12 (1): 26-36.

Yochelson, S., and S. E. Samenow. 1976. *The criminal personality, Vol. I: A profile for change.* New York: Jason Aronson.

Yochelson, S., and S. E. Samenow. 1977. *The criminal personality, Vol. II: The change process.* New York: Jason Aronson.

Yochelson, S., and S. E. Samenow. 1986. *The criminal personality, Vol. III: The drug user.* Northvale, N. J.: Jason Aronson.

About The Author

D aniel Justin Bayse was born in Roanoke, Virginia. He served for seven years in the U.S. Navy, followed by ten years as a member of the Virginia State Police.

In 1983, he entered Florida Baptist Theological College in Graceville, Florida, and received a Bachelor of Theology Degree in 1986. After taking graduate courses in psychology and counseling at Troy State University, he enrolled in Auburn University. There he received a Master of Science in Family and Child Development in 1989 and is presently working toward a Ph.D. in Counseling Education.

Bayse was ordained in 1987 by the First Baptist Church, Dothan, Alabama, and has served as an evangelist specializing in family and prison ministry since 1983. In 1988, he began writing and implementing, on a volunteer basis, Alabama's first three family life education programs for inmates and their families. These programs are the basis of this book.

He was named a Certified Family Life Educator by the National Council on Family Relations in 1988 and received second place in their national "Student of the Year" competition for his work with inmates. He was included in the 1989 edition of *Who's Who In American Christian Leadership*. He is married and the father of one son.

Bayse is a member of the American Correctional Association, the National Council on Family Relations, the Family and Corrections Network, and the American Association for Counseling and Development.

Other related publications from the American Correctional Association

Helping Hands:
A Handbook for Volunteers in Prisons and Jails

Daniel J. Bayse

A practical guide for volunteers in correctional settings. The criminal justice system, reasons for crime, security issues, understanding the criminal personality, communicating with inmates, preventing manipulation, and inmate slang are discussed.

Cage Your Rage:
An Inmate's Guide to Anger Control

Murray Cullen

This self-study workbook helps offenders who have difficulty dealing with anger. Examines what anger is, its good and bad points, what causes anger, and ways of managing it. A valuable tool for inmates serving time within an institution as well as parolees entering the community.

Getting High and Doing Time: What's the Connection?
A Recovery Guide for Alcoholics and Drug Addicts in Trouble with the Law

Edward M. Read, LCSW, CAC and Dennis C. Daley, MSW

A workbook-style guide aimed at giving readers a better understanding of their addiction problems. It explores the definition and causes of addiction and looks at true-life accounts of addicts and substance abusers now in recovery. A useful counseling tool for inmates incarcerated in a facility, and also probationers and parolees.

Considering Marriage
A Pre-marital Workbook for Couples Separated by Incarceration

Mary K. Friskics-Warren

Provides a realistic view of the marriage experience for both partners, and examines what it's like to be married while serving time. Discusses the Christian and Muslim marriage traditions, and explores expectations, communication, male/female roles, and the emotional cycle of incarceration.

To order these or other ACA publications and videos, call 1-800-222-5646. For more information, contact our World Wide Web home page at: http://www.corrections.com/aca